CROSSING TO KILL

CROSSING TO KILL

The True Story of the Serial-Killer
Playground

Simon Whitechapel

First published in 2000 by

Virgin Publishing Ltd
Thames Wharf Studios
Rainville Road
London W6 9HA

Typeset by TW Typesetting, Plymouth, Devon

Printed and bound by Mackays PBKS

ISBN 0 7535 0496 0

Contents

A todos los sufrientes de Ciudad Juárez

'Power is poison.' [Alan Moore. Interview in *The Edge* (see
http://www.users.globalnet.co.uk/~houghtong/edge.htm)]

'Even the devil is afraid of living here.' [Remark of Juárez
inhabitant reported in Charles Bowden's 'While You Were
Sleeping' (*Harper's* magazine, December 1996)]

'Tonight, John Quinones takes you into their world, where
young women desperate for jobs are being stalked by a nameless,
faceless predator . . . You're in the Mexican desert, just a
stone's throw from the American border, on the
trail of mass murder.' ('Silent Screams in Juarez', ABC's
20–20 current affairs programme, Wednesday, 20 January 1999)

'*Te Mereces La Silla Eléctrica*' ('You Deserve the Electric
Chair'). [Headline from *El Diario de Juárez* (*The Juárez Daily*),
reporting the words of a young woman sexually assaulted
by Jesús Manuel Guardado Márquez, alias '*El Dracula*']

'$e^{i\pi} = -1$.' [Leonhard Euler (1707–1803)]

'Regenbogen am Morgen macht dem Schäfer Sorgen;
Regenbogen am Abend ist dem Schäfer Labend.' [Friedrich
Wilhelm Nietzsche (1844–1900)]

'ἐὰν δὲ ἐκπιέξῃς μυκτῆρας ἐκελεύσεται αἷμα.' [*The Septuagint*
(c. 100 BC)]

Acknowledgements

First, I would like to thank Héctor Carreon of the ParaSagrario Consortium for his response to enquiries made by the author and publisher. The Consortium was created in memory of María Sagrario González Flores, a seventeen-year-old girl who was one of the victims of the serial killings in Juárez, and its website can be found at http://www.aztlan.net/ParaSagrario.[1]

However, I wish to stress that neither Mr Carreon nor any other member of the Consortium has seen or approved any part of *Crossing to Kill* before publication, and its contents remain the sole responsibility of the author.

I'd also like to thank Charles Bowden for his help with contacts and for his article on Juárez, 'While You Were Sleeping' (*Harper's* magazine, 1996), which was an invaluable reference and was incorporated into his book *Juárez: The Laboratory of our Future* (Aperture, 1998); the photographers Jaime Bailléres and Julián Cardona of Ciudad Juárez;[2] the other journalists in México, the United States, and elsewhere who have written about the

---

[1] Affiliated to the ParaSagrario Consortium is Casa Amiga, a group working for women's rights in Ciudad Juárez. Donations can be sent to the following address: Casa Amiga, Centro De Crisis, Peru Norte 878, Col. Hidalgo, Cd. Juárez, Chihuahua, C.P. 32312, México.

[2] Señores Bailléres's and Cardona's agent can be contacted at jazzblues@aol.com

serial killings, in particular Tim Madigan for his detailed series of articles; and all members of the Internet community who provided assistance with material, in particular members of the sci.lang.translation newsgroup and Jason Pope and Joe of alt.true-crime.[1] Again, I wish to stress that no one outside Virgin Publishing who helped with the book had any advance notice of its contents, which remain the sole responsibility of the author.

Further thanks go to David M. Mitchell of Oneiros Books,[2] James Williamson of Creation Books, and the former *Headpress* editor David Slater for affording me many valuable insights into aspects of the psychopathic personality; to James Williamson again for supplying a Spanish/English dictionary that has proved very useful during the writing of this book; to the current *Headpress* editor David Kerekes for permission to quote from the Critical Vision compilation *Critical Vision* (1995) and Jesús Ignacio Aldapuerta's short-story collection *The Eyes* (1995); to Rodolfo Compte of Buenos Aires for help with the Spanish; to Richard Wagner, Photographed by Lightning, Psycho-Testudo, and Heydrich for musical accompaniment; finally and particularly, my thanks go to James Marriott of Virgin Books, without whom this book could never have appeared.

Simon Whitechapel, London, 1999

Note: In Mexican Spanish (Ciudad) Juárez is pronounced something like (see-oo-DAAD) HWAA-ress, with the 'h' pronounced like the 'ch' of the Scottish 'loch', German 'Buch', or Yiddish 'chutzpah'.

---

[1] For further details of Joe's true-crime mailing list and Jason's serial killer website, please visit http://members.aol.com/Joe1orbit/MailingList1.html and http://www.btinternet.com/~serial.killer/
[2] For further details of Oneiros Books, please visit http://www.freeyellow.com/members6/oneiros/index.html

Chronology

Cronología f. Ciencia que tiene por objeto determinar el orden y las fechas de los acontecimientos históricos.

Chronology: A science that attempts to determine the order and dates of historical events.

c. 1947. Birth of Abdul Latif Sharif Sharif (sic) in Egypt. Five decades later, at a deportation hearing in the United States, he will testify to a troubled childhood, claiming that he suffered repeated sexual abuse from his father and other male relatives.

1970. Sharif emigrates to the United States, living at first in New York. He begins to establish a reputation for drunkenness and promiscuity that will accompany him for the remainder of his stay in the United States.

1971. Birth of Victor Moreno Rivera, who will later be charged as an accomplice of Sharif.

1973. Birth of Jesús Manuel Guardado Márquez, also later to be charged as an accomplice of Sharif.

3 January 1977. A missing airline hostess called Sandra Miller is found by police just as she dies from a single stab-wound on a roadside in Pennsylvania. Blood and clumps of hair are found in the snow near her home at Flemington, New Jersey, leading the police to conclude that she was violently abducted and driven across the Delaware River to the scene of her death. The police are unable to find the killer, but two decades later, as news of Sharif's crimes reaches them from México, tell the media

that he is now the prime suspect. Sharif was working for Magnesium Electron of New Jersey at the time, and is known to have frequented the same bars as Sandra Miller.

1978. Sharif has been fired from another job in New Jersey for suspected expense account fraud and has moved to New Hope, Pennsylvania. An acquaintance called John Pascoe will later recall his interest in and ability to attract young girls, including, Pascoe claims, under-age ones. The girls often mysteriously disappear from the area having last been seen in Sharif's apartment. Pascoe grows disturbed about Sharif's behaviour, later recalling, among other incidents, a deer-hunting expedition in local woods during which Sharif tortures a wounded buck.

1980. Pascoe and Sharif fall out when Pascoe enters his apartment without permission and finds the meagre possessions of Sharif's latest conquest – 'petite, pretty, with long, light-blonde hair' – still there, despite Sharif's assertion that she had left for good. Sharif orders Pascoe out of the apartment, and as he leaves he sees a mud-caked shovel in Sharif's front porch.

1981. Sharif has moved to Palm Beach, Florida, to work for a company called Cercoa Inc. On 2 May, he rapes a twenty-three-year-old woman called Tracey. Cercoa Inc., which has created a department specially for him, finds the best legal defence team for their wayward but brilliant employee, but on August 13th, on the eve of the trial, he rapes and assaults another woman called Ruth in West Palm Beach. The police there do not pass details of the second rape to their colleagues, and Sharif gains probation for his attack on Tracey and serves only 45 days for his attack on Ruth.

1982. Fired by Cercoa Inc. because of his legal difficulties, Sharif moves to Gainesville, Florida.

1983. A short-lived marriage ends when Sharif beats his wife unconscious, and he places an ad in the *Gainesville Sun* for a live-in housekeeper. A twenty-year-old college student called Lisa answers the ad and moves in on 17 March. Sharif repeatedly rapes and beats her the same night, threatening to kill her: 'I will bury you out back in the woods. I've done it before, and I'll do it again.' He is arrested and imprisoned to await trial.

January 1984. While awaiting trial, Sharif escapes from Alachua County Jail with a group of other prisoners. He is soon recaptured.

31 January 1984. Sharif is sentenced to twelve years for the rape of Lisa. The assistant State Attorney Gordon Groland promises Lisa that on his release he will be 'met at the prison gates and escorted to the plane' for deportation back to Egypt.

October 1989. Sharif is released after serving less than half of his sentence. No state officials are waiting at the prison gates. A fortnight later he is working for Benchmark Research and Technology, an oil company in Midland, Texas. He soon re-establishes a reputation for drunkenness and promiscuity, but simultaneously confirms his reputation as a 'brilliant chemist', helping Benchmark punch well above its weight in the oil business. The United States Department of Energy marks him out for attention and he is photographed shaking hands in his laboratory with the US senator Phil Gramm.

1991. Sharif is arrested for drunk-driving for the second time in Midland and starts attending meetings of Alcoholics Anonymous. Tom Wilson, a colleague from his Florida days, is now working with him at Benchmark and, aware that he should have been deported after the rape of Lisa in Florida, reports him to the US Border Patrol.

1992. Sharif is arrested and a deportation hearing gets under way in El Paso, Texas, separated by the width of the Rio Grande from Ciudad Juárez, México, which has become famous for its foreign-owned *maquiladora* factories employing thousands of young women. At the hearing United States Immigration Judge William Nail hears testimony in favour of Sharif from colleagues at Benchmark and members of his Alcoholics Anonymous group.

28 September 1993. Judge Nail acknowledges the positive testimony but decides against Sharif, citing his recent arrests for drunk-driving as evidence of his continuing tendency to abuse alcohol and undergo 'a remarkable transformation ... much like the principal character in Robert Louis Stevenson's popular story, *The Strange Case of Dr Jekyll and Mr Hyde.*' Sharif's lawyers immediately appeal against the deportation order and Sharif is freed on bail to await the second hearing, also in El Paso. It is during this period that he is believed to have first begun to travel regularly to Juárez for visits to the sleazy nightclub district of Ugarte.

31 October (Hallowe'en) 1993. Sharif meets a woman called Ann at a nightclub in Midland and takes her back to the home he still owns there. He attacks her and rapes her repeatedly till dawn. Faced with a second serious charge against his client, Jack Ladd, Sharif's chief lawyer in the deportation hearings, proposes a deal to the American authorities: if the charges are dismissed, Sharif will leave the United States for good.

May 1994. Before the authorities have responded to the proposal, Sharif acts on his own initiative and emigrates to Juárez to work for Benchmark in one of the *maquiladora* factories.

August 1994. The authorities accept Ladd's proposal and the charges against Sharif are dismissed. Wayne Kinsey, the Benchmark CEO (Chief Executive Officer), later claims that Sharif stopped working for Benchmark a few months after his arrival in México. The corpses of raped and murdered young women have started to turn up in the suburbs of Juárez and the surrounding desert, casting a spell of fear over the city. Many of the victims have last been seen in Ugarte, where Sharif is now a familiar figure, freely spending the money he earns from another well-paid job as he flirts and dances with young women from the *maquiladoras*.

Summer 1995. Sharif is seen frequently in the company of a seventeen-year-old *maquiladora* worker called Elizabeth Castro García, a 'slender, beautiful girl with long, dark hair'.

15 August 1995. Elizabeth Castro García disappears. Her strangled body turns up four days later beside a highway in southern Juárez.

Early October 1995. A young woman called Blanca accuses Sharif of subjecting her to three days of rape and beatings at his home in Rincones de San Marcos, an exclusive district in north-western Juárez. She tells the police that he also threatened to murder her and dump her body in Lote Bravo, a patch of desert to the south of the city where many of the previous murder victims have been found. A few days later she withdraws the charges and disappears, but the Mexican police have now begun to investigate Sharif's links with the rapes and murders of *maquiladora* workers, and learn of his criminal record in the United States. Sharif is charged with the murder of Elizabeth Castro García and held in the Juárez *Centro de Readaptación Social para Adultos*, or the Centre for the Social Rehabilitation of Adults, known for short as the *CeReSo*, where he awaits trial in the notoriously slow Mexican legal system. Following his arrest the rapes and murders have stopped but Sharif continues to insist that he is innocent.

1995–1996. It is later alleged by the Juárez police that during this period Sharif receives regular visits in the *CeReSo* from members of a Juárez street-gang called *Los Rebeldes*, The Rebels, who are led by Sergio Armendáriz, nicknamed *El Diablo*, The Devil.

1996. Sharif is still firmly behind bars but the rapes and murders of young women have started again, throwing the inhabitants of Juárez into a renewed frenzy of fear, mingled this time with anger at the seeming inability of the authorities to solve the crimes.

April, 1996. After tip-offs from the criminal underworld in Ugarte, the police arrest Sergio Armendáriz and the other members of *Los Rebeldes*, accusing them of a conspiracy with Sharif. They allege Sharif has been paying them to rape and murder in an attempt to establish his innocence of the previous crimes. *Los Rebeldes* insist they are innocent of the charge, accusing the police of torturing them into false confessions. Following their arrest, the rapes and murders stop for the second time.

1996–present. Members of *Los Rebeldes* fight legal battles with the authorities over their arrest. Some are released, none have yet been put on trial for the crimes of which they are accused, although the authorities are confident they have sufficient evidence to secure convictions, including bite-marks on the bodies of some of the victims that match the teeth of *El Diablo*.

Autumn, 1997. Victor Moreno Rivera, an American citizen living in El Paso, Texas, and with convictions for drug trafficking, visits the Juárez *CeReSo* to see a friend being held there. He also, the police later allege, meets Sharif for the first time and establishes a friendship with him.

Early 1998. The bodies of raped and murdered young women start appearing again in the desert around Juárez. The city is gripped by renewed terror and the hunt for the criminals becomes increasingly politicised.

18 February 1999. A fifteen-year-old girl later identified only as Susana is raped and assaulted by a man called Jesús Manuel Guardado Márquez, alias *El Dracula* or *El Tolteca*. Too frightened to report the attack to the police at the time, she will later come forward when Márquez appears in the media accused of a similar attack on another young girl.

3 March 1999. Sharif is finally put on trial for the murder of Elizabeth Castro García, is found guilty, and is sentenced to thirty years' imprisonment. This is the maximum possible sentence for murder under Mexican law, which does not possess the death penalty.

18 March 1999. A fourteen-year-old girl later identified only as Nancy stumbles bleeding and weeping into a stranger's home in the desert around southern Juárez. She is taken to the police and tells them that she has been raped and half-strangled by the driver of one of the *maquiladora* buses. He had abducted her when she became the final passenger on the bus taking her home from the *maquiladora* where she has been working for the past three weeks, after passing herself off as a seventeen-year-old with borrowed identification. The bus driver is identified as Jesús Manuel Guardado Márquez, alias *El Dracula* or *El Tolteca*. Unaware as yet of his attack on Susana, the police nevertheless discover he has a previous conviction for sexual assault, but when they set out to arrest him he has already fled from Juárez with his pregnant wife.

March 1999. In hiding in a town called Gómez Palacio, Durango state, a few hundred kilometres south of Juárez, *El Tolteca* attacks his wife and is reported by his sister to the police, who arrest him and, Márquez later alleges, assault him. He is returned to Juárez, where he later alleges he is assaulted by police again. He makes a confession implicating four other men in the rape and murder of *maquiladora* workers: Augustín Toribio Castillo, *El Kiani*, José Gaspar Ceballos Chavez, *El Gaspy*, Victor Moreno Rivera, *El Narco*, and Bernardo Hernando Fernández, *El Samber*. The five men, all of whom worked as bus drivers for the *maquiladora* companies, are nicknamed *Los Choferes*, The Drivers, by the media, and the police claim they have all confessed to being part of another paid conspiracy organised by Sharif from behind bars. Using Moreno as his contact, Sharif has been paying them to rape and murder two young women a month in another attempt to establish his innocence of the first series of crimes. While not maintaining his innocence, Márquez accuses the police of assault; the other four now maintain their innocence and accuse the police of torturing false confessions out of them. Susana has now come forward to report Márquez's rape of her in February. Following the arrest of *Los Choferes*, the rapes and murders in Juárez have stopped for the third time.

March 1999. A scandal erupts in the Juárez media when, as part of the investigations into the alleged conspiracy between Sharif and *Los Choferes*, it is discovered that Sharif is enjoying extraordinary privileges in the Juárez *CeReSo*, including use of a cell-phone on which he has been making regular unsupervised calls to the outside world in pursuit of his claims of innocence. Links are established between Sharif and an American currency-forger called Newton van Drunen, whom he had befriended in the *CeReSo* and who is now serving a sentence in Chicago. Police allege that van Drunen has been sending money to Sharif with which he paid *Los Choferes* to take part in the conspiracy of rape and murder.

April 1999. Seemingly as a direct result of media pressure, the director of the *CeReSo* in Juárez is dismissed and Sharif is moved from Juárez to a maximum security cell in Chihuahua, the capital of Chihuahua state, where, at the time of writing, he remains.

1999–present. The legal and political echoes of this extraordinary series of rapes and murders, charges and counter-charges, continue to reverberate through México and the United States, and include persistent allegations that Sharif had influential friends in Mexican politics and the Mexican judiciary.

1: Slaughter

Matanza f. (1) Acción de matar a una o varias personas. (2) Exterminio, hecatombe.

Slaughter: (1) The action of killing one or more persons. (2) Extermination, great sacrifice.

Count to ten. Say each number slowly, carefully: one, two, three, four, five, six, seven, eight, nine, ten. Then do it again, in Spanish: uno, dos, tres, cuatro, cinco, seis, siete, ocho, nueve, diez.

And again, in Nahuatl (the main Amerindian language spoken in present-day México): cë, öme, ëyi, nähui, mäcuïlli, chicuacë, chicöme, chicuëyi, chiucnähui, ma'tlactli.

Then do all of that – English, Spanish, Nahuatl – five more times.

And each number of the one hundred and eighty will be a destroyed life. The life of a young woman in the Mexican border city of Juárez during the final decade of the twentieth century. A young woman murdered. Often raped. Sometimes tortured or mutilated. Dumped in the nearby desert, or a gutter or alleyway in the city itself. Dozens more young women are missing, presumed raped and murdered in the same way and by the same men.

asesinar v. t. Matar alevosamente

The Spanish word for murder is *asesino*, related to the English 'assassin'. Related too, some say, to the Arabic

1

hašiiš – hashish. The story goes that a fanatical Islamic sect of medieval Syria used the drug to reward and enslave its adherents, sending them forth from its remote mountain fastness to slay, eager to earn the right to return and suck the heavy scent of *hašiiš* into their lungs again.

The inhabitants of Juárez know heavy scents too. The metallic tangs and stinks of industrial pollution from the foreign-owned *maquiladora* factories. Flavoured dusts and grits borne in on the wind from the rubbish-strewn suburbs and the outlying desert. Rotting food and animal carcasses in the city's dumps. The algal reek of the polluted *Río Bravo* – 'The Rio Grande' in English. And, sometimes, cheap perfume mingled with sweat and blood and semen. The heavy scents of a young woman's corpse lying in a gutter or alleyway.

Blood

Sangre f. Líquido rojo que circula por las venas y las arterias de los vertebrados.

Blood: A red liquid that circulates through the veins and arteries of vertebrates.

'*Festinant ut effundant sanguinem innocentem.*' ('They make haste to shed innocent blood.') (Isaiah, lix, 7)

Why?

In Spanish there are two ways of saying it: '*¿Por qué?*' and '*¿Para qué?*'. '*¿Por qué?*' means 'What causes?'. '*¿Para qué?*' means 'What intentions?'.

Crossing to Kill will try to answer both questions. Why have more than one hundred and eighty young Mexican women been raped and murdered over the past decade? Why are dozens more missing? Why has this taken place in one city on the Mexican–American border?

¿Por qué? Imagine a young woman writhing on desert sand with a trident buried in her guts. One prong is Mexican history. One is Mexican Catholicism. One is Mexican politics.

2

History

Historia f. (1) Desarrollo de la vida de la humanidad. (2) Narración verdadera y ordenada de los acontecimientos pasados y las cosas memorables de la actividad humana.

History: (1) Unfolding of the life of humanity. (2) Faithful and ordered narration of past events and memorable happenings in human activity.

México is an ancient land. Its very name comes from an alternative term for the Aztecs in Nahuatl, and its present-day boundaries enclose the territories of all the familiar kingdoms and empires of pre-Columbian history: the Aztecs, the Mayas, the Olmecs, the Toltecs; and most of the unfamiliar ones: the Zapotecs, the Totonacs, the Teotihuacans, the Mixtecs. It is impossible to find definite divisions between these peoples and their languages and cultures: borrowings and mutual influences were innumerable and frequent – particularly in religion. Gods like Quetzalcoatl, Huitzilopochtli, and Tezcatlipoca were known all over the region under varying names, all of them tongue-twisting, no doubt, in a Western mouth. The meanings of these names are no less mind-twisting in a Western head: 'The Feathered Serpent', 'The Lefthand Hummingbird', 'The Smoking Mirror'.

Such surrealism and psychedelia are familiar in Western art and popular music, and may have had the same origin in pre-Columbian Meso-America: the use of mind-altering chemicals. Another shared element of Meso-American religion was (and is) the ritual consumption of psychoactive fungi and herbs, often by the inhalation of their fumes or smoke. Modern botany commemorates the practice in the scientific names bestowed on some of them: amongst the members of the famously (and infamously) psychoactive mushroom genus *Psilocybe* are *Psilocybe mexicana* – Mexican psilocybe, and *Psilocybe aztecorum* – Psilocybe of the Aztecs (*The Encyclopedia of Psychoactive Drugs: Mushrooms: Psychoactive Fungi*, Peter E. Furst, Burke

Publishing, 1988). But the most famous shared element of Meso-American religion was, of course, human sacrifice:

> During the second ritual month of the Aztec year, *Tlacaxipehualiztli* – 'Flaying of Men' – the priests killed human victims by removing their hearts. They flayed the bodies and put on the skins, which were dyed yellow and called *teocuitlaquemitl* – 'golden clothes'. Other victims were fastened to a frame and put to death with arrows. Their blood dripping down was believed to symbolise the fertile spring rains. (*Encyclopedia Britannica*, entry for '*Xipe Totec*' – Nahuatl for 'Our Lord the Flayed One', under 'Aztec Religion'.)

Such deities and their thirst for blood were not forgotten after the Spanish conquest. On the contrary, some were incorporated into the saintly hierarchies of the new religion imposed on the conquered peoples, and the Mayan rain and compass god Chac, for example, lent attributes to Christian saints and took up the Spanish-imported innovation of horse-riding. Another Spanish-imported innovation was an expansion of the ideology and iconography of human sacrifice. Pre-Columbian religion overwhelmingly concentrated on the death and torture of men. The Spanish conquest would change all that.

Religion

Religión f. Conjunto de creencias o dogmas acerca de la divinidad: religión cristiana.

Religion. Collection of beliefs or dogmas related to God or gods: *the Christian religion.*

The *conquistadores* brought another death cult to México. It was called the Roman Catholic Church. Her greatest antagonist, Protestantism, was being born at exactly the same time as the Aztec empire was dying – Luther was excommunicated and his beliefs outlawed in 1521, halfway through the Spanish conquest of México – and she was fighting back on battlefields both of the sword and of the mind. She consciously increased the splendour and appeal of her rituals and architecture, and the new art and sculpture she commissioned began to re-emphasise one of the most ancient and powerful of all psychological archetypes – the violent and painful death of beautiful young women:

St Agatha; represented in Christian art with a pair of shears, and holding in her hand a salver, on which her breasts are placed. The reference is to her martyrdom, when her breasts were cut off by a pair of shears.

St Catharine; a virgin of royal descent in Alexandria, who publicly confessed the Christian faith at a sacrificial feast held by the Emperor Maximinus, for which confession she was put to death by torture by means of a wheel like that of a chaff-cutter.

St Lucy; it is said that a nobleman wanted to marry her for the beauty of her eyes; so she tore them out and gave them to him saying, 'Now let me live to God'. The story says that her eyesight was restored; but her rejected lover accused her of faith in Christ, and she was martyred by a sword thrust into her neck. (All short hagiographies adapted from *Brewer's Dictionary of Phrase and Fable*, E. Cobham Brewer, 1894.)

In Catholic art these virgin-martyrs are represented at the height of their beauty and sexual attractiveness: as slender, long-haired teenaged girls. Like the victims of Juárez:

Todas las mujeres eran muy jóvenes, esbeltas, de larga y osčura cabellera. All the women were very young, slender, with long, dark hair. ('*En Ciudad Juárez Capturaron a los Asesinos de 17 Jóvenes Mujeres*' –

5

'The Murderers of 17 Young Women are arrested in Juárez', Adriana Candia, *El Diario De Juárez*)

The power of both sets of deaths derives, I believe, from the waste it represents: fertile young women are wantonly sacrificed to nourish, on the one hand, the patriarchal religion of a male trinity, and, on the other, the pleasure of a serial-killer, or serial-killers. *Sanguis martyrum semen ecclesiæ*: the blood of martyrs is the seed of the church. And the female workers of Juárez may have had to bleed for the masters of the *maquiladoras*, the foreign-owned factories, in order to bleed for the master, or masters, of the desert. They may have had to prove that they were not pregnant; that they were still fertile:

> Workers at one plant complain of a company rule requiring new female hires to present bloody tampons for three consecutive months. (Charles Bowden, 'While You Were Sleeping'.)

But even more prominent amongst the female arche-types of Catholicism than the bleeding virgin-martyrs is, of course, another young woman. Alongside the *Beatas Lucía y Agata y Catalina*, roasted or pierced, beheaded or sliced, is the *Beata Virgen María*, the Blessed Virgin Mary, very often represented as a slender, long-haired teenaged girl presenting her left nipple to the lips of the infant Messiah:

> In what may be a 'signature' of the killer, the shoes of at least one of the recent victims were placed neatly beside her body, similar to that of four victims last year. Also, the left breast of at least one was mutilated, similar to some of the earlier cases. (SIX NEW SLAYINGS REVEAL THAT KILLER STILL ON THE LOOSE, Mark Smith, *Houston Chronicle*, 30 March 1996)

In Christian doctrine the *Virgo Maria*, the Virgin Mary, later becomes the *Mater Dolorosa*, the Agonised Mother, mind racked and twisted by grief as she weeps over the bruised and blood-encrusted corpse of her grown-up child.

This beauty of female pain and suffering in God's sight has been a constant theme of Catholic teaching, harmonising smoothly with another theme: the beauty of poverty and hard work for one's divinely appointed masters. So well was this doctrine enforced on the native inhabitants of México that the Spanish word *peón*, meaning 'peasant', was taken into English first for an enforced labourer in the southern states of America and then as a generic term for 'any very poor person'. (*Collins Concise Dictionary Plus*). These twin Christian virtues of suffering and poverty also fit very well today with the intentions of México's secular businessmen and politicians and their counterparts in the United States.

Politics

Maquiladora f. Méx. Planta que ejecuta, para una empresa más importante, una de las operaciones del proceso de fabricación de un producto.

Maquiladora. (Mexican Spanish.) A factory that carries out one of the operations in the manufacture of a product for a larger company.

In Spanish a *maquiladora*, with one 'l', is a Mexican factory producing goods for an overseas firm; a *maquilladora*, with two 'l's, is a woman who applies make-up to herself. The two lie side by side in a Spanish dictionary, and come together in reality every working day in Juárez, most obviously when the white buses provided by foreign firms begin to drop off their passengers after work:

Hundreds of those who descend are waiflike teenage girls, wearing bright red lipstick and *maquiladora* smocks. They have come in the past few months from farms and villages in every state in Mexico, some from as far away as Oaxaca or Chiapas in the far south. (WHO IS KILLING THE WOMEN OF JUAREZ?, Tim Madigan, *Fort Worth Star-Telegram*, 16 March 1999)

In 1980, the population of Juárez was 567,000; in 1999, it is estimated at two million, and rising fast. Such growth in an organ of the human body would be regarded as cancerous, and cancerous Juárez certainly is, in another sense:

There's a whole *maquiladora* corridor along the border, with incredible levels of lead in the water, high levels of pollution and toxic waste, and workers working for five dollars a day. (David Barsamian, *Keeping the Rabble in Line: Interviews with Noam Chomsky*, p. 43, words of David Barsamian)

Juárez is perhaps the paradigm of a Mexican border city, separated by the width of the Río Bravo and a heavily guarded bridge and security fences from El Paso, Texas (population 425,000 in 1980; 583,000 in 1999). Juárez is so close to the fabled luxury and wealth of North America – and yet so far. American laws end at the border, and that is why American companies have been pouring across it, eager to take advantage of cheap Mexican labour and lax Mexican laws on pollution and industrial relations. Construction of *maquiladoras* in Juárez has matched the growth in population: there are now said to be three hundred in the city.

Maquiladoras need *obreras* – workers, particularly women. Young women, with nimble fingers, undimmed eyes, and empty purses. For these are the ones who will be prepared to put up with the long hours and harsh conditions of employment. Who will regard the chance to shower at work as a luxury. Who will travel thousands of kilometres and live in slums reeking with sewage for the *chance* of work, let alone its reality. *A quien dan, no escoge*. Beggars cannot be choosers.

And beggars cannot, in México, be other than Amerindian or *mestizo*, that is, of mixed Amerindian and European stock. It could hardly be otherwise, for the overwhelming majority of the population are of this origin – perhaps ninety-seven per cent, according to one estimate (*Encyclopedia Britannica*, entry for 'Mexico').

So it is that the female workers of the *maquiladoras* of Juárez are Amerindian or *mestiza*, and so it is that the rapes and murders of some of them begin to resonate powerfully with a long-standing erotic tradition of Western popular culture: the dark-haired Amerindian beauty in a world of violence and upheaval.

Disney's 1995 movie *Pocahontas* demonstrates the power of the tradition but offers a prettified and saccharine version of it. A much harsher, and specifically Mexican, version demonstrates also the age of the tradition: H. Rider Haggard's *Montezuma's Daughter* (1892) contains a description of a beautiful Mexican princess being stripped naked and strapped to a sacrificial altar with the white man she loves:

> Turning to Otomie I began to bid her farewell in a clear voice, when to my amazement I saw that as I had been served so she was being served, for her splendid robes were torn off her and she stood before me arrayed in nothing but her beauty, her flowing hair, and a broidered cotton smock.
>
> 'Do not wonder, Teule [white man],' she said in a low voice, answering the question my tongue refused to frame, 'I am your wife and yonder [on the altar of sacrifice] is our marriage bed, the first and last.

Though you do not love me, today I die your death and at your side, as I have the right to do. I could not save you, Teule, but at least I can die with you.' (Chapter xxi)

But Rider Haggard's book stands at the beginning of the tradition, which would flourish more rankly in the following century, bearing such mottled, strongly flavoured fruit as:

She went for him with her hands and mouth right away. She cupped his heavy sack in her hands and slid his hard manhood into her mouth slowly, eyes open and watching it disappear inch by inch. When she had as much in her mouth as she could take, she closed her eyes and slid one hand to the base of his shaft, holding it there while she sucked on it eagerly.

He doubted she had learned this in an Indian camp, and surmised that she had been with a few white men before in her twenty-odd years.

'She' being – with long hair 'black as a raven's wing' – the Amerindian girl Katy Little Flower of J.R. Roberts' *The Bounty Women* (1984), the thirty-fifth book in the porn-western *Gunsmith* series. But even as it bore such mottled fruit, the tradition was setting gnarled underground tubers, one of which is unearthed by the American feminist Andrea Dworkin in her book *Letters from a Warzone*, (Martin Secker and Warburg, London, 1988), where she describes a clandestinely distributed 1980s computer game whose object was the capture and rape of Amerindian women.

Such elements of the tradition, growing in underground darkness or overground sunlight, have undoubtedly helped to nourish the interest shown by the American media in the crimes committed in Juárez, which combine all the most unsettling obsessions of American popular culture: sex, race, money . . . and death.

¿*Para qué*?

Sadismo m. Placer perverso que se experimenta ante el sufrimiento de otra persona.
Sadism. Perverse pleasure felt at the suffering of another person.

Muerte y contribuciones. Death and taxes. They are, it is said, always with us. *Violación tambien*. So is rape. Every culture recognises it and almost all, ostensibly at least, condemn it under some circumstances. But some women – prostitutes and the very poor – lack the right to deny their bodies, and all women are vulnerable. But why do men rape? Why are women raped?

There is almost certainly no single, simple answer, and any analysis that offers one must fall by that very fact. But just as there is murder and serial murder, so there is rape and serial rape. Some men rape once, and never again, others rape once, and then twice, and then go on raping until they die. Or are caught and jailed. And then, in prison, they may themselves be the targets of rape.

Research has shown that for some rapists, it is the *suffering* of the victim, not the sex of the victim, that is the trigger of arousal.

See an experiment described in H.J. Eysenck and D.K.B. Nias' *Sex, Violence and the Media*, Maurice Temple Smith, London, 1978, in which imprisoned rapists were aroused by suffering, irrespective of sex, and not by consensual sex. This group will have a preferred sex to target, but in its absence they will turn with almost equal readiness to the other. Just so long as there is suffering in the sexual act. Screams. Tears. Bleeding. This is where rape becomes a blood-red amalgam with sadism. The criminal – or criminals – of Juárez add a third ingredient: death. They rape, and then kill. And this is a riddle. Sex

11

was designed to preserve life, not to end it. How does the sexual instinct become so corrupted inside the mind of a criminal that he can take pleasure in the suffering and death of a sexual partner?

This is the riddle of necro-sadism. And perhaps the answer lies, partly, in overcrowding. In *caging*. When animals – mice, rats, monkeys – are forced together in overcrowded cages, their normal instincts become corrupted or disappear entirely. Females eat their young. Strong individuals torment and even kill the weak. Males discard the rituals of mating and force themselves on unwilling partners. Translate these corruptions of natural instinct into human terms and we have – what? We have these things: infanticide; murder; rape.

Juárez is like a cage. Two million human beings are crowded together on a few square kilometres of land. Food, water, and shelter are scarce and must be competed for. There is a struggle for survival that corrupts and then, in some, destroys the instincts we share with the animals, leaving finally only the most powerful one, the most deeply rooted: the instinct of self-preservation. The instinct to preserve and to *gratify* the self. To seek pleasure. And if you can find pleasure in the destruction of another of those individuals who compete with you for survival, all the better. *Matar dos parajos de un tiro*. Kill two birds with one stone.

And in Spanish just as in English, 'bird' can carry two meanings: feathered biped, and female human being. *Pajara* is a term of abuse for a woman – meaning a tart, a slag, a slut. It is a word used by *machistas*, adherents of *machismo*. Like *péon*, *machismo* is a word used in English, and like *péon*, it came into English from the Spanish of México: '*machismo m. Comportamiento del hombre que se cree superior a la mujer.*'

Which means: 'behaviour of the man who believes himself superior to women'. In Spanish, 'to believe' is *creer*, one letter away from *crear*, 'to create'. And the creed of creation is, of course, that man was created first, that woman was created after him and *from* him. Man is superior to woman by Holy Writ. Woman is inferior to man. This is the teaching of Catholicism, which mingles with and reinforces the *machismo* of México until, in a hot, airless atmosphere of overcrowding and struggle for survival, the mixture ferments and turns sour. Juárez is a poisonous laboratory of the soul where acids are mixed in male hearts and then poured out – seething, steaming, flesh-destroying – on female bodies and lives.

2: Death

Muerte f. Cesación completa de la vida.
Death: Complete cessation of life.

'Society is more interested in a death than in a life.' (Dennis Nilsen, as reported in Brian Masters' *Killing for Company*, p. 183, 1995, Arrow Books)

July dusk in the desert outside Juárez. It is intensely quiet but there is movement, the nocturnal shift of macro- and microfauna taking over from the diurnal. Scorpio is rising on the western horizon. A meteor scratches a brief red line into the face of the zenith, and as though this were a signal a sound begins to bleed into the silence. The sound of an engine. It gets louder quickly, swelling in time with a splash of yellow light in the west that bleaches out Scorpio. The engine noise and the yellow light are coming from a pick-up bumping its way along a little-used road. The movement in the desert has stopped, broken like the silence. Everything is waiting. Music mingles with the engine noise now – fast, up-beat *norteña* from a local station (*norteña* is a form of contemporary folk music characteristic of northern México). When the pick-up stops and the engine is switched off the music carries on, fanning out into the silence and stillness. In the time it has taken for the pick-up to drive out here and stop, dusk has turned into night.

Someone gets out of the driver's seat of the pick-up, leaving the door open. It is a man, dressed in jeans and open-necked shirt. Thick-set, medium height. He walks to the rear of the pick-up and takes down the backboard, tugs a heavy tarpaulin and layers of cloth off a pale heap of something and drags it out. It falls heavily to the desert floor and lies there. The man walks back to the driver's seat, gets in, closes the door, starts the engine up. His arm is hanging out of the window now, banging the door in time to the music as he turns the pick-up and drives back the way he came, hardly bothering to avoid the heap of pale something he left lying on the sand.

It is a naked corpse. A woman in her late teens or early twenties, slender, long hair forming a darker pool of shadow around her head as the headlights of the pick-up pass disinterestedly over her. As the pick-up gets further away Scorpio begins to shine again through the diminishing yellow splash of its headlights, contributing in time to the starshine that just allows her face to be seen. It is swollen, darker than her body, staring up into the sky with unnaturally protuberant eyes. She has been strangled (*complete fracture of the hyoid*, a pathologist might write if her body is discovered in time) and raped (*severe bruising of the labia majora et minora; laceration of the fourchette*). Her legs fell apart as she was dumped and the starshine is glistening on something wet between them. Blood (*O rhesus negative*) and semen (*non-secretor*). Her breasts are gazing blindly up into the sky too (*multiple bruising and scratches*) with dark, blood-encrusted nipples (*base of left mammilla partly bitten through*).

Free of the tarpaulin and cloth she is starting to cool, her bruised and cut skin starting the drop to ambient temperature. There is movement in the desert again. Small eyes and nostrils, smaller antennae, are examining her, interpreting her, dismissing her. Barely 30 m off and 5 m up, however, there are eyes and nostrils that would be very interested in her indeed, only they are switched off for the night. The shapes of their owners can be seen (*Coragyps atratus*, to an ornithologist), hunched against the star-field of Libra atop the blunter, taller shapes of cactus (*Pachycereus pringlei*, to a botanist).

A snake (*Crotalus atrox*) swims by across the sand, scales whispering on the harshness of its grains. The infrared sensors in its head-pits pick out her limbs and torso against the fading background of solar heat and it pauses a second, contemplating a final meal, before realising that the heat-shapes are parts of a larger whole, too large to eat, and dead anyway. It glides on its way, heading for its hole. A few minutes later a scorpion (*Buthus mexicanus*), attracted too by the lingering traces of heat in her skin, climbs atop her right foot. It pauses, seeming to salute its astrological namesake with raised claws, discovers similarly that she is dead, and climbs off.

Then she is left alone beneath the stars. Scorpio reaches its zenith and begins the long fall into the west. Hours pass. The movement increases around her, the nocturnal shift of fauna heading for their holes and lairs, the first representatives of the diurnal shift emerging from theirs. The sky begins to pale in the east. The dark shapes of the *Coragyps atratus* begin to move, heads shifting and peering dimly around them. In another half an hour they will have seen her. It is dusk again, almost exactly twelve hours after she was dumped. Her skin is at ambient temperature now and she is invisible to snakes and scorpions until the sun rises fully. Dusk gives way to twilight, twilight to dawn. The shapes atop the *Pachycereus pringlei* have seen her. They shuffle from foot to foot then take to the air, flapping their wings a few times before relaxing, legs hanging, into the long glide that will land them within easy waddling and hopping distance of her. What was it they were called again? *Coragyps atratus*. Black vultures.

3: Life

Vida f. Conjunto de los fenómenos que concurren al desarrollo y la conservacion de los seres orgánicos.

Life. The set of phenomena that underlie the development and preservation of organic beings.

'The Nightmare *Life-in-Death* was she . . .' [*The Rime of the Ancient Mariner*, Samuel Taylor Coleridge (1772–1834)]

She had been conceived seventeen years and eighty-six days before on 3 July 1981 in a small town outside Coatzacoalcos in Vera Cruz, a province in south-eastern México. Her parents were newly married, her father working as a fisherman on the Gulf of México, often absent for weeks at a time, her mother as a loom-tender in an American-owned textiles factory. She was born on 14 March 1982, a little prematurely. Her mother was back at work four days later, and had difficulty getting time off to attend the christening, where the new-born girl-child was given the names Elena Lidia Matilda Arriaga: Elena for her paternal grandmother, Lidia for her mother's favourite aunt, Matilda for her natal saint.

She was a quiet baby, large-eyed, watchful, and rarely complaining, even at the occasional hunger she experienced when money was shorter than usual. Her mother left her during work hours at the home of a great-aunt, a pious, superstitious woman prone to bouts of drinking and tears, but mostly conscientious in her childminding at other times. The aunt sometimes wondered, amusing the child with a swinging rosary over the cradle, whether this latest of her grandnieces would die quite soon – for she had lost three of her own children, and they had all been quiet and easy to manage, sliding quickly down the dark slopes of disease and malnutrition towards death.

But Elena did not die. Not then. She remained quiet, learning to talk early but rarely using the words she gathered with feminine facility from the lips and tongues of those around her. Another child was born to her parents at the end of the same year, a boy, Hernando, and she seemed content to stay in the shadow cast over her by his noisy, demanding exuberance. By the age of three, she was helping her mother with the care of her younger brother and of the two sisters, María-José, and Conchita, who had been born after him (a further child, another boy, had died in a local epidemic of *sarampión* – measles). Shortly after her fourth birthday, her mother died in a bus crash and her father had to migrate north for work, leaving his four motherless children in the care of the great-aunt. After a year, money stopped arriving from the north, and they never heard from him again, nor ever learned what had happened to him.

She was six before she first attended school, quick to learn, mostly unnoticed by the teachers, but always there to be called upon to teach or comfort a younger child in difficulty. She was often absent, increasingly so during her second and third years, but the school knew of the circumstances at home, with her great-aunt sliding finally into full-blown alcoholism, and no comments were made. Despite her absences she had no difficulties with the work and had she been from a wealthier family she would have been marked already for *universidad* and a career, perhaps, as a bilingual secretary in México City or even Miami or Los Angeles, the zenith of ambition for a peasant girl from a poor region of a poor country.

But the prospect was never mentioned to her, because of course it was almost impossible, and the teachers judged it better to say nothing. They had seen many like her come and go, a few more brilliant, and knew her absences would increase and lengthen until finally she would, unofficially, have left school for good and people would start to forget the thin, quiet girl in clean but shabby clothes who sat on the left of the class, in the sunshine. Once, when she had impressed a rare government inspector with a quick answer to a question, her teacher made a note to give her advice, even offer her help with finding tuition in English, the golden key to advancement, but she was absent the next day, and the next, and the next, and every day after that. She had, unofficially, left school, aged thirteen-and-a-half, and people started to forget the thin, quiet girl in clean but shabby clothes who sat on the left of the class, in the sunshine.

She had left because she had found a job gutting fish at one of the canning firms by the harbour. She had lied about her age, and the man who hired her knew she had lied, but young workers would work harder for less and he was happy to take her on. The job was dirty – stinking – and the smock she wore turned stiff with fish-blood and scales and the sinews and muscles in her wrists and fingers sang with agony for an hour after she finished in the evening. But she needed the money.

For by then her great-aunt was dying in a free hospital run by the Church, and her brother and two sisters were at school. One, Conchita, was doing almost as well as her eldest sister before her, and the hopes of the motherless, fatherless family were centred on her. Hernando, nearing thirteen, slow but strong, wanted to leave school and find work too, but Elena was trying to persuade him to stay on a couple more years, fearful that with money of his own he would fall into drugs, or glue-sniffing. He did not. He did not have time. Like his mother, he was killed in a crash, travelling in a car with friends, late at night. The car had been stolen, but the police made no trouble, for it had been too burnt and twisted by the crash to be recognisable to them or its owner.

In the year after the crash, aged fourteen-and-a-half, Elena managed to find a better job in the warehouse of a *supermercado*, a supermarket. After a week or two she was initiated by older workers into the pilfering that had gone on there for years. She was reluctant, and would only take food, but it helped save a little money for birthdays and for Conchita and her school books. The job lasted two years and then she was sacked with half the rest of the warehouse staff when a new manager arrived and decided on a show of zeal and honesty before reorganising the theft on a more systematic and profitable scale.

Five years into NAFTA – The North American Free Trade Agreement, much criticised in México for lowering wages and destroying jobs – work was hard to find in Vera Cruz, and she had two months of unemployment before she decided to leave the province and travel north to find a job in the *maquiladora* corridor. She was not sure at first which city to try, but she still remembered her mother telling her about the revolutions in the nineteenth century, and the role played in them by Benito Juárez, so she chose the city named after him (she rarely had the money or the time to buy newspapers or watch the *televisión*, so she did not know that Juárez was becoming famous for another reason than its revolutionary namesake). She had to borrow money for the trip and though she found a job almost at once on her arrival in Ciudad Juárez, her first month's wages went on paying off the debt. Then she was able to start sending money directly to Conchita and María, living on as little as possible herself and trying to resist the demands of the new friends she had made that she stop thinking eternally of others and enjoy herself a little. One Tuesday she won something on a twenty-five-peso lottery ticket and went out with her friends to enjoy herself a little.

She was not at work the next day, and the next, and the next, or on any day after that. The cheques stopped arriving in the small town outside Coatzacoalcos, Vera Cruz province, south-eastern México. María and Conchita never heard from her again, nor ever learned what had happened to her. Only the man in the pick-up, and the black vultures, ever knew that.

4: Work

Trabajo m. (1) Ocupación retribuida. En economía política, uno de los factores de la producción. (2) Fenómenos que se producen en una sustancia y cambian su naturaleza o su forma: trabajo de decomposición.

Work. (1) Paid occupation. In political economy, one of the factors of production. (2) Phenomena that are produced in a substance and change its nature or form: *the work of decomposition.*

'Facito aliquid operis, ut semper te diabolus inveniat occupatum'. 'Keep working at something, that the devil might always find thee occupied.' [St Jerome (?347–?420 AD)]

The Latin word for enjoyment or leisure is *otium*, and the opposite of enjoyment is *neg-otium*, business or work. This is an attitude that has lingered in the cultures founded and still influenced by the Romans: those of France and Spain, for example, where 'work' is *travaille* and *trabajo* respectively. The words have a common root, and the French is still close to the English travail, meaning 'painful or excessive labour or exertion'. All three words ultimately come from a Vulgar Latin word meaning 'to torture', *tripaliare*, from the older Latin *trepalium*, an instrument of torture constructed of *tres pali*, three stakes, to which the victim was bound for the attentions of the torturer and his instruments.

In most of the Western world, such a simile – that work is akin to torture – could only be used jocularly or with conscious hyperbole. Work is hard for most people in the West, but it does not usually shorten life and irrevocably destroy health. It can be boring, frustrating, unpleasant, stressful . . . but painful? Agonising? Not in most people's experience. Not in the West. It is often very different in the Third World, and México is part of the Third World. Work there can often be compared to torture without jocularity, without any trace of humour other than the blackest. In México work often shortens lives and destroys health. That is one of the reasons work has been created there by companies from the United States and other countries in the rich West. In México these companies need not concern themselves or their shareholders with such niceties as workers' rights, unless the workers in question are valuable to the company.

The latter is not true of those who work on assembly lines, needing only a clear eye and a steady hand, but it is of those who work to design or invent what those who work on the assembly lines will assemble. These designers and inventors need to have something special, something that – unlike clear eyes and steady hands – cannot easily be found and bought. Abdul Latif Sharif Sharif was one of those who had this special something. It had already helped him find well-paid work long before he arrived in México to work for a *maquiladora* in Ciudad Juárez. It also helped him retain the work he found when he was accused of rape and violent assaults on women:

Sharif was a scientist of inventive genius. US companies stood to make millions from his work and helped find for their problematic employee the finest legal defense available. One Midland, Texas, company hired him from prison, helped him avoid deportation to Egypt, and stood by him as evidence of his terrible nature mounted. ('MONSTER' BEATS THE SYSTEM, Tim Madigan, The *Seattle Times*, 1999)

Before then, in 1981, while living in Palm Beach, Florida, Sharif was accused of rape and assault by a young woman called Tracey, who said she had been given drugged vodka when invited by Sharif to his apartment for a party that turned out to be a *tête-à-tête*. He denied the charges:

> Jim Gambale, the owner of Cercoa Inc. and Sharif's boss, was inclined to believe him. Sharif had been fired from his last job in New Jersey. Something about a padded expense account. But no one questioned Sharif's genius in the laboratory, a chemist who, in the words of one colleague, 'could make a bomb out of Bisquick' (a biscuit mix popular in the United States). Sharif was a great guy. He was being railroaded. It was Gambale who helped Sharif find and pay for the highly regarded Palm Beach defense lawyer, Greg Scott. (*Ibid.*, The *Seattle Times*)

Sharif avoided any serious consequences from this escapade, but ended up in prison shortly afterwards as a result of a nearly identical crime, when, after moving to a new job in Gainesville, Florida, he raped and assaulted a young woman called Lisa on her first night in his apartment as a live-in housekeeper. He was sentenced to twelve years' imprisonment on 31 January 1984, but was out a little less than six years later in October 1989. He walked from prison straight into another well-paid job, this time for Benchmark Research and Technology, an oil company in Midland, Texas. Patents from this period can be found with his name on them in the archives of the US Patents Office, evidence that Sharif's expertise was earning large sums for Sharif himself, and large sums for the company he worked for.

Which, yet again, was prepared to stand by him and back him with the best lawyers when he fell foul of the law once more. The machinery of the US Immigration service had finally begun to move, for Sharif had already committed enough crimes to be deported. A deportation hearing belatedly got underway in El Paso, Texas. The judge finally ordered him deported, but his lawyers immediately appealed and Sharif was released on bail. On Hallowe'en night, 1993, he met a woman called Ann in a nightclub in his old haunt of Midland:

> He talked her into visiting his home that night, then trapped her there, raping her again and again until the sun came up. There were moments when Ann wondered whether she would live to see her children. (*Ibid.*, The *Seattle Times*)

As pointed out elsewhere, the period of Sharif's bail is likely to have been his first prolonged acquaintance with the pleasures available to a man of his tastes in Juárez, just across the Rio Grande from El Paso. Having liked what he experienced in Juárez, Sharif went into voluntary exile there when he was charged with the rape of Ann. In Juárez he took up yet another well-paid job working in a *maquiladora* for Benchmark, and started, the authorities now believe, on the career of rape and serial murder that would see him behind bars yet again, this time seemingly for good in a Mexican prison.

> But for Sharif, life in the gritty city neighboring El Paso would be more Eden than exile, at least at first. Most of the city's two million residents lived in wretched poverty, tens of thousands in cardboard shacks with no electricity or running water. Sharif's home, by comparison, was a spacious two-storey Spanish-style villa with stucco walls and tile roof. He was a brilliant chemist who joined the Juárez gentry of doctors, lawyers, architects and drug lords. (*Ibid.*, The *Seattle Times*)

But Sharif, living there at the apex of the pyramid of work, was more than willing to descend regularly to those at the base of the same pyramid. Young women were preferred for jobs at the lowest levels because, as one BBC report on the crimes put it, 'they tend to be more dextrous and less bolshy than the men'. The report then went on to give an additional reason: young women, without children, still living with their parents, want money to enjoy themselves:

After all week on the factory floor, on Friday night they dress up and go out to the discos. It's their only way to stay sane. Standing in skimpy tops, laughing together they tell you that the small amount of money they earn is for themselves to spend as they want. (Tom Carver, 'Mexico's murder town', BBC, 9 September 1999)

This pursuit of pleasure brought the *maquiladora* workers of Sharif's day into the same environment that, as we have already seen from his meeting with the rape victim Ann, Sharif habitually stalked: the nightclubs and bars of a teeming city centre. In Juárez, nightclubs and bars are most heavily concentrated, as is to be expected, in the central district, and to any present-day inhabitant of the city only three syllables have to be spoken to conjure them: *oo-gaar-té*. Ugarte:

Hundreds of rickety buses rumbled onto Ugarte around the clock, depositing thousands of naïve teenage girls with painted nails and fresh lipstick. They were part of the legion of workers in foreign-owned factories, the *maquiladoras*, girls who made three dollars a day, then stepped from their buses downtown and virtually onto the laps of men who bore them ill. ('MONSTER' BEATS THE SYSTEM, Tim Madigan, The *Seattle Times*, 1999)

26

It seems very difficult to doubt that among these men was a well-groomed, well-dressed, charismatic, charming, highly intelligent serial-killer called Abdul Latif Sharif Sharif. Sharif was as good at both his day job and his night one as a well-groomed, well-dressed, charismatic, charming, intelligent serial killer called Peter Sutcliffe had once been. When Sutcliffe took a job as a lorry-driver with a family haulage firm called Clark's near Bradford, northern England:

> Tom Clark and his son William were soon to overcome any reservations they had about taking on an inexperienced new driver. The new man was quiet and polite and kept the most perfect records they had ever seen ... Very conscientious; a pity all the drivers weren't like him. Four months later, on 5 February 1977, Sutcliffe took Irene Richardson to Soldiers (*sic*) Field, Roundhay Park, Leeds, hit her three times over the head with a hammer, and slashed and stabbed her stomach so badly her intestines spilled out. (*The Yorkshire Ripper: an in-depth study of a mass killer and his methods*, Roger Cross, p. 71, HarperCollins, 1993)

Ciudad Juárez, northern México, would soon be subject to the same bloody reign of terror in the 1990s as the towns of northern England had been in the 1970s and 1980s.

5: Juárez

Ciudad Juárez, c. de México (Chihuahua), puerto en el río Bravo.
Industrias. Comercio. Universidad. Obispado.

Juárez City, city in México (Chihuahua state), port on the Rio Grande.
Industries. University. Bishopric.

Sandwiches. Boycotts. And chihuahuas. Sandwiches are more famous than the man – an eighteenth-century English aristocrat – who gave them their name, as are boycotts. Sandwiches were named for the fourth Earl of Sandwich (1718–92), and boycotts for an Irish land agent called Captain C.C. Boycott (1832–97). And chihuahuas – although these were named not for a man but for a state. Chihuahua is the largest state in México, and sprawls across thousands of square kilometres of desert and mountain, from the borders with the American states of Texas and New México down almost as far as the Pacific coast across from the Mexican state of Baja California.

And the largest city in the largest state in México is Ciudad Juárez. Literally 'Juárez City', named in 1888 for a Mexican political hero, the rebel-leader Benito Juárez (1806–72). Previously it had been known as *El Paso del Norte*: North Pass. For Juárez has always been most famous as a place not to go to, but to go *through*: a crossing-place uniting a convenient mountain pass with a convenient ford of the Río Bravo. And when, after the Mexican–American war of 1847–8, the river became a border, splitting the region in two between a waning

28

México and a waxing America, Juárez itself was split in two: half, on the southern bank of the Bravo, remaining Mexican, half, on the northern, becoming American.

This American half still preserves part of the old, undivided city's name: El Paso. El Paso, Texas, one half-automatically completes, for the city is not particularly populous or famous. Except, perhaps, as a border-crossing, a gateway for Americans to Mexican 'food, shopping, nightlife' (*Northern México Handbook*, Joe Cummings, Moon Publications, 1998). And women. Mexican goods, and Mexican women, are exotic. And cheap:

> The whores are out, sixteen- and seventeen-year-olds. There is no way to tell if they are full-time prostitutes or factory workers making an extra buck. The peso has lost another chunk of its value in the last day or so.
>
> 'How much?' I ask.
>
> She leans into the car window and says the equivalent of fourteen dollars.
>
> 'How long?' I say.
>
> 'How long can you resist me?' she asks with a laugh. ('While You Were Sleeping', Charles Bowden, *Harper's* magazine, December 1996)

Juárez could be regarded as a kind of contact sore, a purulent wound ground out on the border by the rubbing together of American plutocracy and Mexican poverty, of American desire and Mexican desperation. Earlier in the century Tijuana, another city split in two by the post-bellum realignment of México and the United States, had been another kind of contact sore:

> In describing how Carpophorus trained the animals that had relations with women, I used Apuleius and

also the technique employed by the Mexican gentleman I met in Tia Juana (*sic*) who was making 16 mm stag films on the subject. (*Those About to Die*, Daniel Mannix, Panther, London, 1960)

For decades Mexican women have been selling their bodies and their dignity like this in northern border cities, withholding only one thing: their lives. These they will not and cannot exchange for American dollars, and so these have to be taken by force. And *can* be taken by force – and with far greater ease than those of their sisters, white or Latina, in the United States.

These facts have flowed down the gutters and conduits of culture in the United States to create a reeking sludge where American perceptions of México and Mexican women have seeded some startlingly poisonous swamp-flowers of heterosexual male fantasy:

Down in Cunt Valley where Red Rivers flow,
Where cocksuckers flourish and whoremongers grow,
There lives a young maiden that I do adore
She's my Hot Fuckin' Cocksuckin' Mexican whore.

CHORUS

Oh Lupe, Lupe, dead in her tomb,
While maggots crawl out of her decomposed womb.
But the smile on her face is a mute cry for more!
She's my Hot Fuckin' Cocksuckin' Mexican whore.

This is one of a number of songs from an unofficial rugby song website – more follow below. The date given for the song is 1980, but the song itself is, however, doubtless at least a few decades older, for the ready sexual availability of Mexican women on which it predicates its necrophiliac stanzas has long been an important component of heterosexual male American folk knowledge, and can also be found in the most famous of all obscene drinking songs in the English language, 'Eskimo Nell'.

Eskimos are, of course, Amerindians, and so are part of the white male erotic obsession with the dark female, but at the time described by the song Nell is working as a prostitute not in the north but in the south. From internal evidence, it could even be suggested that she plies her trade in Juárez, for the song's anti-heroes 'Mexican Pete' and 'Dead-eye Dick' head south to their nemesis. In the website version their journey is described like this:

> So do or dare this horny pair,
> Set forth for the Rio Grande [i.e. the Mexican–American border],
> Dead-eye Dick with his mighty ***** (*sic*)
> And Pete with his gun in his hand.

'At the height of a blazing noon', they enter a saloon-cum-brothel whose male clientele are 'dagos' and order 'forty whores', presumably also 'dago', to strip:

> Now Dead-eye Dick was breathing quick
> With lecherous snorts and grunts
> As forty ***** were bared to view
> And likewise forty *****.

> Now forty ***** and forty *****
> If you can use your wits,
> And if you're slick at arithmetic,
> Makes exactly eighty tits. (*Ibid.*, *sic omnia*.)

'Maria', a lesser-known song, makes the Mexican *mise en scène* even more explicit:

> Maria, Maria, she's got gonorrhoea,
> She gave it to me, amigo,

31

Oh my amigo,
I will visit the doctor today.

CHORUS

Ay yai, yai, yai,
Si, si senora (*sic*),
Tra la, la la, la la la la la,
Tra la, la la, la la la.

This association of *Méxicanas* – Mexican women – with
disease and corruption is reinforced even further in the
second verse when a woman called Melinda is described as
urinating from a window on to a *sombrero*, the archetypal
piece of Mexican headwear. Such songs are known as
'rugby songs' in the United Kingdom and other white
nations of its Commonwealth, and yet the two examples
given here, with many others in the canon, are clearly
imported from the United States. One can only conclude
that Mexican women have long figured in the fantasies
and sex-tourism of American men, and there is, indeed,
evidence that they have done so at least as far back as the
nineteenth century. They have, however, become even
more prominent in American fantasy and sex-tourism in
the final decade of the twentieth century, as the population
of México has been forced to unprecedented levels of
mobility in the search for work. Many thousands of
Mexican women have headed and are heading north to the
maquiladora corridor, young, naïve, alone, losing contact
with family and friends in the south, taking a succession of
short-term jobs in huge factories and assembly plants, and
so becoming ideal prey for serial killers. Certain questions
inevitably arise. How many women have disappeared who
have never even been recorded as *desconocidas* – unknown
female victims – because their bodies have never been
found? Whose bodies have never even been searched for,
because no one knew they had ever gone missing?

And was knowledge of this killing ground under construction in Juárez what brought Sharif south in the early nineties? In emigrating, after all, he could exchange an American criminal record and the vigilance of the rich, well-resourced, forensically sophisticated American police for the anonymity of a cancerously growing Mexican border city and an overburdened, under-resourced, forensically primitive police force that was unaware of his past.

If so, he was an appropriate figure to take his place in the *Comedia de Terrores*, the Comedy of Terrors, about to play itself out in Juárez under the gaze of the American media. Another aspect of the American relationship with México is its being not just a place to travel *to* but also a place to travel *from*. México is the last stage in a journey from poor, Roman Catholic Latin America to the rich, Protestant United States. But this journey is not undertaken just by people, but also by goods and animals. Goods and animals that are, like people, unwanted by the United States. As the song 'Maria' has already suggested, a constant image of México presented in the American media is that of a source of infection and contamination: the infection and contamination of drugs and of almost Biblical plagues of animals:

Natives of the upper Paraguay River floodplain where Brazil, Argentina, and Paraguay meet, red fire ants (*Solenopsis invicta*) first [appeared in the United States] in the 1930s. They soon proved to be among the insect world's fastest and fiercest colonisers . . . A mound can be up to a yard high and five feet in diameter, linked to a wider tunnel system and housing hundreds of thousands of ants . . . Children have died from multiple bites [and, in] infested areas, between thirty and sixty per cent of the population are stung each year. (*Why Things Bite Back*, Edward Tenner, p. 111, Fourth Estate, London, 1996)

'Infested areas' of the United States are mostly those that have borders with México. An even more famous Mexican emigrant to the United States is, however, a species whose arrival was anticipated with dread for more than two decades. One of the earliest examinations of the threat it posed coupled it explicitly with other famous Latin American exports:

> The banana boat *Cubahama* . . . Six a.m. on a humid August morning . . . A US Customs launch idled off the port stern, watching for any suspicious activity . . . The Customs Bureau had been tipped off that there would almost certainly be cocaine on board [but] this time the contraband would not be cocaine . . . At seven a.m. sharp, the US Customs team boarded the *Cubahama* . . . Inspector Denis Bracken jumped down inside [the hold]. Suddenly there was a scream and a loud buzzing sound . . . Bracken was waving his arms frantically and running wildly, trampling boxes of bananas . . . Captain Paul Keough, who was in charge of the search party, ran to Bracken, now lying face down in the hold . . . He turned [him] over to try mouth-to-mouth resuscitation, but drew back in horror.
>
> Bracken's face was swollen to twice its normal size and marked with huge red welts. His lips were bulbous, grotesque. As Keough opened Bracken's mouth he saw [the killers] crawling on his tongue and down his throat. They had flown into Bracken's mouth when he screamed for help. (*The Killer Bees*, Anthony Potter, p. 1, Grosset & Dunlap, New York, 1977. The cover of this book has a stark black-and-white image of . . . a wasp.)

Three Latin American exports are here combined in one narrative: bananas, cocaine, and a deadly hybrid species of

Apis mellifera that is notorious throughout the world as the 'killer bee' and that was created in Brazil by cross-breeding of native species with an aggressive import from Africa. Although fans of the late Peter Cook might find killer bees more laughable than frightening, they are in fact no joking matter for inhabitants of the regions they breed in, and would be better called not *Apis mellifera*, the 'honey-bearing bee', but *Apis letifera*, 'the death-bearing bee'.

And yet the narrative just quoted is fiction, a scene from a journalist's imagination presenting how the first citizen of the United States to die at the stingers of this new Latin American export might do so. Bananas ... Cocaine ... Killer bees ... All implicit, deliberate, designed references to the origins of the threat. Non-fiction refers to the origins of the threat not contrivedly, but contingently, and yet is even more explicit:

> After futile efforts to create Central American barrier zones, more African bees were found near Hidalgo, Texas, in October 1990. In July three years later, an eighty-two-year-old farmer, the first US casualty of the invaders, died from dozens of stings after poking the wrong beehive with a stick in an abandoned house in the border town of Rio Grande City, Texas. (*Why Things Bite Back*, Edward Tenner, p. 134, Fourth Estate, London, 1996)

'Hidalgo' ... 'Rio Grande City' ... 'Border town' ... After these references, the origin of these alien, killer bees hardly needs setting out in cold print. Texas – a Mexican name truncated and remarried to its origins in the culinary and cultural adjective 'Tex-Mex' – accounts for more than half of México's border with the United States, and there is a better than even chance that any unwanted 'invader' making its way north from Latin America will appear first in Texas, having crossed directly from México.

The association of México with death and suffering is, then, a long-standing element of American perceptions of their southern neighbour, lying eternally ready to be fanned into crackling, fuming life by new reports of some deadly aspect of Mexican life or culture, such as the crimes being committed in the border city of Juárez. And yet it is possible to question whether the reports of rape and sex murder that began to filter out of México were new to *all* the citizens of the United States.

6: Rebels

Rebelde adj. y s. Que se rebela. Que se niega a obedecer a la autoridad legitima.

Rebel(lious). Noun (and adjective). One who rebels. One who refuses to obey legitimate authority.

The word 'rebellion' has a strong taste in the mouth, sometimes sweet, sometimes bitter, for the speakers of any language, but particularly for speakers of Mexican Spanish. The very existence of México was won by rebellion, the rights of her people fought for and sustained by it, her heroes and folk myths forged and tempered by it. The taste of rebellion is sweet in Mexican mouths, and sweet in Mexican reality. Above all in the north, in the state of Chihuahua, whose hero of heroes is Francisco 'Pancho' Villa (1877?–1923), bandit, womaniser, and rebel.

Something of all this must have been in the minds of a group of youths from Juárez when they formed a gang and chose the name for it. The name they chose was *Los Rebeldes* – The Rebels. *Los que se niegan a obedecer a la autoridad legitima* – those who refuse to obey legitimate authority. But that is a definition from a Spanish dictionary in both senses: a dictionary of Spanish published in Spain. One published in México might not stress that authority was legitimate. And anyway, it is better 'to reign in hell, than serve in heav'n' (*Paradise Lost*, Milton, Book 1, line 261). Particularly when the hell you reign in is self-created, and you are not the one to suffer in it.

Juan Jorge Contreras Jurado, 'El Grande' – 'Big Guy' – was twenty-three years old when he made his declaration at 10:30 a.m. on 15 April 1996.

'El Grande' said he was a worker in a *maquiladora* and came from San Pedro de las Colonias, Coahuila state.

In his declaration, the detained man confesses to being a member of the gang of *Los Rebeldes* and gives a detailed account of his participation in the crimes committed in Lomas de Poleo, Juárez.

The following is part of his testimony that forms part of the investigation undertaken by Judge Quinto de lo Penal.

'The first Saturday in March, 1996, at three in the morning, I was inside the dance hall La Tuna, located on Ugarte Street, drinking a beer, when El Diablo – "The Devil" – and Carlos Barrientos Vidales, alias "Charly the Dancer", came in.

'A short while after, El Sinaloa, also known as "El Chapito", came in, and later José Luis Reyes came in.

'I said to El Chapito or El Sinaloa, or maybe to Carlos Armando Molina Mariscal, that I was off back home, to which he said, okay, and so we all went off in a Ford LTD Crown Victoria.

'But because Carlos Armando Molina Mariscal, who was driving, did not go in the direction of my house, I asked them why they were not taking me home.

'El Diablo told me that first they were going for money to his girlfriend's place. The only thing I knew about her was that she was the dancer in the Faustos bar but now I know that she called herself Lucy and lived in the hotel Río de Janeiro. Later when we got to the hotel, El Diablo and Charly the Dancer got out of the car and went into the hotel and came back after about ten minutes.

'I saw that Charly the Dancer was carrying Lucy in his arms and that she was tied up and gagged and because of that I got out of the car with the intention of getting away but, when he saw me doing this, El Diablo said to me, "We're going to have some fun with her and if you do not come I will sort you out."

'We drove off down Mariscal Street going from north to south, till we came to where they sell snacks for a *peso*. Maybe before we got to Ugarte Street, we came across Héctor, who has only got one leg and who I now know is called Héctor Raymundo Olivares Villalba.

'El Diablo threatens him, saying, "Get in or I will sort you out," so Héctor got into the car in the back seat, staying on the left-hand side.

'El Diablo said to El Chapita, "Go that way," meaning the Anapra side of the street. We were getting drugged up with cocaine at the time.

'El Diablo used one of his fingers to try and make Lucy take some coke, but she did not want to and pushed herself to one side, so El Diablo does not make a fuss about it and snorts the cocaine that he had on his finger.

'On the drive, El Diablo said to us, "When we get there we are going to rape her," so I asked why and El Diablo said to me not to be a coward.

'When we got there, Charly the Dancer got Lucy out and El Diablo immediately pushed him off her, like the two of them had got out of the car straight away, and then they put her on the ground, face-up.

'Charly unbuttons her pants, which were a kind of whitish tweed colour, and pulls them off her and then takes off her blouse and pulls her knickers down one of her legs.

'Lucy was half-conscious and El Diablo dropped his pants and his underpants past his knees and then got on top of Lucy, opened her legs, and then he raped her.

'Because Lucy struggled, El Diablo started to hit her with his fists until she stopped struggling, and he stayed penetrating her for about fifteen or twenty minutes.

'After El Diablo finished, Charly the Dancer and El Chapito did the same.

'After they had both finished, El Diablo said to me, "Fuck her as well, do not be an arsehole," so I dropped my pants and underpants, but I turned Lucy face-down and grabbed hold of her waist and she stayed face-down and that was how I raped her.

'El Diablo, when he saw that I had finished, came up to me and said, "Get off her, I am going to fuck her again."

'Then El Diablo started to strangle her and we all got into the car.

'El Diablo was the last to get into the car. He got behind the wheel and we asked him about Lucy, so he said to us, "She has been sorted out," so I asked him why he had done it and he told me that, "There will not be any hassle, she does not have any relatives."

'He [got out again and] stayed there to deal with Lucy's body and the rest of us went back the way we had come. We left Héctor on the corner of Mariscal and Ugarte Street and I got out at the Cathedral. I also want to say that about a year and a half before I was introduced by Sergio Armendáriz Díaz, El Diablo, to someone who he said was called George, who I went on seeing and hanging out with there sometimes. I have found out now that he is an Egyptian and is called Sharif Sharif, and about a month ago I went to visit him in the Centre of Adult Rehabilitation, better known as the *CeReSo*, and he gave me an envelope of money and told me to give it to El Diablo.

'I also want to say that I went to see George, or Sharif Sharif, because El Diablo threatened me. He said, "Go and see George and pick up a packet. If you do not do it, I will sort you and your wife out, because I know where you live. When you get to the *CeReSo* read this bit of paper and say that your name is what is on it, everything is sorted out."

'I do not remember what name I used to get into the *CeReSo*. I went there and picked up the envelope and then went to the Marimar pool hall, on Ugarte Street, where I had already arranged to meet El Diablo at five in the afternoon, and that is what happened. When I handed over the envelope of money to El Diablo, he opened it and put the money in a bag and I saw that it was in one-hundred-dollar bills, and I reckoned up that there was about four thousand dollars.

'When I gave the money to El Diablo he said, "Okay, get lost," and I went straight home to see that my family was alright.' n.b.: Some words in the original text of this and the following confession have been changed because of the coarseness of the descriptions and out of respect for the reader. The text issued by the Public Ministry was also changed for publication in a newspaper, with due regard to its content.

The member of *Los Rebeldes* known as 'El Mocho' described the murder of Rosario García Leal, whose case was the one that allowed the police to establish the identity of the suspects. Héctor Raymundo Oliveres Villalba, 'El Mocho', was born in Ciudad Juárez and at the time of his arrest was working as a singer in dance halls in the city centre. The file created by the Office of Preliminary Investigations states that he was eighteen years old at the time of his statement, but afterwards his family proved that he was a minor and he was released.

'I am a member of the gang called "The Rebels" who come together in [clubs in] the city centre, most often in Tuna, Joe's Place, Fiesta, Divers, and Gilbert's, sometimes in Alive.

'The time I am telling you about, the sixth of December, 1995, a person who I now know is called Juan Jorge Contreras Jurado, alias "El Grande", told me between nine and eleven in the evening that he had been the same day to the *CeReSo* [the detention centre in Juárez] and had a meeting with someone called Sharif by arrangement with a guard, the two of them giving the guard I do not know how much.

'Next day I was outside the Tuna club, in Ugarte Street, next to Copel [a shop], in the city-centre, it would have been sometime between eight and nine in the evening. A white car stopped there, an Oldsmobile, a four-door, with tinted windows and an antenna on the boot shaped like a boomerang or airplane, with El Grande; El Diablo, who I now know is called Sergio Armendáriz Díaz; Charly *(sic)* El Chero; Fernando 'Ferna' Rubén Guermes Aguirre; Gerardo 'El Gera' Fernández Molina; as well as someone else whose name and nickname I did not know, but I now know that he is called José Luis, on board.

'The person behind the steering wheel was José Luis, with me next to him, and next to me Gerardo or "El Flaco". In the back behind the driver was El Grande, with Charly in the middle, and El Diablo next to him.

'I also want to say that on the floor in the back of the car there was a girl who had her mouth gagged and her hands tied behind her back, so that it looked as if she was handcuffed, but she really had her hands tied with a shoe-lace, because she had the shoe-lace missing from one of her shoes, and she could not speak, she could only try to speak or shout.

'I asked El Diablo what the hell was going on and then he told me that we were only going to have a bit of a chat-up "over there", meaning Anapra [a district of Juárez].

On the drive there all the guys were snorting cocaine and after about an hour and twenty minutes' driving, Charly tried to make the girl take some, like with his forefinger and thumb he wanted to put the stuff up her nose, but the girl would not let him, so the guys were hitting her.

'José Luis went on driving without saying where, except that before there had been this fried-chicken stall and I knew the area now. When the car stopped, Gera got out and went to the boot and I do not know what he took out, because just then I went to the front of the car to urinate and the lights of the car were off, which meant the place was very dark.

'Next José Luis got out, and Grande and Charly, and then they pulled the girl to the middle of the seat and turned her face upwards and lifted her legs, and while I got out to urinate they started to take her clothes off.

'Once she was stripped they lifted her legs and José Luis held her underneath, just above her knees, and with his male member out and erect. Then he started to put his hands underneath a dark blouse she was wearing and stroked her breasts and put his member into her.

'Then José Luis spent about fifteen minutes raping her, while the rest of us told him he should stop pestering her.

'Then, once José Luis was finished, Charly came up, dropped his pants below his shins, and turned the girl over.

'That was when José Luis told me to collect her clothes. The rest went off about 7 m from the car and began to dig a hole near a mezquite bush that was there.

'Because Charly had finished raping the girl, El Diablo went over to where the bundle of clothes was and got Charly out of the way and it was Charly who buried the bundle in the hole that they had made.

'When El Diablo finished raping the girl, he and Charly got the girl down on the front-seat passenger's side of the car and that was when El Diablo said, "Let's get it over with," and between the two of them they lifted her and went off with her into the darkness about 7 m almost in the direction where the clothes had been buried.

'Then José Luis and Gerardo went after them and I saw that the girl was moving her head like she was going to pass out and then I lost sight of them, so I went after them and could get close enough to see that Charlie (*sic*) and El Diablo had put her on the ground.

'Then José Luis bent down and gave her a slap and then gave her like five punches and at the same time he was squeezing her throat and the girl was moving like she was suffocating and making a noise like she needed air, until she stopped moving.

'Then all of us started to kick her all over her body, and then Gera, Charlie, and then El Diablo started to tear at her with their hands and then they dug a hole about 60 cm wide and deep, I do not remember, but the girl fitted into it exactly.

'Then we covered her up with soil and stamped the soil down with our feet, at the same time smoothing it over.

'Then we went back to the car and from there we drove back to the city centre. We went to the wine bar El Nacional, on the corner of Ugarte and Mariscal and, as I was getting out, José Luis said to me, "Do not say anything because if you do we will sort you out the way we have already told you we would."

'I recognise the girl I have told you about in a photograph of Rosario García Leal, from the Philips *maquiladora*.'

Rebels and devils. Rebels and a 'Devil', at least. The nicknames and slang and straggling syntax of the confessions all add to their power. To their ring of truth. But are they true? No one knows. That *Los Rebeldes* were a gang of young criminals seems reasonably certain, but there are many gangs of young criminals in Juárez – in México – in the world. And some of these gangs do indeed rape and abuse women. But few of them, surely, then make a habit of strangling and burying their victims, all of this done for money paid by a convicted rapist already behind bars.

And the members of the gang have accused the police of torturing confessions out of them, and shown the marks of it. Their lawyers have also pointed out that there is little evidence against them. True, but what there is, the prosecutors retort, is very strong. One of the gang was confronted with it by a presenter from ABC, the American Broadcasting Company, during 'Silent Screams in Juárez', a *20–20* special on the Juárez murders:

John Quinones [voice-over]: Two and a half years ago, authorities rounded up what they thought was a gang of serial killers known as 'Los Rebeldes', led by this man who called himself 'El Diablo'. Police say the gang tortured seventeen women, brutally assaulting them on this concrete slab before murdering them. Several of the girls had bite marks all over their bodies. We visited El Diablo in a Juárez prison and showed him a picture of one of his alleged victims.

[On camera] Do you recognise this woman? *¿La conoces?* The police say you killed her. You raped her, tortured her.

Sergio Armendáriz, 'El Diablo': No.

John Quinones: No? Investigators say your teeth perfectly match the bite marks that were on her breast.

Sergio Armendáriz [through translator]: Those famous bite marks. They do not match.

John Quinones: Those are not your teeth?

Sergio Armendáriz: No.

John Quinones [voice-over]: But back at her forensics lab, Dr Rodríguez, the medical examiner, says these imprints, the bite marks, leave no doubt that it was 'El Diablo' who tortured at least three of the victims. Authorities say they're confident they will convict him in those murders. But what's troubling to this community is that even while 'El Diablo' has been in jail, more than fifty other women have been raped and murdered. (Transcript of 'Silent Screams in Juárez', ABC's Wednesday, January 20, 1999 transmission of *20–20*)

But is this *prueba odontológica* – 'dental proof', as Spanish puts it – unassailable evidence of Armendáriz's guilt? No, not *unassailable* evidence. México has always been notorious for official corruption, particularly in the police and judiciary, and more sophisticated forensic science must sometimes have meant nothing more than more sophisticated ways for suspects to be framed. But even on the supposition – and it seems, admittedly, a strong one – that 'El Diablo' did leave teeth-marks on the bodies of young women while he was raping them, this does not prove that he was working with a gang. Still less does it prove that he or the gang were working for Sharif Sharif, being paid by the corpse to help him establish his

innocence. The police, under pressure to stem a blood-red
tide of sex murders, may simply have decided that one
rapist would help them to seal the case against another.
Armendáriz was arrested with his confederates, the story
of Sharif's machinations from behind bars invented, and
acquiescence in it beaten into the gang.

For the simple fact remains that the arrest of *Los
Rebeldes* did not stem that blood-red tide: the murders
stopped for a time and then continued until *another* gang,
also allegedly in conspiracy with Sharif, were arrested.
Then the tide reached a high-water mark and seems, so
far, to be lapping there, rising no more. The questions,
however, continue to flow. Would the police have
invented the story of a conspiracy between Sharif and *Los
Rebeldes* when it would so easily be undermined by the
continuing murders? Perhaps, perhaps not. Perhaps the
police had picked up rumours of a conspiracy between
Sharif and an outside group, and thought, when they
arrested *Los Rebeldes*, that they had arrested this outside
group. When *Los Rebeldes* refused to confess, they were
made to confess. If so, it would be a familiar story: the
police, believing they have the guilty parties without the
evidence necessary to secure a conviction, decide to
invent the necessary evidence. Under this reading, *Los
Rebeldes* are a kind of Mexican Guildford Four or
Birmingham Six (famous cases in Britain of suspects
convicted on fabricated or badly flawed evidence), and the
police may have been just as shocked as the public when,
with all members of the conspiracy apparently behind
bars, the bodies of raped and mutilated young women
began to turn up again on the desert outskirts and the
building-lots of Juárez. Month after month after month
after month.

Until the arrest of that other gang, *Los Choferes*. The
Drivers.

Thread

Hilo m. Hebra larga y delgada que se forma retorciendo cualquier materia textil.

Thread. Long, thin fibre produced by twisting some textile material.

'Behold, *when* we come into the land, thou shalt bind this line of scarlet thread in the window which thou didst let us down by . . .' (Book of Joshua, 2, xviii)

'Scarlet thread' is a Biblical phrase from the Book of Joshua, used to describe how a 'harlot' of Jericho and her family escape the otherwise indiscriminate massacre that follows the capture of the city by the Israelites:

> And they utterly destroyed all that *was* in the city, both man and woman, young and old, and ox, and sheep, and ass, with the edge of the sword.
> But Joshua said unto the two men that had spied out the country, 'Go into the harlot's house, and bring out thence the woman, and all that she hath . . .' (6, xxi–xxii)

'Scarlet thread' is used in a context of death in the Book of Joshua, and so translates smoothly and easily to a Book of Juárez. All serial killers may be said to weave a scarlet thread into the tapestry of life, and the moment they make a final, fatal mistake may be said to be the moment when the thread begins to unravel – when it is seized, tugged, begins to come loose and reveal the interconnections and hidden patterns of the crimes.

But the crimes of Juárez seem to have revealed not one scarlet thread but at least two, perhaps three: the thread woven by Sharif himself; the thread perhaps woven by a gang of Sharif's hirelings, the young psychopaths of a street-gang called *Los Rebeldes*; and the thread far more certainly woven by another group of Sharif's hirelings, the older men of an unofficial gang christened by the media

Los Choferes, The Drivers. The moment when the last of these threads began to unravel was perhaps late on 13 March 1999 – a Saturday – when:

A fourteen-year-old female employee of the Motores Eléctricos maquila was found barely alive on a ranch near the Pemex plant in the southwest part of Cd. Juárez. The assassin fortunately did not complete his crime, leaving the young girl for dead.

Nancy, as she is known, had been severely beaten, raped and strangled, however when she lost consciousness the alleged perpetrator, Jesús Manuel Guardado Márquez, 26, a maquila bus driver, assumed she was dead and abandoned her. (*Frontera NorteSur*, April, 1999)

Guardado had a *nombre de apodo* – a nickname. Two of them, in fact. *El Tolteca*, The Toltec, and *El Dracula*, Dracula. After his arrest, which came about when, in hiding, he beat up his pregnant wife and was reported to the police by his sister, his confession led the authorities to other men and other nicknames: Augustín Toribio Castillo, José Gaspar Ceballos Chavez, Victor Moreno Rivera, Bernardo Hernando Fernández – 'El Kiani', 'El Gaspy', 'El Narco', 'El Samber' – Kiani, Gaspi, Druggie, St Bernard. Another act was about to open in the Comedy of Terrors created by Sharif in Ciudad Juárez, though, as I have suggested before, not all the players in the rest of the play were necessarily recruited from México.

7: *Sinergia*

Sharks

*Tiburón m. Nombre dado a los peces selacios de cuerpo fusiforme y
aletas pectorales grandes cuya boca, en la parte inferior de la cabeza,
tiene forma de media luna y está provista de varias filas de dientes
cortantes.*

Shark. Name given to selachian fish with streamlined bodies and large
pectoral fins whose mouths, in the lower part of the head, are
half-moon-shaped and filled with rows of cutting teeth.

About ten years ago, a survey was conducted to establish which word
had the greatest impact on the greatest number of people. Researchers
tested words like 'rape', 'death', 'murder', 'sex', 'love', 'snake', 'poison'.
To their surprise, it was the word 'shark' which aroused the public's
emotions more than any of the others. (*Great Shark Stories*, Valerie and
Ron Taylor, 1978)

Blood in the water. In the open sea it can be a death knell,
drawing sharks from great distances to participate in an
uncouth, thrashing circle-dance centred on the writhing
body of the victim – a feeding frenzy.

Translate this into the world of human beings, retaining
one of the terms: blood. Blood on the streets. In the free
media it can be a dinner-bell of income, drawing
journalists from great distances to participate in an
unseemly, squabbling circle-dance centred on the con-

torted body of the victim. Or the bodies of the victims. Particularly if the victim or victims are female.

This is what has happened in Juárez. Female blood was spilt on the streets there, and in the dust of the surrounding desert. The scent of it travelled very far, wafting south through Chihuahua state to México City and continental Latin America, north across the border to the United States and Canada, west and south across the Pacific to Australia, New Zealand and Japan, east across the Atlantic to Europe and the United Kingdom.

The following appears courtesy of the 9 September 1999 online edition of the BBC news:

> Mexico's murder town. Bodies of young girls keep turning up. Tom Carver reports from a town on the Mexico–US border where the murder rate of young women is horrifically high ... 'It was around the beginning of 1995 that the police belatedly realised that a serial killer was haunting the unlit squatter camps like Anapra that ring Juárez. The bodies of young girls kept turning up.'

But were these journalists and their tape-recorders and camera lenses all that the scent of fresh female blood brought to Juárez? For consider that journalists do not work to feed merely their own appetites for death and pain, but also the appetites of their audience. All those millions watching, listening, and reading in the United States, being told of baffled police unable to protect the young and vulnerable women of a city just across the border in México. Blood in the water. Blood in the media. Victims to be had for the taking. Would it be surprising if one or more serial-killers certainly at work in the deep south of the United States pricked up their ears and wanted to learn more? If one or more of them dug out an interstate map and idly calculated how long it would take to drive to El Paso, Texas, and the border crossing to Juárez? If one or more of them decided that it was time to take a short vacation down Mexico way?

Synergy

Synergy n. The working together of two or more drugs, muscles, etc., to produce an effect greater than the sum of their individual effects.

Jesus and Elvis are, it is said, the only human beings well enough known to everyone to be referred to by just their first names. *Aficionados* of true crime cannot quite match this with individuals, perhaps, but they can with couples. Two couples so far. Ian and Myra. Fred and Rose.

Perhaps a third couple began to be added to this infernal pantheon of anti-heroes when a bleeding woman, wearing only a 'padlocked metal collar' (Associated Press, 1999), stumbled from a mobile home in Elephant Butte, New Mexico, with a tale of three days of enforced sexual torture and bondage. Ian and Myra. Fred and Rose. David and Cindy?

In the future perhaps, but today they must be identified by their full names: David Parker Ray and Cynthia 'Cindy' Lea Hendy. Ray stares out from his police identification photo like an ageing school caretaker, with no hint of his depraved tastes in eyes lined and pouched by the passage of fifty-nine years of hitherto unremarked life. Hendy, if anything, seems even more ordinary: blonde, plump, a thirty-nine-year-old woman who seems about to slide unprotesting into middle-age, and long, slow, comfortable years of retirement: TV, conversation, European holidays, grandchildren.

The testimony of their victim – and the two others who have come forward so far – contradicts all that more than a little. More than a lot. The naked woman who escaped in the padlocked collar told the police of three days of torture during which Ray chained her to a bed and molested her with 'sexual devices', attached wires to her breasts and passed agonising jolts of electricity through her body, and bound and suspended her from the ceiling of the mobile home while he whipped her with a 'leather object'. Hendy, meanwhile, stood guard cradling a revolver and threatening to shoot the victim if she tried to escape.

Having charged Ray with 'kidnap and criminal sexual penetration' and Hendy with 'kidnap and accessory to criminal sexual penetration', the police searched the makeshift torture chamber and emerged with a *smörgåsbord* of sexual psychopathology.

Anatomy books, medical books 'and a chart depicting what appears to be methods of sexual torture and bondage' that were reportedly found in the trailer known as the toy box, along with 'photographs depicting women in various stages of bondage', a large coffinlike box and a diorama in a glass and wood case that contains 'dolls posed and painted in different positions depicting bondage and sexual sadism'. One affidavit said the coffinlike box was about seven feet long and had carpeting inside. It also had ventilation holes, 'so that a person could be secured in the box and at the same time kept alive for an extended period of time.' (*Albuquerque Tribune*)

More disturbing even than these, however, were maps of the nearby Elephant Butte Lake with 'X's marking various points along the shoreline and on the island of Kettle Top, and about one hundred videotapes. The last, of course, raises immediate echoes of a duo from a side-gallery of the Sex Criminal Hall of Fame: the American 'Vietnam veteran' Leonard Lake and, from Hong Kong, his 'accomplice' Charles Ng, who together abducted three women and kept them as their 'sex slaves' in a specially built torture chamber beneath their cabin near Wisleyville, in Calaveras County, California. The three women were murdered when their captors finally tired of them, as were the two young children abducted with their 'sex slave' mothers. (See *The Serial Killers: a study in the psychology of violence*, Colin Wilson and Donald Seaman, Virgin Publishing, London, 1990.)

As also proved true of Parker and Hendy, Lake and Ng had videotaped their torture of the women, informing one that she would 'wash for us, clean for us, fuck for us'. Lake's fantasy, revealed in a journal discovered surrounded by chains and hooks in the torture chamber, was that of a 'woman who does exactly what she is told to do and nothing else. There is no sexual problem with a submissive woman. There are no frustrations – only pleasure and contentment.' (*Ibid.*, ch. 7.)

An audio-tape discovered in Ray's mobile home has revealed the same turn of mind in this other couple. Used in the 'indoctrination' of his victims, it informed them that they were 'going to be kept naked and chained up like an animal and used and abused any way we want to' (*Albuquerque Tribune*). The voice, positively identified as Ray's by the New Mexico State Police investigator John Briscoe, then goes on to talk of using Phenobarbital and sodium pentothal on women 'to erase memories and make them susceptible to hypnosis'. There are echoes here of Jeffrey Dahmer, the 'Milwaukee Cannibal' who experimented with trepanning and injections of bleach into the brains of his victims in an attempt to create a perfectly obedient sex-zombie.

Homosexual Dahmer, however, operated alone: Ray seems to have operated not merely as half of a heterosexual couple but also, like Frederick West, as a kind of godfather of rape, sexual torture, and, it is believed, serial murder: his thirty-two-year-old daughter Glenda 'Jesse' Ray and a twenty-seven-year-old acquaintance, Dennis Roy Yancy, have been charged alongside him and Hendy; Ray *fille* with participation of her father in twelve separate counts of kidnap, sexual torture, and conspiracy; and Yancy with the murder of a twenty-two-year-old woman called Marie B. Parker, who had disappeared without trace from an Elephant Butte bar in 1997.

The investigation of Ray's activities, still in its early days, seems to be following a familiar trajectory: the fortuitous and highly fortunate escape of an intended victim; the arrest of the accused and the issuing of firm denials of wrongdoing from his quickly hired defence lawyer; the searching of the home of the accused and discovery of items suspicious in themselves and offering clues to the truly damning evidence: the graves of 'as many as fourteen people'. The police are now searching for these in the 'arroyos' – the beds, sometimes seasonally dry, of a river or stream – of Sierra County, calling upon the assistance of 'ground-penetrating radar and cadaver-sniffing dogs'.

Those familiar with the Moors Murders or the 'House of Death' at Cromwell Street, Gloucester, could provide parallels for each of the steps taken by the investigation so far, and it seems perfectly possible that 'David and Cindy' will, very early in the third millennium, join 'Ian and Myra' and 'Fred and Rose' as instantly recognisable onomastic icons of twentieth-century sex-murder. Already forensic psychologists are finding patterns in what is known so far of Ray's behaviour that point to his fitting the profile of a typical serial killer. One characteristic of the serial killer is that he will wish to revisit the graves of his victims, reliving the excitement of the crimes and feeding a ghoulish delight with a secret knowledge that only he and his accomplices possess. Ian Brady and Myra Hindley did this both literally and photographically, when Brady photographed a smiling Hindley hugging a puppy atop a child's grave dug into the turf of the bleak moors that overlook Manchester. So far Ray seems to have done it only literally: as already mentioned, an 'X' on one of the maps discovered by the police in his mobile home marks an island called Kettle Top in Elephant Butte Lake. From the windows of his mobile home, Ray only had to raise his eyes to see this island.

Even more characteristic of the serial killer is, however, a penchant for the keeping of souvenirs of the victim:

> FBI profilers believe Ray, 59, kept items from the victims, including jewellery, hair or fingernails ... The profilers say people who commit serial crimes collect such trinkets and keep them in a cache so they can relive the experiences. (DA: HENDY SAID RAY KILLED UP TO 14, *Albuquerque Tribune*)

Is it here that the crimes in Elephant Butte, New Mexico, intermesh with the crimes in Ciudad Juárez, Chihuahua? Suly Ponce, the head of the Special Investigator's Tribunal in Juárez, has drawn the media's attention to a strange feature of some of the murders discovered there so far. She has remarked of some of the victims that:

> 'They had no panties. None. They could have all their other clothes – shoes, socks, stockings, bra. But no underpants.' (THE DEATHS THAT HAUNT JUÁREZ, Mary Beth Sheridan, *Los Angeles Times*)

It seemed that a serial killer in Juárez had been collecting souvenirs of his crimes, and that he, like Ray, had a fetish about female hair:

> Victims [in Juárez] were in their teens or early 20s, slim and petite, almost always with long dark hair. (SIX NEW SLAYINGS REVEAL THAT KILLER IS STILL ON THE LOOSE, Mark Smith, *Houston Chronicle*, 1996)

But could this collector of sex-souvenirs and trichophile – hair-fetishist – in México be the same collector of sex-souvenirs and trichophile as in New Mexico? In short, could David Parker Ray have been responsible for some of the crimes in Juárez?

On geographical grounds alone, the answer must be in the affirmative. Nowhere in New Mexico is very far from Texas or the Mexican border, but Ray committed his crimes, and is said to have buried his victims, in Sierra County, in eastern New Mexico, almost on the state boundary with Texas. This put him – and Hendy – within very easy striking distance of El Paso and the crossing to Juárez: a couple of hours' comfortable driving there, a couple of hours' comfortable driving back.

And hair-fetishism and the collection of sex-souvenirs are by no means the only darkly disturbing echoes to reverberate between the accounts of the crimes in Elephant Butte and Juárez. One of the women to survive Ray's attentions, tracked down by the police through a 'distinctive swan tattoo on her right leg' that was visible on one of the videos found in Ray's home, has testified that:

> 'I remember him telling me he was into a satanic group. He said members of the group had been watching me and they wanted me as a sex toy.' (DA: HENDY SAID RAY KILLED UP TO 14, *Albuquerque Tribune*)

There are two echoes of the crimes in Juárez here. The first is the tattoo that allowed Ray's victim to be identified. One of those accused of the crimes in Juárez was similarly identified by a tattoo:

> His identifying characteristics were confirmed by the picture released by the authorities [in Chihuahua], such as two tattoos on his arms, a rose and hands

joined in prayer with an inscription that reads 'My Mother Carmen'. (*El Diario de Juárez*)

And what is the second darkly disturbing echo raised by the testimony of the swan-tattooed victim from the account of the crimes in *El Diario de Juárez*? It is this:

The motive of the crimes continues to be unclear, but various theories suggest that they are connected with a traffic in human organs, the white-slave trade, or . . .

Or '*ritos satánicas*'. Satanic rites.

8: Satan

Satanás o Satán, jefe de los demonios, espíritu del mal.

Satanas or Satan, chief of demons, spirit of evil.

ἐθεώρουν τὸν Σατανᾶν ὡς ἀστραπὴν ἐκ τοῦ οὐρανοῦ πεσόντα. 'I beheld Satan as lightning fall·from the heaven.' (The Gospel of St Luke, x, 18)

Satanism. The worship of Satan, 'chief of demons, spirit of evil'. And arch-rebel. In México, a nation forged by rebellion, that makes him a figure of special, particular power. To swear allegiance to Satan is to swear allegiance to the first and greatest of rebels, and to join in a rebellion against the Lord of the Universe. And, of course, in a rebellion against His earthly representatives: the Roman Catholic Church.

For if the true piquancy and *frisson* of Satanism is only possible in a society heavily influenced by some form of Christianity, the expression of Satanism is always conditioned by its origins in Roman Catholicism. The United States, for example, is a Protestant nation, and yet the symbol of Satanism there, as in Roman Catholic México, is the inverted crucifix, despite the fact that the crucifix – a cross, sometimes bearing the nailed, tortured body of Jesus – is not something upon which Protestantism has ever chosen to place much emphasis.

For Protestantism, another rebellion against the Roman Catholic Church, rebelled by negation and extirpation; Satanism rebelled by *inversion*. Compare two cases:

Protestant and Satanic attacks on a Christian church. During the English Civil War of the seventeenth century and the Commonwealth that followed it, extreme Protestants raided churches in search of the symbols of Roman Catholicism. Where and when they found such symbols, they destroyed them, smashing statues with hammers and axes, whitewashing religious paintings, tearing out rood-screens and altar-rails. Their strategy was *iconoclasm* – literally, the breaking of icons.

The strategy of Satanism might therefore be described as *iconomachy*, literally a war with icons. But that 'war with' bears two senses: it is a war against, and a war by means of. Satanists do not usually destroy the 'icons' of a Christian church: the crucifixes, the altar and its paraphernalia, the hymn books and missals. Instead, they corrupt them, co-opt them to an opposite end. In short, they *invert* them. Satanism is Roman Catholicism inverted – Roman Catholicism in negative. The Holy wafer is at the heart of ritual in both religions, but where Roman Catholicism honours and elevates it, Satanism degrades and defiles it. Where the Roman Catholic mass is a preserve of patriarchiality, the Satanic mass is served upon the naked body of a woman in whose vagina the Holy wafer will be inserted for commingling with the semen of the celebrant Satanic priest, who tradition holds must also be a defrocked Roman Catholic priest. Where the sacred blood of the Roman Catholic mass is subtilised into symbolic wine and partaken of in reverent sips, the sacred blood of the Satanic mass is literal blood, partaken of in greedy gulps from a chalice held beneath the slashed throat of a child. Or of a virgin, a young woman with an unbroken hymen between her thighs. For where Roman Catholicism celebrates the *life* of a virgin – the Virgin Mary – to the point (for Protestants, beyond the point) at which she threatens to overshadow her son Jesus Christ, Satanism celebrates the *death* of a virgin. In short, where there is white in Roman Catholicism, there is black in Satanism; where there is black in Roman Catholicism, there is white in Satanism. All this is concentrated and distilled in those two Satanic symbols: the *crux inverta*, the inverted crucifix, and the *virgo immolata*, the sacrificed virgin.

These facts of history and psycho-culture underlie and resonate within the claims that '*ritos satánicos*' are involved in the Juárez murders. Young women, many of them literal virgins, are kidnapped, raped and tortured, treated with extreme violence and contumely, before being strangled or stabbed to death and *buried*. In this last fact we find another echo of anti-Christian ritual, for the inhabitants of pagan Latin America, like those of old pagan Europe, would consecrate and protect buildings by the sacrifice of human beings whose corpses were then buried in the foundations.

As time went on, this sacrificial ritual (in the same progression that saw the literal blood-drinking that underlies the Eucharist transmuted into symbolic wine-drinking) was undertaken with animals instead. Perhaps in Juárez we have seen a return to the older, purer ritual, for much of outlying Juárez is occupied by building lots, ideal for the burial of murder-victims whose graves will soon be covered by cement and steel. But can we extrapolate from this to the existence of some Satan-worshipping building contractor, hiring men to protect his investments by the murder and burial of young women beneath the foundations?

Such an extrapolation seems doubtful, even (perhaps certainly) ridiculous, but there is no need to make it, for there are easier alternatives. We could suppose the existence of an allegorical spirit of ancient evil brooding above the psychogeographic landscape of Juárez, nourished by the pain and misery of its inhabitants and sliding tendrils into the receptive unconsciousness of men like Sharif and 'El Tolteca'. The tendrils bloom into the consciousness of these men with ideas: the idea of the rape and murder of young women, the idea of their burial in the harsh sand of empty or half-constructed building lots.

For parallel ideas do not necessarily indicate a common origin. Instead, they can indicate common conditions. Iron heated and pounded behaves similarly everywhere in the world; minds wounded and twisted produce similar psychopathologies everywhere in the world. Rape and murder have been found in every culture and at every time, and their expression in ritualistic form may presuppose only particular, unconnected corruptions of a general human nature, not an underlying network of shared history and tradition. The ritual of 'foundation burial' may have arisen spontaneously and independently many times around the world, and may re-arise spontaneously and independently wherever the conditions are right. In Juárez the conditions may have been right: the sexually provoking presence of young women, the ready availability of burial space.

Perhaps we could read into the ritual an even deeper significance, stretching beyond even the most general human nature into our evolutionary past: many carnivorous animals bury uneaten portions of their slaughtered prey as a precaution against scavengers and to avoid alarming still-living members of the prey species. Perhaps Sharif and his confederates have resurrected this ancient instinct, dredging it up from the ancient centres of the brain devoted to the most basic patterns of behaviour: sex and feeding.

This would explain too the bite-marks found on the bodies of some of the victims. Like re-triggerable fragments of an outmoded code buried in a rewritten computer program, ancient instincts are buried in the human brain, quiescent – *repressed* – under normal conditions, but always ready to be re-triggered by psychosis and induce the anomalous behaviour of an attack by biting from a creature whose teeth are no longer adapted to it. It is difficult and inefficient for a human being to inflict life-threatening injuries on another human being by biting, and the appearance of this behaviour amongst some rapists seems to represent a psychological atavism: the re-emergence of an ancestor's behaviour in a modern descendant.

The rituals of Satanism could be viewed as a deliberate, conscious attempt to re-awaken these ancestral instincts, to provoke the omophagy – the eating of raw flesh – that was seen in the ancient rites of Dionysus and Bacchus. The Satanic mass is a kind of inverted behavioural therapy of deconditioning that uses the drinking of fresh human blood to accustom its participants to the breaking of the ultimate dietary taboo: cannibalism. And yet the drinking of blood is, for some, an end in itself: the beverage of choice for such archangels of the Satanic hierarchy as the vampire-king Count Dracula.

The Transylvanian legend of Dracula was taken up, adapted, and transmitted to the rest of the world by the Irish novelist Bram Stoker (1847–1912), and it and its connotations are as well known in México as anywhere else. So it was that Spanish-speaking readers of the Juárez newspaper reports of the arrest of a gang of bus-drivers for rape and murder would not have been puzzled by the nickname attached to one of them. Guardado Márquez is known both as 'El Tolteca' – the Toltec – and as 'El Dracula'. In Spanish the vowels and consonants of the latter have appropriately pure, monophthongal European values: draa-koo-laa. The first two syllables, in fact, raise an echo from an ancient European text: '*Et ecce draco magnus rufus*'. This is the Latin of what was once the only lawful form of the Bible in Catholic Europe, and can be rendered in English like this: 'And behold a great red dragon'. (The *Revelation* of St John the Divine, xii, 3.)

Dracula: draco. Dracula: dragon. And the dragon is, of course, a Biblical symbol of Satan, found both in the New

Testament and in the Old. Dracula is a dragon, and dragons are famed in such hagiographies as that of St George for their propensity to demand virgin sacrifice. Guardado Márquez, 'El Dracula', was an ancient word made modern flesh, a dragon sacrificing virgins to himself and his own pursuit of pleasure.

How did Márquez acquire his *apodo vampírico*, his vampiric nickname? Newspaper reports do not tell us, but perhaps there was a sense of something sinister about him, a whiff of a particular evil that was redolent of the legend of the vampire-king and his atavistically long and pointed canine teeth. And the men who christened Márquez with this sobriquet must have already been attuned to its anti-Christian, Satanic resonances, for they live in a city named for an anti-Christian rebel:

> Santa Anna was overthrown in 1855 by Benito Juárez, whose liberal reforms included many anti-clerical measures ... In 1862, Miramon [a former president of México] appealed to Empress Eugénie, consort of Napoleon III, saying that steps must be taken against Juárez and his anti-Christian policies. (*The Hutchinson Softback Encyclopedia*)

This French intervention brought about another war and another victory for Juárez, sealing his status as a folk-hero and encouraging, perhaps, the choice of a border city for his onomastic memorial. Ciudad Juárez, facing the United States across the Río Bravo, bears in its name a defiant challenge: the name of the rebel who faced down foreign interference and intervention directed from Paris, the Vatican City, and Washington.

With unconscious irony the outside world, seeing México through American eyes, refers to 'Juárez' as just that, unaware that it is confusing a city with a man. In México, Juárez must be Ciudad Juárez, Juárez City, for

Mexicans, in another piece of unconscious irony, are respectful of their rebel-heroes, even adoring of them. Their chief political party, winner of an unbroken string of national elections, is the *Partido Revolucionario Institutional*: the Institutional Revolutionary Party. Perhaps this oxymoron can be seen as a symbol of México's endemic corruption. The concepts of revolution and rebellion have become simply another propagandistic tool by which the powerful exploit the masses for their own enrichment and pleasure, and the ring of names like Juárez, a folk-hero of México's historic quest for freedom, acquires a flat, sour note in popular Mexican discourse.

This corruption of rebellion would fit well with the legend of Satan, whose defiance of God was inspired by the lust for personal advance: 'To reign is worth ambition, though in hell:/Better to reign in hell, than serve in heav'n'. (*Paradise Lost*, Milton, lines 260–1.) To institutionalise revolution, as México has done, and to honour rebels and revolutionaries in the names of your cities is to contradict the very concept one wishes to honour, and the message received by the youth of México can only be a distorted one: rebellion is not for the good of others but for the good of oneself, not to overturn power alone, but to overturn power in order to become powerful oneself.

The message spoken by the final two syllables of 'Ciudad Juárez' across the Río Bravo then becomes not a defiant challenge but a sardonic chuckle. And the first to hear this chuckle will be, of course, the inhabitants of El Paso, Texas. Perhaps this helps to explain a man who is probably the most famous son of the Texan city:

One of the most recent of these so-called 'high-scoring' serial killers was Richard Ramirez, alias 'The Night Stalker' – twenty-eight years of age, unmarried, a drifter and satanist (*sic*) from El Paso, Texas. In the fifteen months between June 1984 and August 1985 the Night Stalker murdered thirteen people and sexually assaulted several others in the suburbs of Los Angeles . . . Men were shot or stabbed as they slept. The women were beaten, raped and sexually abused, regardless of age: most were murdered by strangulation, stabbing or shooting. Their children (of both sexes, some as young as six) were either sexually assaulted in their homes, or abducted, to be raped and sodomised before being turned loose on the streets, miles away. All Ramirez' attacks were marked by extreme cruelty; on one occasion he gouged a woman's eyes out. He 'signed' some of his murders by sketching in lipstick a pentagram – a five-pointed star, often associated with satanism – at the scene of the crime, either on the victim's body or the wall above. (*The Serial Killers: a study in the psychology of violence*, Colin Wilson and Donald Seaman, Virgin Publishing, 1990)

There is an immediate echo here of Victor Moreno Rivera, 'El Narco', the Druggie, a member of *Los Choferes*, the bus drivers who the Mexican authorities said have been paid by Sharif to rape and murder in his stead:

The first to speak with reporters was Victor Moreno Rivera. The American citizen, twenty-eight years old, [said] that he had been imprisoned in Doña Ana county for smuggling marijuana into the United States and for robbery, which was why he decided to settle after nearly a year in Ciudad Juárez.

'I came to work here so I did not have to pay a monthly fine of forty dollars, and I began to work cleaning cars. A little later I went to work selling cars that I brought from El Paso, and that is what I have been doing for the past six months.' (*El Diario de Juárez*)

Like Richard Ramirez, 'El Narco' was twenty-eight years old on his arrest, a Latino American citizen, familiar with El Paso, and accused of rape and murder. He is accused of being Sharif's contact with the outside world, travelling regularly to the *CeReSo* to hand over evidence of the crimes and receive envelopes of money to be handed out to the remainder of *Los Choferes*.

9: Slice

Cortar v.t. Separar por medio de un instrumento cortante.
Slice. Transitive verb. Separate by means of a cutting instrument.

An electron microscope can reveal the tiniest details of structure in a plant or animal cell – with one great disadvantage. The cell can no longer be living when it does so. It must be treated, prepared, bathed in toxic chemicals, and the stream of radiation with which the electron microscope plucks its secrets from it would kill it anyway. Scientists can see in exceedingly fine detail what a cell looks like, but not how it works. They see a snapshot, not a film.

Murder is like an electron microscope – revealing the tiniest details of life – but murder offers more than a snapshot. The investigations that take place after a murder can cover days of the victim's life, preserving details that would otherwise be lost among the forgotten debris of history. Who, for example, would have bothered to record the day-to-day lives of prostitutes in a working-class district of nineteenth-century London? Who, that is, if those prostitutes had not been victims of Jack the Ripper?

No one, it seems likely, but those prostitutes *were* the victims of Jack the Ripper, and their day-to-day lives *were* recorded. Similarly, who would be bothering to record the lives of the *maquiladora* workers and bar-girls of Juárez if they were not falling victim to a serial killer or serial killers? Again, no one, it seems very likely. But those *maquiladora* workers and bar-girls are falling victim to murder, and their lives are being recorded. Sometimes after their deaths. At autopsy:

Case 16, 30 July [1996] – Rocío Miranda Aguero: Rocío Miranda Aguero, 28 years old, manageress of the nightclub Top Capos, was found by children in a 200-litre drum full of corrosive acid, with only her hands and feet remaining undissolved. She was identified by her silicone [breast-] implants. She had been abducted by 17 people. In the same house there were a female servant and a two-month-old baby, the daughter of the murdered woman, both of whom were miraculously saved by hiding. [This is taken from the ParaSagrario website, as are the other 'case study' quotations which follow.]

There, in seventy-three words of terse, sinewy forensic Spanish, is a slice of Juárez life, paradoxically fixed and preserved and magnified by an act of enforced death. The report is like a prose-poem, its phrases almost as corrosive on the emotions and sensibilities of the reader as the acid Rocío Aguero was submerged in and devoured by.

And more, much more, can be inferred than is explicitly stated. The 'silicone implants' that enabled the identification of Aguero's otherwise almost entirely dissolved corpse suggest a strong American influence on Juárez – an influence easily confirmed by reference to foreign tourist guides for the city:

When visiting Ciudad Juárez, bear in mind that it has the highest consumer price index in México . . . Many everyday consumer items are US Goods brought in from El Paso. In spite of the relatively high cost of living, the city has México's fifth highest US expatriate population – more than 28,000 at last count. (*Northern Mexico Handbook*, Joe Cummings, Moon Publications, 1998)

It is another piece of circumstantial evidence for the involvement of a home-based American citizen in the Juárez murders. In another Mexican city or town, further south perhaps, more inaccessible, an American might stand out, be noted and remembered by bar tenders or hotel workers, street vendors or school children whom the police could then question and obtain a description from. In Juárez there are too many Americans for this to happen. An American serial killer could come and go as he pleased in the reasonable confidence that he would not stand out even if memories were jogged by a *direct* link with the death of a woman. Examine another slice of Juárez life paradoxically fixed and magnified by the act of murder:

Case 25, 21 September [1998] – A woman has her throat cut with a knife in the Juárez Hotel. She was Dutch [according to] documents found in a pillow-case and was found under the bed stripped naked. It is calculated that she had been dead 14 hours. The room had been rented by a man of North American appearance who has not yet been traced.

Note that phrase: 'a man of North American appearance'. Citizens of the United States are recognisable as such in México, but in a city like Juárez, home to a large expatriate American community and visited by many American tourists, recognising someone's nationality on sight is not the same as remembering that someone clearly when he or she is out of sight.

So who was that 'man of North American appearance'? A first-time, one-off murderer, brought to the crime in a fit of rage or drunkenness, fleeing the scene in remorse and horror? The nature of the woman's death would suggest otherwise: slitting a woman's throat is not the usual means adopted by a first-time murderer. It suggests a familiarity with extreme violence, bespeaks someone ready to engage in what the Spanish calls '*guerra a cuchillo*': war to the knife. (An answer supposedly given by José de Palafox (1780–1847) to a request for surrender at the siege of Saragossa in 1808. Palafox's original words were probably *guerra y cuchillo*, 'war and the knife', but the meaning – that he would fight to the last resource – is little altered by the change.)

The nakedness of the murdered woman and her nationality are also suggestive of more than a one-off murder. Nakedness implies sex, and sex and death imply some form of psychopathology in the killer. And the woman's nationality? It implies that she was almost certainly a stranger to Juárez herself, very likely a newcomer, with no close friends or relatives to press the police for a solution to her murder. If one were an American serial killer looking for a victim in Juárez, a Dutchwoman, citizen of a small country thousands of kilometres away, would be almost perfect, particularly at that stage of the wider killings. By 21 September 1998, Mexican women would have been becoming less and less accessible to serial killers. Even young and naïve *maquiladora* workers from the south, now far from family and friends, had feminists and political activists working hard on their behalf, forcing the state authorities and *maquiladora* companies to take measures for their employees' safety:

Factories have started issuing pepper spray to female employees. The government has done sweeps to find underage employees like the young survivor ['Nancy']. It has also demanded that bus drivers be tested for drugs. (THE DEATHS THAT HAUNT JUAREZ, Mary Beth Sheridan, *Los Angeles Times*)

71

And consider that the previous murders must have operated a kind of natural selection amongst the young women of Juárez, eliminating the easiest targets, the most foolish and reckless, the most desperate of those who conformed to what seems to have been the killers' ideal victim profile: young, slender, *guapa* (attractive), and with long, dark hair.

Foreign women very rarely turn up in the list of victims compiled by the ParaSagrario Consortium, and perhaps the Dutchwoman – still unnamed – represented the first of what would have been an increasing trend, the target of a putative American serial killer who had crossed to kill in this Satanic playground of death: Juárez, the rebels' city named after a rebel in a country of institutionalised rebellion.

But at the time of writing, the serial rape and murder of young women in Juárez seems to have stopped. *Los Choferes* are behind bars and the abused and mutilated bodies, or the skeletal remains of abused and mutilated bodies, are no longer turning up in the empty building lots of Juárez or in the surrounding desert. But does this prove that the serial killers responsible are all behind bars? No, it merely *suggests* it. But, as I have stressed elsewhere, serial killing is a 'profession' that places a premium on intelligence and cunning, and one or more of the serial killers responsible may have decided to transfer his attentions to the women of some other city in some other region.

10: Charisma

Carisma m. Don espiritual otorgado a grupos o individuos. Fascinación, gran prestigio del que gozan algunas personas.

Charisma. Spiritual gift granted to groups or individuals. Fascination, special power possessed by some people.

In his posthumous book *Vom Kriege* (1833) – *On War* – the Prussian general Karl von Clausewitz (1780–1831) outlined the four types of officer and their respective values to a commander. The best kind of officer was, he said, one who was intelligent, but lazy. He will obey orders efficiently, and act on his own initiative when necessary, but not otherwise. After him came the stupid and lazy officer, who will obey orders and never try to act on his own initiative. After him came the intelligent and industrious officer, who will try to improve on the orders he is given, and will act on his own initiative whenever he can. Last of all came the stupid and industrious officer, who is disastrous in all ways.

Apply this reasoning to the serial killer. Suppose we take the concept of 'best' here to mean 'best for society'. The best kind of serial killer would be, then, the stupid and lazy one. He is likely to be caught after his first crime, without having had the chance to kill again (and so, of course, will never become a recognised serial killer). After him comes the stupid but industrious serial killer. He will be caught easily, but may have had time to commit several murders during the time the police are hunting for him.

73

After him comes the intelligent but lazy serial killer. He will kill for a long time, and may never be caught, but being lazy will not kill very many. Last and worst of all – for society – comes the intelligent and industrious serial killer. He too will kill for a long time and he too may never be caught, but whether he is caught or not, he will kill very many.

Sharif was the last kind of serial killer: intelligent and industrious. His were the best of crimes, and the worst of crimes. The best for the sex-criminal *manqués* who cheer men such as him on from the sidelines, the worst from the point of view of society. No one knows how many women Sharif has killed in Juárez, and no one knows whether Sharif killed only in Juárez, and only in Juárez after he emigrated to work there for a *maquiladora*. After the first two of the rapes he committed in Florida and Texas, he should have been an automatic candidate for deportation from the United States as an undesirable alien.

But Sharif committed two rapes, then went on to commit more, and the United States Immigration Service only undertook proceedings against him in 1993, when he was employed by Benchmark Research and Technology of Midland, Texas. The deportation hearing took place in a city in the same state, a couple of hundred kilometres further east and nearer the Tex-Mex border. In fact, right *on* the Tex-Mex border.

The move to México had been Sharif's idea, Benchmark CEO Wayne Kinsey said in a recent interview. Sharif had become familiar with Ciudad Juárez during his deportation hearings in El Paso, just across the Rio Grande.

Sharif was not imprisoned during the later stages of the hearing, and was at liberty to come and go as he pleased when his presence was not required in court. Accordingly, he must have come and gone in a way many inhabitants of El Paso do, back and forth across the Rio Grande, from El Paso to Juárez, back again from Juárez to El Paso. As one American tourist guide remarks of Juárez:

'For residents of neighboring El Paso it's a destination in its own right for food, nightlife, shopping, and greyhound and horse racing.' (*Northern Mexico Handbook*, Joe Cummings, Moon Publications, 1998)

Food, shopping, greyhound and horse racing. And nightlife:

There seemed a strange stillness over everything; but as I listened I heard as if from far down the valley the howling of many wolves. The Count's eyes gleamed, and he said, 'Listen to them – the children of the night. What music they make!' Seeing, I suppose, some expression in my face strange to him, he added, 'Ah, sir, you dwellers in the city cannot enter into the feelings of the hunter.'

That is chapter two of Bram Stoker's *Dracula* (1897), but the Count is wrong. Some dwellers in the city *can* enter into the feelings of the hunter, because some dwellers in the city are also hunters. And they do not even need to leave the city to hunt. Or want to leave it. For there can be a *música de la noche*, a 'music of the night', in the city as well as deep in the Transylvanian forests, though, like the selenolatric song of wolves, it is a music whose beauty only a particular kind of mind can appreciate:

'He demonstrated how two of them would grab the victim by the neck and strangle her between them, often until the vertebrae cracked,' Carmona said. He said, 'That made such a nice cracking sound.' (FORENSICS EXPERT STRUGGLES WITH WORK, Mark Stevenson, Associated Press)

The man who thought the cracking of female vertebrae 'made such a nice cracking sound' was Jesús Guardado

75

Márquez, El Tolteca, the leader of the bus drivers hired by Sharif, whose own tastes in music remain veiled. Sharif certainly, however, must have been exposed to yet another 'music of the night', for during his trips to Juárez from El Paso and the deportation hearing there:

> Sharif would soon discover Ugarte Street, the seedy strip a few blocks from the mission square in the bustling downtown, the place in Juárez that was a sexual psychopath's dream.
>
> On Ugarte and nearby streets, rough taverns like Joe's Place, Tuna Country, Casino Deportivo, and Noa-Noa's tumbled one unto another – lairs of the street gangs who ran the area's drug trade and prostitution. Hundreds of rickety buses rumbled onto Ugarte around the clock, depositing thousands of naïve teenage girls with painted nails and fresh lipstick. They were part of the legion of workers in foreign-owned factories, the *maquiladoras*, girls who made $3 a day, then stepped from their buses downtown and virtually onto the laps of men who bore them ill. ('MONSTER' BEATS THE SYSTEM, Tim Madigan, The *Seattle Times*, 1999)

As the egregious American heavy-metal band Guns'n'Roses once proclaimed: 'Welcome to the Jungle'. After his emigration to Juárez, Sharif became a predator of this jungle, a big cat, a jaguar, glossy-coated, sheathing razor-claws in velvet pads, supremely confident in his primacy and his ability to hunt down his prey by cunning and charisma:

> On Ugarte, Sharif was taller than most. He spoke halting Spanish. And in a world of blue jeans and T-shirts, Sharif favored expensive watches and gaudy jewelry, silk shirts and turtlenecks, sports coats and

dress shoes. (A MONSTER EXPOSED Tim Madigan with Juan Antonio Ramos, The *Fort Worth Star-Telegram*)

This sartorial elegance and regard for personal appearance will be familiar to readers of Anthony Burgess's *A Clockwork Orange* (1962), whose literally and onomastically lawless anti-hero, Alex, is also noticeable for his concern for appearance and cleanliness. Yet Anthony Burgess was not inventing the characteristics of his ultra-violent protagonist. A link between, on the one hand, a cat-like obsession with personal hygiene and grooming and, on the other, a propensity to extreme violence is found not only in the fictional Alex but also in real psychopaths and serial killers such as Dennis Nilsen, who is described in Brian Masters' *Killing for Company* as:

> tall and slim, slightly stooped, with ... thick brown hair. He habitually wore dark trousers and a pale grey tweed jacket, blue shirt, dark blue tie [and was] clean and tidy ... he wore rimless spectacles and was clean-shaven.

It was also found in Peter Sutcliffe, the Yorkshire Ripper:

> All the same she [Carol Jones, an early girlfriend of Sutcliffe's] was happy to be out with him, a smart, clean, always tidy beau, who didn't swear and never showed any sign of violence ... because the bathroom was to one side of the house it was noticeable that when Sutcliffe did get out of his old clothes to go out it took him a long time to prepare himself; he would pay particular attention to his hair. (*The Yorkshire Ripper: an in-depth study of a mass killer and his methods*, Roger Cross, HarperCollins)

As is described elsewhere, the attraction of women to men is mediated by evidence of success. Serial killers, pop singers, and athletes are all successful, and one way their success manifests itself is in their prominence. They are noticed, observed, talked about. Only the last of these might seem to happen to serial killers before their arrest and imprisonment, but that is in fact not necessarily so. Many serial killers are prominent before their arrest and the attendant publicity. It is merely that they are not identified as serial killers before their arrest. The same underlying insecurities and abnormalities as drive them to acts of rape and murder also often drive them to positions of prominence in business and at work:

> The management [of Clark's, a haulage company near Bradford, northern England] had been so impressed with Sutcliffe, regarding him as possessing all the virtues required by the best lorry drivers, that he was chosen to appear in a promotional brochure for the firm. He is shown, hair in place, beard neatly trimmed as usual, behind the wheel of 'Wee Willie' [his lorry], and a giant enlargement of the photograph was given pride of place in the entrance to the firm's offices. (*The Yorkshire Ripper: an in-depth study of a mass killer and his methods*, Roger Cross, HarperCollins, 1993)

But Sharif and Sutcliffe shared more than just this concern for their appearance and professional ability. Like Sharif, Sutcliffe had charisma, and a charisma that women found attractive. Susan Kelly, a typist and switchboard operator who was the only female working at Clark's while Sutcliffe drove a lorry for the firm, had, according to Roger Cross, always been struck by his pleasantness, his politeness, and particularly by the fact that she never heard him swear, something of a record among lorry drivers.

This is echoed again by the Sharif case. During his trial for rape in Palm Beach, Florida, Sharif was represented by a defence lawyer called Greg Scott. Scott knew of the violence and sexual nature of his client's crimes, and yet found himself unable to resist his charisma.

But Scott also couldn't help being charmed by his client. Sharif was personable, funny and intelligent. He always treated Scott with respect. Criminal lawyers are used to dealing with the dregs of society. That in no way seemed to describe Sharif.

And, in a sense, it was not the way to describe Sharif. Language and the instinctive systems of belief on which it is based mislead us in our relations with other human beings. 'Sharif' is a personal name, and we suppose that a personal name somehow attaches to a permanent entity: a body and mind that may change radically over time, but will do so slowly, in response to plainly visible influences from their environment. Similarly, we suppose that changes in a body and mind taking place over short periods of time will be related by simple steps to some factor in the environment.

It is suspected, for example, that Sharif had been raping and murdering women long before he emigrated to México, and one former acquaintance called John Pascoe has told of how he met a young girl in Sharif's apartment in New Hope, Pennsylvania, in 1980: he described her as 'petite, pretty, with long, light-blond (*sic*) hair, and wearing a tube top and blue jeans'. The girl then disappeared, but she had strangely left her few possessions behind in the apartment. Pascoe pointed this out to Sharif, who:

> realised then that Pascoe had been in his place
> without him knowing. He flew into a rage. 'If you
> ever do that again . . .' Sharif screamed. 'Get out!'
> Pascoe wasn't about to argue, and hurried for the

door. It was on his way out that he saw a new shovel, caked with fresh mud, standing against a wall on Sharif's front porch. ('MONSTER' BEATS THE SYSTEM, Tim Madigan, The *Seattle Times*, 1999)

Sharif's rage is easily explicable, whether or not he had actually murdered and buried the girl, for the privacy of his home had been intruded upon without his permission or knowledge. There was a clear stimulus and it evoked a clear, comprehensible response.

Examine now another example of Sharif's behaviour, when he was living in Midland, Texas, and, on 31 October – Hallowe'en night – 1993, invited a woman called 'Ann' back to his house:

It was a large, beautiful place in a new neighbourhood on the edge of town. They entered through the garage, and when Ann asked to use the bathroom, Sharif pointed the way. He was waiting outside when she came out, and punched her when she refused his advances. He called her a whore and bitch, and raped her.

Then he poured her a glass of orange juice, chatting amiably, until his rage swelled back up. She said he raped her again and again until the sun came up, each attack interspersed with kindnesses, causing Ann to arrive at the same metaphor used a month earlier by Judge Nail [in the deportation hearing]. Sharif was first Dr Jekyll then Mr Hyde, a monster not content to attack her body. Sharif seemed to need to mess with her head, too. ('MONSTER' BEATS THE SYSTEM, Tim Madigan, The *Seattle Times*, 1999)

Set this alongside the description, from the same source, of his behaviour during the multiple rapes he committed on a woman called 'Lisa' in Gainesville, Florida:

Several times during her ordeal, she wished Sharif would go ahead and kill her, too, would get it over with. But then, after hours when his rage rose and fell like some evil tide, he stopped. It was as if someone had finally found the handle to shut off a faucet of venom. 'Oh, I've hurt you,' he said. 'Do you think you need to go to the hospital?'

Sharif's volcanic rage and the sexual violence accompanying it are not easily explicable: what is repeatedly inflaming them and then quenching them? Why are they interspersed with 'kindnesses'? Why does the series of violent sexual and physical attacks in Florida end with the utter incongruity of an offer to take the victim for medical attention? The victim called 'Ann' in Texas was puzzled by the same questions, and her memories of the culture she inhabited provided her with a metaphor to encapsulate this puzzlement and the questions evoking it: Sharif was a 'Jekyll and Hyde'. 'Jekyll and Hyde' is another fictional creation that is, like Dracula, more famous than its creator, for it forms a narrative eminently suitable for translation to an easily digestible couple of hours on the cinema or television screen. The force of the narrative of Jekyll and Hyde, like that of Dracula, is most powerfully conveyed through the medium of vision: to see the transformation on the screen is more affecting than to read of it:

Late one accursed night, I compounded the elements, watched them boil and smoke together in the glass, and when the ebullition had subsided, with a strong glow of courage, drank off the poison.

The most racking pangs succeeded: a grinding in the bones, deadly nausea, and a horror of the spirit that cannot be exceeded at the hour of birth or death. Then these agonies began swiftly to subside, and I came to myself as if out of a great sickness. There was something strange in my sensations, something indescribably new, and, from its very novelty, incredibly sweet. I felt younger, lighter, happier in body; within I was conscious of a heady recklessness, a current of disordered sensual images running like a mill race in my fancy, a solution of the bonds of obligation, and an unknown but not an innocent freedom of the soul. I knew myself, at the first breath of this new life, to be more wicked, tenfold more wicked, sold a slave to my original evil; and the thought, in that moment, braced and delighted me like wine. I stretched out my hands, exulting in the freshness of these sensations; and in the act I was suddenly aware that I had lost in stature. (*The Strange Case of Dr Jekyll and Mr Hyde*, Robert Louis Stevenson)

Robert Louis Stevenson (1850–94) is confronting questions about the mysterious mutability of human nature, and answers them in his book in satisfying narrative. Dr Jekyll drinks a potion and is transformed into Mr Hyde. There is an external stimulus (albeit internally assimilated) and an externally visible response to it. Mr Hyde's moral nature, fed by the invisible springs of the soul or brain, is changed from that of Dr Jekyll, and this change is accompanied by a change in *physical* nature. Jekyll and Hyde are not truly one person, but two, as distinct in body and name as they are in character. We are satisfied by this resolution of the difficulty because it matches our expectations of human nature: that radical moral or behavioural changes in a single individual do not take place easily or quickly or without some clear reason.

The real-life narrative of Sharif does not answer the difficulty. The Sharif raping 'Ann' and the Sharif offering her a glass of orange juice are distinct only in moral and behavioural nature, not in name and body, and we can see no clear reason for the transition from one to the other, let alone for the way in which this takes place quickly and repeatedly over the period of a single night.

That may be, however, only because we are not observing the situation in sufficient detail. Unless we are medically trained our perceptions of other human beings tend to be only skin-deep. Literally skin-deep. A beautiful woman is called 'beautiful' because of the way our eyes receive and our brains analyse light-rays from the surface of her body. We forget that, in one Christian saint's anti-erotic phrase, she is also a 'sack of dung': there is a great deal of physiological activity going on beneath her skin that our eyes and brains do not perceive. But this is true not just of beautiful women, and it is true not just of activities related to 'dung'. Beautiful women, like all human beings, have brains, but under normal circumstances we observe what is going on in those brains only by indirect means: by changes that are, again, visible at the surface: in the skin and musculature of the face, for example.

But what if we observe under circumstances that are not normal? What if we could have observed Sharif's behaviour with 'Ann' not just with our unaided eyes and ears, but with scientific instruments too? Suppose that he had electrodes attached to his scalp as he underwent the transition from Sharif à la Jekyll to Sharif à la Hyde, and back again. We would then have seen, I suggest, the underlying neurological basis of his behaviour, and might even have been able to predict when the transition from one moral and behavioural state to another would take place *before* there was any visible sign of it at the surface of Sharif's body. And before Sharif himself was aware that the transition was about to take place.

But what is it that we would have seen under these special circumstances? Presumably, radical changes in the pattern or level of electrical and chemical activity in Sharif's brain: the neurological equivalent of a storm replacing the neurological equivalent of a calm summer's day, and *vice versa*. And yet would we not have merely replaced one mystery with another in making this more detailed observation? The question still remains: why would these changes have taken place? To answer that, we would, I suggest, have to undertake a more detailed examination still of Sharif's brain and its functioning. There are more sophisticated instruments now available than scalp-electrodes and the electroencephalogram, and they offer highly detailed, two-dimensional images of the living brain: X-ray CT, NMR, and PET scans for example (unpacked, these acronyms mean X-ray Computed Tomography, Nuclear Magnetic Resonance, and Positron Emission Tomography, respectively). With these newly developed techniques or others that will surely become available in the near future, the electrical and chemical activity of Sharif's brain could be examined in minute detail to reveal, I suggest, some organic dysfunction in his brain responsible for these transitions from Jekyll to Hyde, from Hyde to Jekyll. Perhaps the neurological systems that in a normal adult male channel sexual behaviour in socially acceptable ways are missing or weakened or damaged in some way in Sharif. Perhaps sexual stimuli are conveyed to and activate inappropriate regions of his brain, such as the centres responsible for anger and aggression.

The same proposed analysis applies to many more sex-criminals than Sharif. Remember Peter Sutcliffe and the female typist who was struck by 'his pleasantness, his politeness, and particularly by the fact that she never heard him swear, something of a record among lorry drivers'. Swear-words are a sign of anger or frustration, but Sutcliffe did not use them in everyday life. There was, in other words, something wrong with the systems within his brain controlling anger and aggression. We need not, however, take up the hydrological metaphor offered by Freudianism, and assume his anger was repressed until it became too powerful to control. Sutcliffe almost always released his anger and gave vent to his aggression under special circumstances, and there are very few records of his manifesting his underlying psychopathology in a setting other than that of a red-light district or a dimly lit city street after dark. Here is one of these rare records from Laurie Ashton, a friend from Sutcliffe's time as a grave-digger:

'I began to realise that Peter was staring straight ahead, totally motionless, like in a trance, for quite a few minutes; then suddenly he took hold of the handle of his glass, stuck it up in the air and crashed it down on the table. There was beer and bits of glass everywhere.' (*The Yorkshire Ripper: an in-depth study of a mass killer and his methods*, Roger Cross, HarperCollins, 1993)

Yet even in this description there is no clear indication of what Sutcliffe truly was and was capable of, and I suggest that the Freudian analysis of his behaviour is wrong: there was no mysterious, mindless fluid collecting in the vesicles of his brain, rising in volume and pressure until it burst forth in a murderous geyser of blood-lust. He smashed a beer-glass in that public house, did not attack anyone, let alone a woman, and when he did attack women, it was only certain women under certain circumstances, and the attacks, however violent, followed a kind of grammar of psychopathology:

In a paroxysm of rage he stabbed her again and again, some 18 times, in her breasts and chest, her stomach and the area of her vagina – fierce slashing swipes, a terrible burst of rage which relented only when the vilified body was almost unrecognizable. (*Ibid.*, p. 95)

The wounds described here were *purposeful*, aimed at particular parts of the female body, directed by a brain efficiently absorbing and assimilating sense-data about the environment in which its owner's body found itself. Sutcliffe was not an obvious psychopath: few serial killers are. If they were, they would find it difficult to find victims and to avoid attention from the authorities once they had found them. This is not to say, however, that there is nothing objectively abnormal about serial killers such as Sutcliffe and Sharif. If, as well as the clean, regular-featured face with its neatly trimmed beard, Sutcliffe's prostitute-victims could have seen the functioning of their prospective client's brain, they might have recognised him for the psychopath he was, noting the quickening flicker of neuro-electrical and neuro-chemical rhythms that were prognostic of a red, oncoming rage. And some of Sutcliffe's victims, prostitutes and otherwise, almost certainly never even saw him, perhaps never even heard him, being attacked from behind in dim light or darkness with overwhelming force.

But even now there is no readily available means of clearly monitoring the neurological activity of those with whom one comes into casual contact. We rely, sometimes mistakenly, on the indirect evidence of facial expressions and the voice. As well, of course, as the eyes.

11: Eyes

Ojo m. Órgano de la vista: tener algo ante los ojos. – El ojo humano consta de tres membranas: la esclerótica, que le protege y forma delante la córnea transparente; la coroides, que se prolonga y forma la iris, horadada por la pupila; la retina, sensible al excitante luminoso, unidada al encéfalo por el nervio óptico, y sobre la cual se dibujan las imágines.

Eye. Organ of sight: 'to have something before one's eyes'. – The human eye consists of three membranes: the sclerotic, which protects the eye and forms the transparent cornea at the front; the choroid, which extends and forms the iris, pierced by the pupil; the retina, which is sensitive to light and attached to the encephalus by the optic nerve, and over which images are formed.

He arrived in the city at dusk. The coloured lights of the traffic signals seemed to be crystallising out of the thickening darkness, to left and right, everywhere. Like eyes, opening on his coming. (*The Eyes*, Jesús Ignacio Aldapuerta)

Poner el lobo a guardar las ovejas. Set a thief to catch a thief. Literally, the Spanish would be translated 'Set a wolf to guard the chickens'. There are several other ways to express this idea in Spanish: *Para un pícaro, otro mayor; a pillo, pillo y medio; poner la zorra a guardar las gallinas*; or the literal translation *ponga un ladrón para coger a otro ladrón*. To understand a psychopath, go to another psychopath. To understand the behaviour of the psychopathic chemist Abdul Latif Sharif Sharif or the psychopathic lorry-driver Peter Sutcliffe, go to the psychopathic writer Jesús Ignacio Aldapuerta, the *soi disant* 'Andalusian de Sade' whose most famous – or infamous – work is called simply *Los Ojos – The Eyes*.

There is an extremely ancient tradition in Mediterranean culture of what English most famously describes by the borrowed Italian term *malocchio*: the evil eye, or the eye that by its mere gaze can cast a spell of misfortune or disaster. Rumoured possession of the evil eye is sufficient to cause someone to be shunned or avoided, even when it is acknowledged that the individual in question is quite innocent of any conscious evil intent. The Italian *littérateur* Mario Praz (1896–1963), for example, the author of a definitive study of literary decadence called *The Romantic Agony* (1933), was a harmless scholar but was said to have acquired the evil eye by his close acquaintance with the œuvre of the nefarious Marquis de Sade (1740–1814) and his *confrères*.

Whether Praz ever included Aldapuerta in his minute and punctilious studies in literary decadence remains unrecorded, as does whether Aldapuerta himself was in possession of what the Spanish call the *mal de ojo*, 'the evil eye', but there is no doubt that Aldapuerta was conscious of the maleficent power of the gaze, whether literal:

I sat and gazed at her.

She was, I would guess, about nine or ten years old, puppyfat-less with malnutrition and disease. I can't remember very much else about her, not even what her face looked like, only that her skin was very clean because of the post-choleric sweating. Perhaps I should remember more, because I stared at her a very long time, nearly an hour, but you must remember that I was thinking at the same time. [Jesús Ignacio Aldapuerta, 'Handful', p. 39 of the 1995 Critical Vision (Stockport, Cheshire) edition of *The Eyes*.]

Or metaphorico-allegorical:

It was two or three in the morning. He had felt the glass in front of his face grow cool, cooler, cold. The cars came less frequently, and sometimes the giant green cyclops eye of the traffic signal glowed on him for minutes at a time. (*Ibid.*, p. 9)

Or another way:

Cradling her in two hands, he walked over to the flak-hole in the fuselage wall. The moon rode beneath him, a negative pupil in a giant eye of water. He sat down on the edge of the hole, legs dangling over kilometres of emptiness, and waited, dandling the head in his lap like a child, for the impulse to come to push himself and her out and down to the black, unending sea. (*Ibid.*, pp. 24–5)

These describe, respectively, an obese paedophile gazing at the child-victim he is about to rape, strangle, and *eat* whole; a crash-fetishist psychopath waiting for a twin-car collision that will deliver a severed female head to him for sexual play; and an experimental-rocket-aircraft-fetishist psychopath already in possession of a female head and about to commit suicide by leaping from an aircraft several thousand metres into the sea.

In the first passage, Aldapuerta, drawing doubtless on his own psychopathology, implicitly recognises the subconscious nature of the maleficent gaze: the paedophile cannot clearly remember what the girl looks like, for just as his mind has been overthrown and conquered by the will to ill, so his brain has been swamped by the rhythms of an impending surrender to violence and sexual perversion. The second extract from *The Eyes* is interesting for the additional reason that it is taken from a story that mentions goats.

Goats have long been associated with Satanism and the anti-Christian occult, and usual explanations of this association have concentrated on their feral nature and a possession of horns that links them ex- or implicitly with pagan deities like Pan – goat-horned, hoofed, and with shaggy-furred lower limbs – and Dionysus, lord of intoxicating ivy and vine. I suggest here, however, that an additional caprine characteristic has been overlooked: their possession of disturbing eyes. Goats, unlike any other common domestic herbivore, have slitted, vertical pupils in what are often unsettlingly golden or tawny eyes.

Their eyes are, in short, like those of cats, and we can easily see an association between the great cat *Panthera onca*, or the jaguar, and the crimes committed in Juárez. The gaze of a jaguar or other predatory animal is unsettling because it is scrutinising, probing, supplying information to a brain whose centres of instinctual aggression and attack are activated. Examine now ocular narratives from the lives of Sharif and Sutcliffe. First Sharif, and information from 'Lisa', a victim raped and assaulted by him in Gainesville, Florida, and John Pascoe, his acquaintance in New Hope, Pennsylvania. It was there that Sharif threatened to kill her if she screamed. It was there that Sharif said he had done it before, and promised to kill again. Lisa had no doubt, then or later, that he spoke the literal truth. She saw the evil in his eyes. Was it Pascoe's imagination, or did Sharif become even more sinister as the months passed? There was the way he lovingly fingered his huge, red-handled hunting knife, the look of madness that sometimes came into his eyes.

Now to Sutcliffe, and information from Gerry Douglas, a Glaswegian whose family Sutcliffe, before his arrest, had befriended using the false name of 'Peter Logan':

Gerry Douglas, young and unemployed, looking like a down-at-heel George Best with a wife and three children, was later to reveal an amazing incident involving Pete Logan. 'One night Pete was at my mammy's house,' Gerry remembers, 'and my brother

William said to him, "Pete, you know your eyes look evil tonight. I don't know what it is." Pete just looked at him and said, "Well, I am the Yorkshire Ripper." We all had a laugh.' (*The Yorkshire Ripper: an in-depth study of a mass killer and his methods*, Roger Cross, HarperCollins, 1993)

What these observers of Sharif and Sutcliffe were seeing, I believe, was a gaze controlled and directed by a brain in attack-and-aggression mode – a brain operating at an instinctual, animal level yet still possessing human intelligence and insight. If one were to take a metaphor from metaphysics or religion, one might almost say that Sharif and Sutcliffe were *possessed* by the spirit of a predatory animal. This idea that men can be so possessed is found all around the globe and on every continent. In the Old World, for example, the most prominent predator was the wolf, and men behaving like Sharif or Sutcliffe have long been known as lycanthropes: wolf-men: werewolves. In Latin America, another predator is more prominent, and so in place of werewolves anthropologists find the universal concept of the 'were-animal' taking a different but closely related form:

The natural jaguar is a predator whose appearance and behaviour, in the inventive hands of the shaman, is raw material for elaborating an infinitely malleable concept of man-animal and shaman-jaguar transformations. Differences in age, knowledge and predisposition mean that the jaguar concept may be interpreted differently by individuals and tribes ... The Desana Indians ... possess at least three different interpretations of jaguar symbolism: some say that the 'were-jaguar' is simply a human who has been snuffing [*Anadenathera peregrina*, the psychoactive plant known as] *viho*; others take the identification of the shaman with a jaguar at face value, by saying that a man merely puts on a jaguar skin; whilst others proffer the opinion that the 'jaguar' is neither a skin nor a real jaguar, but an 'essence' or 'state of mind', which enforces the individual to act like a jaguar. (*People of the Jaguar: The Living Spirit of Ancient America*, Nicholas J. Saunders, Souvenir Press, 1989)

Does this not cast light from a different angle on to the behaviour of Sharif and *Los Choferes*, allowing us to see fresh facets of their psychopathology? What they did was 'natural' in one sense, but wholly unnatural in another. It is natural for a predator like the jaguar to prey upon human beings, particularly for it to prey upon the weakest and most vulnerable of them. It is wholly unnatural for a *human being* to prey upon human beings like this, even more especially for a *male* human being to prey like this upon *female* human beings. It represents a warping, a crippling, a truncation of the neurological systems of intra-species sociability and compassion that seem to operate among all mammalian groups and that have reached their highest state of development among human beings.

And yet we arrived at this discussion of the interrelation of the animal and human behaviour by taking a false step, when we moved from the slitted, vertical pupils of the goat to the slitted, vertical pupils of cats. For the jaguar, like other great cats, has *round* pupils rather than slitted, vertical ones, which are characteristic of the smaller species of the family *Felidae*. What the eyes of great cats like the jaguar have in common with those of their smaller cousins is this:

Jaguars, like all cats, possess a dense layer of light-gathering cells at the back of the eye called the *tapetum lucidum* [literally, the 'shining carpet'].

Whilst this enables them to see better in the dark and be more efficient predators, it also means that their eyes appear to glow in the dark when a light is placed in front of them. (*Ibid.*, p. 161)

The eyes of jaguars are, in other words, like *mirrors*:

Eyes are full of metaphorical significance for native Amerindians: they enable shamans to perceive the otherwise invisible spirits, they are linked closely to mirrors and ideas of reflection and they emit tears, which are often seen as analogous to rain and so linked to the concept of fertility. (*Ibid.*, p. 95)

Mirrors were an integral part of pre-Hispanic culture in Central and South America – remember the god Tezcatlipoca, the 'Smoking Mirror' – and have exercised a powerful influence on Latin American art and culture to the present day. Mirrors reflect and distort, fooling the eye into believing that right is left, left is right, here is there, there is here. These concepts allow us to add another allegory to the collection we will gather in the course of this book. The crimes in Juárez, I suggest elsewhere, could be described as a *Comedia de Terrores* – a Comedy of Terrors. They could also be described as a *Laberinto de Espejos* – a Labyrinth of Mirrors.

Who is innocent? Who is guilty? Who knows whom, who paid what to whom, who took orders from whom? There seems certainty only at the centre of the labyrinth, where Sharif waits like the Minotaur, bellowing his defiance and rage down the twisting, mirror-lined corridors that snake back and forth but lead always in his direction. And yet even Sharif shares, in a small way, in the shifting, shimmering uncertainties of the case, like a face thrown back from the curved surface of a sideshow mirror or a *mesa* seen far off through distorting kilometres of sun-scalded desert air. What is Sharif's full name? One can find several versions in the American and Mexican media: Sharif Abdul Latif Sharif; Sharif Abdel Latif Sharif; Abdel Latif Sharif Sharif; Abdel Latif Sharif; even – probably a 'Freudian' slip – Omar Latif Sharif and – surely a typographical error – Abdel Latif Sahif Sharif. And yet the meaning of the one element that remains constant – Sharif – throws us back into the allegory of the *Comedia de Terrores*, the Comedy of Terrors. Sharif is a serial rapist and killer, and yet in his mother tongue, Arabic, his name means 'noble', *šariif*, from a verb meaning 'to be exalted', *šarafa*. [From the etymology given for 'sherif' (*sic*) in the *Concise Oxford English Dictionary*.]

12: Drugs

Droga f. Cualquier sustancia medicamentosa natural o sintética de efecto estimulante, deprimente o narcótico.

Drug. A natural or synthetic medical substance with a stimulating, depressive, or narcotic effect.

All languages seem to have a tendency to shorten long words in common use. In English, omnibus – a Latin word meaning 'for everyone' – became bus. In Latin American Spanish, *narcotraficante* – drug-trafficker – became *narco*. Druggie. But there is an irony in the word, for *narco* literally means 'numb', and Latin American *narcos* typically prefer stimulating cocaine to numbing heroin.

But, they might ask, why should it be otherwise? For cocaine is a Latin American drug, produced from a Latin American plant with a Latin American name: *coca*, or *kuka* in the Amerindian Quecha language of Peru. Cocaine comes from what in the classificatory language of international science is called *Erythroxylon coca*, meaning 'red-wood coca'. The Greek prefix *erythro-* turns up again in another scientific term: erythrocyte, meaning 'red blood cell'. Here nomenclature echoes reality, for a great many red blood cells have been spilt over red-wood coca. There are huge sums of money to be made from its cultivation, harvesting, and conversion into snow-white cocaine. And of course, as the Bible puts it, the love of money is the root of all evil. (First Timothy vi, 10.) In the case of cocaine this root puts forth an evil of tropical luxuriance, heraldically profuse, poisonously green, thornily glittering.

Take, for example, the 'War on Drugs' waged by the government of the United States for so many years. This has been, literally, a killing joke. Leslie Cockburn's *Out of Control: The Story of the Reagan's Administration's Secret War in Nicaragua, the Illegal Arms Pipeline, and the Contra Drug Connection* describes how, to finance the freedom-fighters of the Contra-Sandanista resistance in Nicaragua, weapons and cash were flown to Central America from US Air Force bases on American soil. The book then goes on to describe how drugs were flown back from Central America to Air Force Bases on American soil. And should the hypocritical stench of that particular phase of the 'War' ever begin to fade, point your nostrils – cautiously – towards another. An ongoing one. The complicity of American chemicals industry in the drugs trade:

> Heroin is impossible to control by indirect means. . . . Cocaine is a different matter, and it should be possible to stop its production because it requires a few essential chemicals to extract it from coca leaves and refine it. Cocaine production in Columbia is probably in excess of 1,000 tons a year, and this requires the importation of 20,000 tons of organic solvents, which is 15,000 tons more than legitimately required by industry. Along the way to the final snowy white powder, the process requires the solvent methyl ethyl ketone, and the oxidizing agent potassium permanganate. Columbia imports over a third of all the methyl ethyl ketone shipped from the USA to South America. Clearly much of this is destined for the cocaine laboratories. The Colombian authorities are also trying to control diethyl ether, which can be used in place of methyl ethyl ketone,

and have not issued an import licence for this solvent since 1987. However, the police seize almost 1,250,000 litres (250,000 gallons) of it a year when they raid cocaine labs, and estimate that each year ten times this amount is imported into the country illegally. (*Molecules at an Exhibition: Portraits of intriguing materials in everyday life*, John Emsley, Oxford University Press, 1998, Gallery 3A)

Nature abhors a vacuum, and the vacuum created by American consumption of cocaine sucks the drug north, some of it by air and sea, but, particularly since an American 'crackdown' on direct exports, most of it overland, through Panama, Costa Rica, Nicaragua, Honduras, Guatemala, and El Salvador, until it reaches México, the final reservoir in which it will be stored before it is released on to the market of the United States. Some shipments of cocaine take to the sea at this point, carried off the Yucatán Peninsula across the Gulf of México and the Caribbean to Florida and Louisiana, Miami and New Orleans. Many other shipments, however, continue overland to the border and cities like Juárez. Juárez is the drugs capital of north-central México, the power-base of a giant cartel once run by a druglord called Amado Carillo Fuentes, who was described by one DEA report as being:

extremely well connected within the MFJP. Reporting in March 1993 indicates that Amado Carillo Fuentes possesses MFJP Jefe de Grupo credentials for the special investigations section and has a gold colored MFJP badge. (From a 'Secret DEA summary of the cartels and their link to Gonzales (*sic*) Calderoni', PBS Online)

The DEA, many readers will already know, is the American Drug Enforcement Administration; the MFJP, somewhat fewer readers will already know, is the Mexican Federal Judicial Police. The drug-dealer Fuentes, incredible as it may seem, had official accreditation as a drug-policeman. But he could hardly have been described as a *lobo con piel de oveja* – a wolf in sheep's clothing – because wolves and sheep are hard to distinguish in the world of Mexican drug-trafficking. Just as they are hard to distinguish in the world of Mexican politics: the Mexican president Carlos Salinas fled the country in 1995 just ahead of charges for corruption and complicity with the drugs cartels. The tougher regime that followed supposedly led to the demise of Carlos Fuentes, who is said to have 'died while undergoing surgery to conceal his physical identity' (*Northern Mexico Handbook*, Joe Cummings), although he was already famous for his lack of a physical identity: 'No one knows what he really looks like'. (WHILE YOU WERE SLEEPING, Charles Bowden.)

By then, however, he was long established as a popular hero, one of the underworld figures known, in seemingly conscious imitation of the Mafia term *capo*, as *jefes*, 'bosses'. And just as there is a Mafia *capo di cappi*, a capo of capos, so there is a narco *jefe de jefes*, a boss of bosses. The title was borrowed for the name of an album by the northern Mexican band *Los Tigres del Norte*, whose name literally means 'The Tigers of the North', though *tigres* means 'jaguars' in Latin America. The album recorded by these 'Jaguars of the North' consisted of nineteen *corridos* – ballads – but of a particular kind: *narco-corridos*. Though the genre and musical idiom are entirely different, the inspiration is the same as it is in gangsta-rap: the lives of *narcotraficantes y pandilleros*, drug-dealers and gangsters. Lives that are often nasty, brutish, and short, but that are idealised by many of the youths of cities like Juárez, who are further encouraged by official disapproval of *narco-corridos* to see men like Carlos Fuentes as avatars of past Mexican rebels: rising from the people to inhabit a phantasmogoric world of extreme glamour, extreme wealth, and extreme violence.

For the profits to be made from any illegal drug – and Fuentes was said to be earning two hundred million dollars a week at the height of his power (WHILE YOU WERE SLEEPING, Charles Bowden) – encourage violence among the rival criminals trafficking in it, but trafficking in cocaine is much likelier to encourage violence than any other drug. Many traffickers are also users, and users of cocaine experience a deadly mix of emotions:

> Taking cocaine produces a brief and immediate period of intense well-being, exhilaration and euphoria. This can be followed by feelings of agitation, anxiety or fear, and even hallucinations when the user feels threatened.
>
> Large doses cause sleeplessness, hallucinations, tremors and convulsions. Paranoid delusions can lead to violent behaviour. Respiratory troubles, digestive disorders and sensations of insects crawling on or under the skin occur. The pupils become dilated, and heart rate and blood pressure increase. (*Drug Warning: an illustrated guide for parents and teachers*, David Stockley, Macdonald Optima, 1986)

Those initial feelings of euphoria and wellbeing unbalance the judgment and encourage the taking of risks, and the succeeding feelings of anxiety and paranoia encourage a swift resort to violence when those risks fail to come off. Combine this with the already violence-prone *machista* culture of México, and you have a recipe for spiralling murder rates: male on male, and male on female:

> 2 February [1999] Just days [after the death of another woman], a 17-year-old woman, eight months pregnant, was murdered, and her stabbed body was

found on 9 February, partially buried in a patio under construction at her home in Cd. Juárez. It is believed that her boyfriend, also 17, murdered and buried her on 2 February before hanging himself the next day.

José Luis Durán Estrada, allegedly a drug addict, told his family before his suicide that his girlfriend, Paulina León, had left their home to visit her mother, however the family found that strange since she had not packed any of her clothes. Estrada's brothers found her buried body a week later, and the cause of death was reported as shock due to loss of blood.

14 February On Valentine's Day ... Elsa América Arreguán, 22, mother of a six-month-old and a two-year-old, and five months pregnant, was shot to death at the door of her home in Cd. Juárez by two men who had asked for her husband, David Campa López. América was a victim of regular beatings by her husband, according to her mother. Campa is allegedly a drug addict. There are suspicions that the crime may be some type of drug trafficking revenge or that the bullets were intended for Campa. Two suspects remain in custody. (Ann Marie Mackler, editor, *Frontera NorteSur*, March 1999)

These are examples of the female deaths that have continued since the arrest of *Los Choferes*: violent, bloody, but not accompanied by rape or sexual mutilation. They are isolated, fragmented evidence more of a society's psychopathology than of an individual's.

But recall part of the confession of one of *Los Rebeldes*:

'On the drive there all the guys were sniffing cocaine and after about an hour and twenty minutes' driving "Charly" tried to make her take some, like with his forefinger and thumb he wanted to put the stuff up her nose, but the girl would not let him, so the guys were hitting her.' (*El Diario de Juárez*)

Here cocaine is working as part of Mexican gang culture: *macho*, violent, self-gratificatory. Even if this particular incident in this particular confession is, as I have already suggested, a fabricated one, it must be based on experience, must have rung true with the gang member or police officers who fabricated it. Coke and violence. Coke and murder. Coke and rape. They go together like Jesus and Mary. For if drugs can warp the mind, so can culture. Particularly that aspect of culture known as religion.

13: The Egyptian

Egipto, Estado del NE. de Africa. Las regiones desérticas ocupan el 97 por 100 del territorio egipcio.

Egypt. State in the north-east of Africa. Desert occupies ninety-seven per cent of Egyptian territory.

'*Nonne tu est Ægyptius, qui ante hos dies tumultum concitasti, et eduxisti in desertum quatuor millia virorum sicariorum?* Art thou not that Egyptian, which before these days madest an uproar, and leddest out into the desert . . . men that were murderers?' (Acts, xxi, 38. I have followed the Authorised Version's translation here except for the change of 'wilderness' to 'desert')

The cultures of Ancient Egypt and Ancient México, as has been pointed out by the Norwegian adventurer and historian Thor Heyerdahl in his travelog *The Ra Expeditions* (1967), show many strange and thought-provoking parallels: pyramids; worship of the sun, stars, and anthropomorphised animals; funerary mummification; hieroglyphs; papyrus boats. Modern Egypt and modern México show fewer parallels, but one very large one remains: desert. Egypt and México – particularly northern México – are places whose cultures have been shaped by heat, sand, and dust. In some ways, Abdul Latif Sharif Sharif must have felt he was coming home when he came to Juárez to take up well-paid work for Benchmark Technology and Research. He must have felt this because he is an Egyptian.

Today he is *the* Egyptian – *el egipcio*. He has earnt this status by becoming the chief suspect for the Juárez serial killings. For some, including his defence lawyer, this is evidence of Mexican xenophobia. Serial murder, the police have claimed, is not a Mexican crime: it is something foreigners do. Americans, or naturalised Americans, like Sharif, *el egipcio*. After all, America is a Protestant country, Egypt a Muslim one, and surely neither is anything like Catholic México.

Surely? Not so surely. Islam recognises Christianity as being, like itself, a Religion of the Book. Christianity's book is the Bible:

And He [Jesus] shall set the sheep on his right hand, but the goats on the left ... Then shall he say unto them on the left hand, Depart from me, ye cursed, into everlasting fire, prepared for the devil and his angels. ... And these shall go away into everlasting punishment. (Matthew xxv, 33–46)

Islam's book is the Qur'an:

What will be of the companions of the left hand? [They will be] in the midst of a fierce blast of fire and in boiling water ... and in the shades of black smoke ... [They] shall surely taste of the tree of Zaqqum ... and drink boiling water on top of it: indeed, [they] shall drink like diseased camels raging with thirst! [*The Holy Qur'an*, Surah, LVI 41–55 trans. Abdullah Yusuf Ali (1946). The 'tree of Zaqqum' (*sic*) is a 'bitter and pungent tree described as growing at the bottom of Hell, a type of all that is disagreeable' (note to Surah xvii, 60)]

These cultural echoes are not coincidental, for Islam was built on a foundation of Christianity just as Christianity was built on a foundation of Judaism. A religion exists to perpetuate itself, and it makes no difference that it should do so at the expense of the psychological health of its adherents. Indeed, damaging the psychological health of its adherents is one of the most effective ways for a religion to increase its hold over them: it is the unbalanced who need priests (and *imams*), just as it is the sick who need doctors.

For surely the sadistic gloating seen in Christian and Muslim descriptions of the torments of Hell must have an unbalancing effect on those who are exposed to them, particularly in childhood. If God or Allah sees fit to apply His infinite wisdom to the task of devising ingenious ways of torturing guilty human beings through all eternity, can it be good for human beings to try their humble best to emulate Him?

The answer, for many Christians and Muslims, has been that it *is* good – so long as the cause is just and righteous, of course, and the tortured human beings guilty of the requisite crimes. Such as the crime of being female:

The government of Afghanistan is declaring war against women. The situation is so bad that an editor of *The Times* compares the treatment of women with the treatment of Jews under the Third Reich. Since the Taliban took power in 1996, women have had to wear a *burqua* (tunic) and have been beaten and stoned in public for not using the required clothing, even if it is just not using the mesh that covers the eyes. A woman was beaten to death by a group of fundamentalists when she accidentally did not cover her arms while driving. Another was stoned to death when trying to leave the country with a man who was not her relative. Since 1996, women [have not been] permitted to work or to appear in public unless they are accompanied by a male relative; women professionals such as teachers, translators, doctors, lawyers, artists and secretaries have been forced to leave their work and are confined to their houses. The resulting cases of depression are at an epidemic level. Women prefer to take their lives rather than live under such conditions. The houses where there are women have to have the windows painted so they can never be seen from outside. They have to use silent shoes so they can never be heard. Women fear for their lives if they commit the most minimal wrong. Because they are not able to work, those who do not have male relatives or spouses are dying of hunger or begging even though they have degrees ... In one of the scarce hospitals for women, a reporter found immobile bodies, wrapped in their tunics, unable to talk, eat or to do anything other than to die slowly. Others have become crazy and are found rocking in a corner or crying, mainly out of fear. (Revolutionary Association of the Women of Afghanistan)

The Taliban referred to here are, of course, Muslim fundamentalists (although it should be noted that the concept of 'fundamentalism' cannot be applied to Muslims in the way that it can to Christians or Jews). Some Muslim apologists would defend the actions of the Taliban on the grounds that they are trying to restore the fundamental dignity of women in their proper, God-ordained sphere of the family and the home. The hollowness of this defence can be seen from a story that emerged from Afghanistan earlier, when the Taliban – as the freedom-fighting *Mujáhidín* – were fighting for victory against a puppet government propped up by the atheistic Soviet Union. The story told of a:

young woman living in the Shahrara district of Kabul in early 1994. Her husband had been killed in a bomb attack. She had three children of between two and nine years old. One day she leaves her children to go and find some food. Two Mujahideen armed guards arrest her in the street and take her to their base where 22 men rape her for three days. She is allowed to go. When she reaches her home she finds her three children have died of hypothermia. She has now lost her sanity. (AFGHANISTAN: THE WORLD'S DIRTY SECRET, *Amnesty Journal*, Jan/Feb 1996)

This is an example of what can happen when the sexual repression enforced by Islam on men is given opportunity for release. Other, less extreme examples can be found in the harassment faced by Western women in Muslim countries like Pakistan: the West is, in the perfervid imagination of the sex-starved Muslim male, a paradise of sexual delights, and Western women the concomitant ever-available *houris*.

Ever-available in every way. After all, Allah has ordained that, to her husband, a Muslim wife should be sheer tilth: 'Your wives are as a tilth to you; so approach your tilth when or how you will.' (Surah ii, 223.)

'Tilth' is 'that which is to be tilled', 'till' being a metaphor for the act of penetrative sex, and Fatima Mernissi's *Women and Islam: An Historical & Theological Enquiry* describes how this verse has been used to justify the sodomising of Muslim women by their husbands. There is, however, no little theological controversy about this verse, with some holding that it refers merely to variants on vaginal sex, and Mernissi's judgment is that the 'no-holes-barred' interpretation is a piece of self-serving Qur'anic exegesis by men and yet another example of the oppression and abuse of female minds and bodies that flourishes in male-dominated Islam.

But sodomy is a sexual practice that has flourished in Islamic countries not only against women. Islam has always restricted the access of the sexes to one another, and when the female sex is not available to the patriarch, the male sex will serve almost as well for this form of sex:

Sharif would be his own star witness [during the hearing to deport him as an undesirable alien], insisting during emotional testimony that his mistakes were long behind him. Therapists were helping him work through the trauma of his Egyptian childhood, of being sodomised as a child by his father and other male relatives, Sharif said. ('MONSTER' BEATS THE SYSTEM, Tim Madigan, The *Seattle Times*, 1999)

Doubtless this is how sodomy has persisted in Islamic culture for millennia, as each generation's crop of male victims becomes sowers of the next generation's crop. For a male to be humiliated and psychologically and physically scarred by the act of anal rape by other males may, as we see elsewhere, be a potent ingredient in the creation of a male-on-female rapist. This certainly seems possible in the case of Sharif, for it could be argued that Egyptian sodomy was exported by one Muslim male for use against the Catholic women of México. And not only the fully grown women:

The body of Irma Angélica Rosales Lozano, 13, was found in a vacant lot near the Luis Olague colonia on the southwest side of Cd. Juárez. She was raped vaginally and rectally, and suffocated with a plastic grocery bag. She had been released from work at Electrocomponentes de México, a nearby *maquila*, the same morning she was found dead. It is believed she had been dead for only a few hours when she was found which indicates that this crime happened in broad daylight. Semen was found in her body which has provided some leads in solving the crime. (BORDER REACTS TO 184 MURDERED WOMEN, Anne Marie Mackler, *Frontera NorteSur*, March 1999)

This particular murder took place after Sharif's arrest, but anal rape is believed to have been a characteristic feature of the sex-murders he is accused of and was, while still free, capable of committing. This *modus operandi* would naturally, if the police claims of an outside conspiracy are to be believed, have been adopted by the proxies he appointed to continue the murders in his name. These proxies would have been Christians, but with attitudes towards women that had been similarly warped by their religious upbringing. Examine, for example, an interesting theory to emerge (albeit jocularly) from the work of an American government commission on the effects of pornography in the United States:

> [The campaign against pornography was more difficult] in Los Angeles, where the porn industry fought back through Beverly Hills lawyer John Weston, representing the Adult Film Association. Weston had done a little research of his own: why, he wanted to know, was the Commission worried about pornography when most serial killers in the United States actually come from rural, right-wing, fundamentalist protestant backgrounds, where their reading matter would have been mainly limited to the Bible in their early years? 'Would one literally extrapolate from that undeniable fact that the Bible or formal fundamentalist protestant theology inculcates within its adherents the desire or necessity of serial killing? I think not.' (*Soft Core: Moral Crusades against Pornography in Britain and America*, Bill Thompson)

But why not? Though it was invented jocularly, there seems no reason for the theory not to be applied seriously. There may well be a causal link between the reading of the Bible and the sex-murder of women, for a constant theme of the Bible is that of the sexually wanton woman who must be punished for her misbehaviour:

Thus saith the Lord God: Because thy filthiness was poured out, and thy nakedness discovered through thy whoredoms with thy lovers ... I will judge thee ... And I will give thee blood in fury and jealousy ... [Thy lovers] shall strip thee also of thy clothes ... and leave thee naked and bare ... and they shall stone thee, and thrust thee through with their swords ... I will do these things unto thee, because thou hast gone a whoring [sic] after the heathen ... Thou shalt be filled with drunkenness and sorrow, with the cup of astonishment and desolation ... Thou shalt drink it and suck it out, and thou shalt break the sherds thereof, and pluck off thine own breasts: for I have spoken *it*, saith the Lord God. (Ezekiel xvi, 36–40 & xxiii, 30–34)

In the Bible one can find a psychotic harping on the promiscuity and lust of women, startlingly expressed in these verses from Proverbs:

xxx, 15; The leech has two daughters, saying, 'Give! Give!' Three things are insatiable, and a fourth that never says, 'That is enough.' xxx, 16; Hell, and the mouth of the womb, and the earth that is never filled with water, and fire truly never says, 'That is enough.' (Translation of the Catholic *Vulgate*, or Latin Bible)

The 'mouth of the womb', or *os vulvæ*, is, of course, the vagina. These Biblical messages about female nature are found in all modern versions of the Bible, but there are additional messages in the Catholic Bible, which incorporates the Jewish Apocrypha and includes another indirect but unmistakable reference to the insatiable greed of the vagina:

A headstrong daughter must be held with a tight rein,
or she will find opportunity to bestow her favours . . .
No stake but she will make fast by it, no arrow comes
amiss to her archery. (Ecclesiastes, xxvi, 13 & 15)

This is the delicate mistranslation of the prudish
Catholic writer Mgr Ronald Knox (1888–1957), renowned for his scholarship but unable, apparently, to
recall here that the Graeco-Latin word *pharetra* should be
translated not 'archery' but 'quiver'. When the word is
translated correctly, it becomes obvious that Ecclesiastes is
describing the woman's desire for her vagina to be
penetrated by a penis – the 'stake' and the 'arrow'.
It is easy to imagine that such Biblical verses – the
'plucking off' of breasts, the 'tight rein' for would-be
promiscuous young women – could become converted in
the mind of a psychopath into divine commands for the
mutilation and asphyxiation of female sinners:

Also, the left breast of at least one was mutilated,
similar to some of the earlier cases . . . She was raped,
vaginally and rectally, and suffocated with a plastic
grocery bag. [BORDER REACTS TO 184 MURDERED WOMEN,
Anne Marie Mackler, *Frontera NorteSur*, March
1999. (Note, too, that Knox's 'tight rein' is also a
paraphrase.)]

When Sharif emigrated to Juárez, he brought the
psychopathology of one daughter of Judaism, Islam, into
a region steeped in the psychopathology of another,
Roman Catholicism. The mix was potent, seething,
corrosive, lethal, and destined to eat out permanent scars
in the psychic landscape of northern México. Or so
Sharif's arrest and conviction for the murders of young
women would seem to force us to believe. This Egyptian
immigrant Sharif, the police and media of Juárez

proclaimed, was guilty of these horrifyingly brutal, radically un-Mexican sexual crimes.

And the belief in his guilt can only have been confirmed when it was discovered that Sharif had previous convictions for rape and sexual assault arising from his stay in the American states of Florida and Texas: in 1981 he was sentenced to forty-five days' imprisonment for 'assault and battery' in North Palm Beach, Gainesville, Florida, and in 1983 he was sentenced to twelve years' imprisonment for rape in Gainesville, also in Florida. After serving six years of this sentence, he was again released early, and was sent by the American company he worked for to supervise the setting up of a *maquiladora* in Juárez. In other words, he raped in the United States, was imprisoned, released, began to rape again in the United States, was imprisoned, released, and began to rape yet again, in México. But this time he also began to murder.

Or did he? For here we need to pause and examine a little-discussed and less-publicised point of statistical jurisprudence. Is the probability of Sharif's guilt strengthened by the discovery of his previous convictions for sexual violence and assault? At first glance the answer clearly seems to be yes. But is it? In fact, the answer is not so simple. One needs to distinguish between these two questions: Given that Sharif is the man responsible for the sex-murders in Juárez, how likely is it that he has a history of rape and sexual violence against women? And: Given that Sharif has a history of rape and sexual violence against women, how likely is it that he is the man responsible for the Juárez sex-murders?

Whatever the probability given for question one, the probability given for question two must be lower. To see why, examine these parallel questions: Given that someone is Mexican, how likely is it that he or she speaks Spanish? And: Given that someone speaks Spanish, how likely is it that he or she is Mexican?

In this recast form, the underlying propositions lose their initial obscuring emotiveness and become exercises in logic and mathematics. It is more likely that a Mexican speaks Spanish than it is that someone who speaks Spanish is a Mexican. Similarly, it is more likely for someone who is a sex-murderer to have convictions for rape than it is for someone who has convictions for rape to be a sex-murderer. The likelihood of Sharif's guilt is not greatly increased by the discovery that he has a history of rape and sexual violence against women. No one, for example, would regard a failure to discover such a history as greatly increasing the chances of his innocence, and Sharif's previous convictions remain circumstantial evidence of his present guilt, even in the face of claims made by a previous victim. An American victim:

> Then, in March 1983, a 20-year-old college student answered Sharif's ad for a live-in housekeeper. Sharif attacked the woman, Lisa, on her first night in his house – punched, choked, kicked and raped her. And that night, there was a particularly sinister element to his behavior. To Lisa, he bragged of killing other women and burying them; he threatened to kill her if she tried to escape. ('MONSTER' BEATS THE SYSTEM, Tim Madigan, The *Seattle Times*, 1999)

Such evidence must still be regarded as circumstantial, like other facts about him, including, strangely, his intelligence and, not so strangely, his taste for a combination of strong drink and low company:

> 'I meet the wrong people when I'm drinking and I go to the wrong places.' (SIX NEW SLAYINGS REVEAL THAT KILLER STILL ON THE LOOSE, Mark Smith, The *Houston Chronicle*, 30 March 1996)

Sharif's own words. The pleasure and the sense of release brought by alcohol depend on its effects on the brain. It relaxes and dissolves inhibitions. It also, in Shakespeare's words, 'provokes the desire', but 'takes away the performance'. (Macbeth iii, 28.) The desire of what? As Shakespeare might also have put it: the desire of venery. Venery is an interestingly ambiguous word in this context, for it means both 'sexual indulgence' and 'hunting'. Drinking heavily provokes a desire for one kind of venery that, impossible to satisfy, may transmute into the other. How many drunken men, frustrated by their inability to achieve the gratification of sex with a woman, have turned instead to the gratification of violence against a woman? The erectile tissue of the penis is not under conscious control: a man cannot bring about an erection by a simple act of will. But by a simple act of will he can create a fist, or pick up a bottle, use it to enact the second kind of venery, and discover that he is then able to enact the first.

Was this Sharif's discovery? Alcohol has played a part in rape and serial murder for as long as either has been recognised, sometimes used to release the inhibitions of the victimiser, sometimes used to enfeeble the victim:

> And Lot went up out of Zoar . . . And he dwelt in a cave, he and his two daughters . . . And the firstborn said unto the younger, 'Our father *is* old, and *there is* not a man in the earth to come unto us after the manner of all the earth . . . Come, let us make our father drink wine, and we will lie with him, that we may preserve the seed of our father.' (Genesis xix, 30–32)

Lot broke the taboo on incest by being drunk, just as, as Brian Masters' *Killing for Company* describes, Dennis Nilsen broke the taboo on murder by being drunk. Drink

113

seems very likely to have nurtured Sharif's psychopathology, perhaps even to have created it in the first place. Again we can see the lie in the claim that rape and murder can be pursued from a rational assessment of the pleasure to be gained from them. For rape and murder to take place there must be a psychopathic substrate, a temporary neurological imbalance brought about by a single bout of drinking, perhaps, or a permanent neurological imbalance brought about by the explosive physiological damage of a blow or fall, or the slow-burning chemical insult of prolonged drinking to excess.

It is the second, permanent kind of abnormality that underlies the behaviour of the serial killer, the criminal who rapes and murders not once but many times over an extended period. Sharif's brain was and is abnormal: I believe this to be objectively verifiable fact. And yet his brain is also a highly efficient one: Sharif, as we shall shortly see, has been described as a *mucho muy inteligente señor*: a very intelligent man.

But what of his intelligence? How is this evidence for his crimes? It is evidence for his crimes because above-average intelligence has been found to be a feature of a certain class of serial killer, perhaps best exemplified by Theodore 'Ted' Bundy (1946–89). Biologists have long observed that predators are more intelligent than their prey: cats are more intelligent than mice; wolves more intelligent than deer; predatory human beings more intelligent than the many, many species they prey upon – including the species to which they themselves belong, *Homo sapiens*.

Yes, it seems. Serial killers – those who make almost a profession of murder – have in some sense to be more intelligent than their victims. More cunning, certainly, but also, in the case of serial killers like Bundy and, perhaps, Sharif, more intelligent in the strict sense. Because they have to outwit not only their victims, but also the authorities, their employers, their families, their friends and acquaintances. Bundy was not a psychopathic drifter, but a psychopathic professional: he held down a good job while he raped and murdered. He could not allow his secret inner life to become suspected by those around him, or his secret inner life was over. (Perhaps, in the end, that was what he wanted: to carry out his final killing spree he is known to have deliberately moved from a state where murder did not carry the death penalty to one, Florida, where it did.)

And there are in fact some chilling parallels between Bundy and Sharif, almost as though the two were contemporaneous avatars of some misogynistic deity of blood and murder:

Bundy: Bundy scoured university campuses, student rooming houses and youth hostels searching for 'look-alike', attractive female victims. (*The Serial Killers*, Colin Wilson and Donald Seaman, p. 7, Virgin, 1990)

Sharif: The six most recent cases involve girls, ages fifteen to seventeen, who closely match the physical description of the nine earlier victims. All fifteen victims were in their teens or early twenties, slim and petite, almost always with long dark hair. (Mark Smith, The *Houston Chronicle*, 1996)

Bundy: His *modus operandi* was to use guile, plus his undoubted surface charm, to lure them to a waiting car. On 14 July 1974 he abducted two girls on the same day – Janice Ott and Denise Naslund – from Lake Squammish Park. Both were approached by a good-looking young man with his arm in a sling, who asked for help in lifting a boat on to the luggage rack of his car. (*The Serial Killers*, Colin Wilson and Donald Seaman, Virgin, 1990)

Sharif: In general, Sharif attacks women while on dates or approaches them, gives a fake name and states that his car is disabled. [Capt. Sadie] Darnell [of the Gainesville Police Department, Florida] wrote to [US Immigration Judge William] Nail on 6 November 1992. 'Once they are within his span of control, he physically attacks them, beating them severely, usually in the face, and rapes them. The [victims] were all verbally and physically abused. The detectives stated the victims were terrified, and said Sharif threatened to kill them.' ('MONSTER' BEATS THE SYSTEM, Tim Madigan, The *Seattle Times*, 1999)

Bundy: After his second escape from custody, Bundy deteriorated into a drunken, disorganised 'blitz' type of serial killer. (*The Serial Killers: a study in the psychology of violence*, Colin Wilson and Donald Seaman, Virgin Publishing, London, 1990)

Sharif: Not all of Sharif's colleagues, past or present, were so enamored [of him]. Tom Wilson had worked with the Egyptian chemist for three years in Florida, witnessing both Sharif's technical acumen and the spiral into drunkenness and violence that in 1984 led Sharif to be imprisoned for sexual battery . . . Twice in his first three years in Midland [Texas], Sharif was arrested on drunk-driving charges, but bosses chalked that up to difficulties adjusting from prison. Sharif insisted he had become sober after the last arrest in 1991, and was dutifully attending therapy and several meetings of Alcoholics Anonymous a week. ('MONSTER' BEATS THE SYSTEM, Tim Madigan, The *Seattle Times*, 1999)

Bundy: His background was far from normal. Theodore Robert Bundy was an illegitimate child, born in November 1946 to a respectable and religious young secretary, Louise Cowell, in a home for unmarried mothers in Philadelphia; his mother has always refused to disclose the father's identity. The child was left alone for several weeks before being taken into the home of his grandfather ... When his mother decided to move to Tacoma (Washington), Ted was miserable at losing the only father he had ever known. (*The Serial Killers: a study in the psychology of violence*, Colin Wilson and Donald Seaman, Virgin Publishing, London, 1990)

Sharif: Sharif would be his own star witness [during the deportation hearing in El Paso], insisting during emotional testimony that his mistakes were long behind him. Therapists were helping him work through the trauma of his Egyptian childhood, of being sodomized as a child by his father and other male relatives, Sharif said. ('MONSTER' BEATS THE SYSTEM, Tim Madigan, The *Seattle Times*, 1999)

And it seems highly likely that many would-be serial killers are arrested and imprisoned before they can become 'serial', after one or two murders, being too clumsy to sustain a career that will lift their body-count of victims into double or even high single figures. Bundy and Sharif, then, embody a kind of psychopathic Darwinism, representing a survival not merely of the sickest but also of the brightest, the most able, of their monstrous kind. This perhaps has some relation to a strange phenomenon observed of murderers and serial killers after their arrest: that they receive fan-mail from many women, and even offers of marriage. The offers are sometimes accepted. On the same true-crime website on which one can find a self-claimed former fiancée of Sharif Sharif requesting up-do-date news of him, one can find the following message from the wife of a man born a stone's-throw from Juárez in El Paso, Texas:

This is Doreen Ramirez. After viewing several websites pertaining to my husband, Richard – including yours – I feel compelled to inform you that I am appalled to read the inaccuracies and, in some cases, outright lies, about my husband and myself. People who do not even know either of us are spewing outrageous opinions which they are passing off as facts, when it is patently clear they know nearly nothing about Richard's case. I appeal to all intelligent persons not to believe everything which is being presented about Richard in the media. The facts of his case ultimately will confirm that Richard is a wrongly convicted man, and I believe fervently that his innocence will be proven to the world. Thank you. (http://www.mayhem.net)

The phenomenon of women – even, as in this instance, intelligent and literate ones – being attracted to famous men is familiar with male sports stars and entertainers, and has been explained there in sociobiological terms by the evolution of a female instinct to mate more readily with 'successful' males.

Even when these successful males will not remain with the woman in question and allow her to use their success to protect her offspring. This may be because success is an indirect guarantee of genes for intelligence or dominance. The success of a serial killer seems likely to be an indirect guarantee of both: the intelligence to obtain victims and escape, at least for a time, the legal consequences, and the dominance to wish to murder in the first place. Distasteful as it may seem, serial killing can, like sport or popular music, be regarded as a career, a profession, in which there are famous successes and unknown failures.

This would explain well the interest Sharif has attracted from at least one female correspondent to the same Internet site just quoted from. Is the story she tells true, or a fantasy? Try and decide for yourself:

I found your site on the Internet while looking for information on the above subject which I know as Sharif Sharif. I was engaged to this man before he was sent out of the United States and got in trouble in México. I have had no contact with him for a very long time. When I knew him I had no idea he had ever been in prison anywhere. He suddenly broke off our engagement after a meeting he had in Houston, Texas, which I later found out had to do with his deportation and a law suit against him and the company he worked for. I now know that he served 6 years in Gainesville, Florida, but was also convicted of a crime before that. I would like to know the whole story about him. What all he has done in the past, everything. I never suspected anything with him. He was always very good to me and my family. Since his arrest in México I have been finding out more and more things I didn't know. Can you give me more information on his crimes or tell me where I can get this type of information? I would really appreciate it. (http://www.mayhem.net)

If the story is true, then perhaps she was attracted to Sharif because of another kind of success he displayed: he has been described as a 'brilliant chemist', with 'registered patents' for inventions made while he was working in the United States. The claim about his registered patents is certainly true:

United States Patent 5,565,513, 15 October 1996

Method and composition for delaying the cross-linking of water-soluble polymer solutions

Abstract

A stable, non-aqueous liquid suspension of delayed boron cross-linkers comprises an anhydrous boron compound or a sparingly soluble borate suspended in a mixture of mineral spirits (commonly termed as naphtha) and a resin. Anhydrous boron compounds suitable for suspension include, but are not limited to, anhydrous borax, anhydrous boric acid, or a mixture of both the anhydrous borax and anhydrous boric acid. Sparingly soluble borates suitable for suspension include, but are not limited to, alkaline earth metal borates, alkali metal borates, or a mixture thereof. The mixture between the mineral spirits and resin produces a mineral spirits–resin solution. Alternatively, the mineral spirits may be replaced with a suitable oil which forms an oil–resin solution when mixed with the resin. The oil–resin solution suspends the anhydrous boron compound or the sparingly soluble borate to produce a stable, non-aqueous liquid suspension of delayed boron cross-linkers.

Inventors: Kinsey, III; E. Wayne (Odessa, TX [Texas]); Sharif, Sharif (Midland, TX); Harry, David (Midland, TX)
Assignee: Benchmark Research & Technology, Inc.
Appl. No.: 495180
Filed: 27 June 1995

Sharif's name can be found on other patents registered at the United States Patents Office, and the income he is said to receive from them has been implicated in the charges of conspiracy brought against him after his arrest and conviction in Juárez. It has also been implicated in the *escandal de sus privilegios* – in the scandal of his privileges:

Before this he [the procurator González Rascón] described a television programme that had been transmitted live the previous morning in the border region, during which he received a call directly from Abdel Latif Sharif Sharif that interrupted an interview he was holding with the special prosecutor Sully Ponce. (*El Diario de Juárez*)

It is possible that Sharif had been watching the programme on the colour television in his cell and, displeased by some point made during the interview, had rung Rascón on his cellphone to protest. Possible, but unlikely: would Sharif have drawn attention to his possession of a personal phone in so glaring a fashion? No, more likely Sharif was unaware that the programme was underway (or was unaware that it was live), and simply availed himself of one of the many privileges he had while incarcerated in the *CeReSo* in Juárez: the ability to make unmonitored calls from his cell to the outside world.

When this came to the attention of the media and outside authorities, an investigation was undertaken and revealed the following list of items in Sharif's cell:

Photograph albums, newspaper and official clippings about the murder of women in Ciudad Juárez ... Two beds, one of them a double bed, the other a single, as well as a microwave oven, air-conditioning, a heater, a clothes-locker and wardrobe ... 14 video-cassettes, a cupboard set into the wall, a colour television, a video-recorder, a table, chairs, a tape-recorder, a bath with shower, a washbasin, a lavatory, kitchen utensils, and a place to keep them.

The Egyptian had been using a cellphone to communicate with the outside world, above all as means of communication to debate with the state authorities. (*El Diario de Juárez*)

The list seems to convert the tale of Juárez's serial killers into a *Comedia de Terrores* – a Comedy of Terrors. A black comedy of bloody terrors. Sharif, mass-rapist and mass-murderer, was living considerably better in prison than the girls and young women he had preyed upon outside:

I am standing by the Carranza sisters' cardboard shack in a part of Juárez called Anapra. They moved to the shanty town about ten months ago, when three years of drought ended their lives in a village in Durango [in central northern México]. A half-dozen murdered, mutilated, and raped girls have been found about a hundred yards from their shack, and this frightens the teenage girls. Each morning they rise at 3:30 a.m., cook over bits of wood, and have some coffee. After a cold *tortilla*, they walk out into the darkness with their few possessions (a pan, a plate, knife, fork, spoon, and cooking oil) and bury them secretly in a hole; otherwise they will be stolen while they are gone . . . The fifteen-year-old girl is a welder at 160 pesos a week (about \$21.62 at current exchange rates). Bus fare consumes about half her salary. (*While You Were Sleeping*, Charles Bowden)

What was Sharif's income when he was free? What is it now? Another twisted laugh can be raised by another fragment of information about his life behind the bars of the Juárez *CeReSo*:

Fellow prisoners said they saw Sharif selling fruit juice and that he asked 1,500 pesos for orange-squeezing equipment. (*El Diario de Juárez*)

But this would have been small beer – small orange juice – beside what he may have been able to earn in other ways:

The general attorney's office of Chihuahua will send the Federal Bureau of Investigations (known by its initials in English as the FBI) and other investigatory authorities in the United States information about the correspondence conducted between, in Juárez, the convicted Egyptian Abdul Latif Sharif and, in the North-American state of Illinois, Newton Van [Drunen], who is serving a sentence for forging American currency. (*El Diario de Juárez*)

Another twisted laugh in the Comedy of Terrors is that the Chihuahuan authorities first had no idea that Sharif was keeping an archive of documents in his cell, and then had no idea of their contents, for they were written *en inglés y árabe* – in English and Arabic. Nonetheless, the female special prosecutor, Suly Ponce Prieto, was confident that nothing incriminating would be found amongst them:

'We are examining what the gentleman had, but he is no fool, on the contrary he has shown that he is an extremely intelligent man, so I do not believe that he might hold any evidence that could incriminate him.' (*El Diario de Juárez*)

But what of the things that seemed direct evidence of, at worst, Sharif's guilt or, at best, of his psychopathology: the photographs of women murdered in Juárez? They, at least, needed no translation, and seemed to indicate that Sharif had been gloating in his cell over the crimes – and perhaps more than gloating.

But this *mucho muy inteligente* man had an excellent excuse for owning the photographs:

Sharif, however, said that he has become 'obsessed' with finding the serial killer himself. 'It is become a personal thing and I have studied everything I can about the murders while in jail,' he said. 'If the police and prosecutors would let me, I would like to help find the true killer.' (SIX NEW SLAYINGS REVEAL THAT KILLER IS STILL ON THE LOOSE, Mark Smith, *Houston Chronicle*, 1996)

In the same interview he suggested that the killer might be a police officer easily able to gain the confidence of young women, and that the renewed outbreak of murders might be because the killer was 'mad' that 'they have given me all the attention'.

And this was said, of course, *before* the arrest of *Los Rebeldes* and *Los Choferes*. Sharif seems to combine very dark sexual tastes with a very dark sense of humour. And with a criminal ingenuity that startled even the hardened investigators of the FBI, who announced that:

'The present case sets a precedent, because it is the only time on record that a sex-murderer has paid not one but two groups of people to commit sex-murders ... A sex-murderer gets pleasure and realises his fantasies by committing crimes, so when Sharif paid for the murders of young women he realised his fantasies, as well as seeking to prove his non-existent innocence.' (*El Diario de Juárez*)

Another feature of the Mexican newspaper reports about Sharif is the continual stress laid on his *otherness*: he is referred to as *el egipcio*, the Egyptian, or as *el extranjero*, the foreigner. Perhaps the slowness with which the police and state authorities reacted to clear and mounting evidence that the crimes had not ended with his arrest is explained by the conviction that with a plainly guilty foreigner in custody, such un-Mexican crimes could *not* be continuing. Before Sharif's arrest, for example, explicit statements had been made to this end:

> One of those who offered his help during the investigation last fall – Rene González de la Vega, a criminologist with the México City Police Department – was quoted by some newspapers as saying serial killings are 'not a trait of the Mexican character'. (Mark Smith, *Houston Chronicle*)

While *El Diario de Juárez*, one of the main newspapers in Juárez, revealed that:

> That the murderer could not be Mexican was the initial hypothesis followed by the sub-procurator's office.

This belief seems to linger in media representations of those subsequently arrested: the name of Jesús Manuel Guardado Márquez is never introduced without his nickname 'El Tolteca', the Toltec, which is then the way he will be referred to in the rest of the article. The admixture of Amerindian blood in the Mexican population is reduced in the north, whose indigenous tribes have preserved a stricter sequestration than those of the south, and the sobriquet marks Márquez out as an outsider, a screen on to which the citizens of Chihuahua can project their particular form of a general Mexican racism.
El Tolteca remains irreducibly Mexican, however, but within even the culture of native Mexicans the name of the Toltecs has an exotic resonance, redolent of the commingled fumes of steam, smoke, and blood:

> It was not the Aztecs, however, who invented human sacrifice on the central plateau of the Mexican sierra. They partly inherited and partly assumed the mantle

of a far more shadowy culture, known as the Toltecs
... Their principal city was Tula ... chiefly famous
today for its reconstructed temple-pyramid of
Quetzacóatl, the Plumed Serpent ... Gruesome
indications of Toltec rituals are to be found carved on
a series of stone panels and free-standing stone
sculptures ... Marching across the upper and lower
registers [of the pyramid] are a series of jaguars and
pumas or coyotes. Alternating rows depicted crouch-
ing eagles tearing and eating the flesh of human
hearts. It could be that these carnivorous creatures
were fed human hearts after the victim's sacrifice, or
they may be metaphorical representations of Toltec
warrior castes dedicated to the jaguar or eagle. In
other words, the Toltec warriors of the jaguar or
eagle conquered and 'ate' their enemies, just as the
real jaguar eats its prey. (*People of the Jaguar: The
Living Spirit of Ancient America*, Nicholas J.
Saunders, Souvenir Press, 1989)

And even if 'El Tolteca' did not have these associations
clustered around his *apodo*, his nickname, and was pure,
mainstream Mexican, the newspaper reports are always
careful to stress his subordination to *el egipcio*, *el
extranjero*, the Egyptian foreigner Sharif:

Sharif is identified as the mastermind of the seven
murders and rapes of women committed by 'El
Tolteca', 'El Narco', 'El Samber', 'El Kiani', and 'El
Gaspy.' (*El Diario de Juárez*)

In Spanish, Sharif is the *autor intelectual*, literally the
'intellectual author', of crimes committed by 'El Tolteca'
and the others as *autores materiales*, literally the 'material
authors'. There is an ironic echo here of the Aristotelian
theology of St Thomas Aquinas (1225–74), with its causes

126

material, formal, efficient, and final. (See, for example, Bertrand Russell's *History of Western Philosophy*, ch. xix, 'Aristotle's Metaphysics'.) And yet no, there is more than that: the Mexican judicial system, like everything else in Mexican culture, is saturated with the influence of Roman Catholicism, and the most influential philosopher in Roman Catholicism is St Thomas Aquinas.

In either case, the irony arises from the fact that concepts from Catholicism are being applied to Sharif, for it is with Sharif that the indigenous racism of México commingles with a racism imported centuries before from Spain. Doubtless Mexican newspaper reports would be stressing the *extranjería*, the foreignness, of Sharif if he were Colombian or Peruvian, but if he were Colombian or Peruvian, he would at least be Catholic. Sharif is not only *extranjero*, but also *extra ecclesiam*: not only foreign, but also heathen. Many place-names in México, as elsewhere, commemorate historical events, but some place-names in México commemorate more than Mexican history. Travel downstream from Juárez on the Río Bravo and you will sooner or later come to the state of Tamaulipas and a city called Matamoros. This literally means 'Kill-Moors', or 'Killer of Moors', a hero-name passed down from the Middle Ages and *la Reconquista*, or Reconquest, of Catholic Spain from *los moros*, the Moors, a generic term in Spanish for Muslims.

Like Juárez, Matamoros (and an identically named city in the state of Coahuila) is named for a rebel-hero, the priest Mariano Matamoros, who was born in 1770 and died of bullet wounds in 1814. Whether attached to a person or a place, however, the name retains its transparent anti-Muslim meaning in modern Spanish, commemorating the violent prejudices of a violent past. (*Matamoros* is now used colloquially in Spanish with the sarcastic meaning of 'bully' or 'braggart' according to *The Cassell's Spanish Dictionary*, eds Anthony Gooch and Angel García de Paredes, Cassell, London, 1978.) Sharif is a Moor, a Muslim, a heathen foreigner representative of the wholly other, not a *matamoros*, but a *matador moro*: not a Moor-killer, but a Moorish killer.

This concept – *matador moro* – carries the resonance almost of a myth or fairy-tale, a bogey-figure with which women might threaten their misbehaving children, something catching and amplifying the folk-memories transmitted to the Mexican psyche in the Spanish language, where *hay moros en la costa* – 'there are Moors on the coast' – is still used as a phrase of warning or caution. And Sharif, an ageing chemist, embodies something of this resonance of myth or fairy-tale. He has been presented in the Mexican media as an ogre, a creature capable of casting a spell of fear merely by his presence, merely by a silent glance:

> I was told that on the Monday when they [the accused bus drivers] were in the cells, the gentleman [Sharif] took the trouble to pass behind them very suggestively. He did not say anything to them but looked at them as if to say 'Here I am' ... It was plain to anyone, but especially to them – and they showed every moment that they knew it – that if they talked and said what had happened, they knew that Sharif was going to end up killing them ... Victor Moreno Rivera, 'El Narco', was the one who most showed his fear towards the Egyptian. (*El Diario de Juárez*)

But is this account, given by the special prosecutor Suly Ponce, to be trusted? It fits very neatly into the half-completed jigsaw she and the police are presenting to the public. For Rivera was, of course, the one whom Sharif first befriended on trips made by Rivera to the *CeReSo*, who was first offered money to kill four young women a month, who negotiated the figure down to two, who smuggled 'intimate garments' to Sharif as tokens of successful rape and murder, who knew *el egipcio* best and might be expected to react most strongly to the unspoken threats in this deadly criminal's foreign eyes.

But if men react to Sharif's presence with fear, women seem to have reacted in other ways. As pointed out before, Sharif, like many other serial killers, has a perverted aura of success and dominance that some women find very attractive. In fact, Sharif, even more than his lieutenant Jesús Marquéz, is reminiscent of another ageing, deadly foreigner: the Transylvanian Count Dracula, who similarly evoked fear in men and fascination in women:

Mina Harker's Journal, 22nd September

I was looking at a very beautiful girl, in a big cart-wheel hat, sitting in a victoria outside Guilano's, when I felt Jonathan clutch my arm so tight that he hurt me, and he said under his breath, 'My God!' . . . He was very pale, and his eyes seemed bulging out as, half in terror and half in amazement, he gazed at a tall, thin man, with a beaky nose and black moustache and pointed beard, who was also observing the pretty girl. He was looking at her so hard that he did not see either of us, and so I had a good view of him. His face was not a good face; it was hard, and cruel, and sensual, and his big white teeth, that looked all the whiter because his lips were so red, were pointed like an animal's. (Chapter XIII)

A tall man with a moustache who is able to cast a spell of menace by his mere presence:

Sharif bolted from his chair, towering over shorter guards who nervously reached for their guns. He was a large, menacing presence who filled the room, a man completely in control, against whom even the prison director seemed cowed . . .

'Man, you're pretty,' said Sharif, as he introduced himself to the girls. The tall, ruggedly built guy with short, dark hair and a mustache often followed up with an invitation. 'How about coming over to my place for a drink?' ('MONSTER' BEATS THE SYSTEM, Tim Madigan, The *Seattle Times*, 1999)

These are, respectively, a description of Sharif on trial for murder in Juárez and a description of him flirting with young American girls when he lived in New Hope, Pennsylvania. Examine further the startling facts uncovered by the inquiry into Sharif's relations with *Los Choferes*:

The director of the Centre for the Social Rehabilitation of Adults [or *CeReSo*] said that . . . the first person who had visited the foreigner in prison was a woman called Carolina who was signed in on the 15th of October, 1996 . . . The majority of those who come to the *CeReSo* to visit Latif Sharif are women and sign in as female friends of his. (*El Diario de Juárez*)

The Spanish is *se registran como sus amigas* – 'sign in as female friends of his': as female friends of a man imprisoned for the rape, torture, mutilation, and murder of an unknown number of other women. There is even a possibility that they came to prison to have sex with him: remember that among the items found in his cell during the investigation into his privileges were: 'Two beds, one of them a double bed, the other a single'.

The tale of Sharif's privileges seems to have become conflated as it travelled around the world, and one South African newspaper even reported that he: 'enjoyed extraordinary privileges in Ciudad Juárez's notorious *CeReSo* jail, including a fax machine, two cellphones and a water bed for conjugal visits' (The *Cape Times*, 17 May 1999.)

But the possibility that the women did indeed come to the prison to have sex with Sharif raises the further possibility that they were not *amigas*, but *putas*: not girlfriends, but whores. Sharif may have been hiring prostitutes to visit him in prison. After all, he had a cellphone to make unsupervised calls on whoever he chose, and an income from, at the very least, the sale of orange juice and orange squeezers to fellow inmates. Another scene unfolds in the Comedy of Terrors whose second act – setting: a prison; our Egyptian anti-hero is ushered into a cell – descends into farce as news of Sharif's extraordinary privileges fights for media attention with the news of his hired accomplices *Los Choferes*. When the prison authorities were grappling with the accusations levelled at them by journalists and reporters, one of the accusations they took special care to refute was that Sharif could ever have stored mementoes of the crimes in his cell after they had been smuggled to him by Victor Rivera Moreno. He could not have concealed intimate feminine garments in his cell because:

'We frequently make searches of the cells, and one of the things we watch out for most is that the prisoners do not have any female clothes, because they can disguise themselves as a woman and escape – it happened once – and definitely we have never found any,' the director of the *CeReSo* assured the media. (*El Diario de Juárez*)

But it would seem a very thorough female-impersonator who went to the trouble of acquiring female underwear before his escape bid. If he was suspected and searched for proof of femininity, the fact that he was wearing knickers and a brassière would surely be far less interesting to guards than what he was concealing beneath them. And dwell too on the picture painted by the director of the *CeReSo*: one of the guards regularly and minutely examining Sharif's cell, shifting microwaves, colour televisions, video-recorders, video cassettes, tape-recorders, and clothes lockers as they search for something suspicious, something out of place in the cell of a dangerous criminal in Juárez's notorious *CeReSo* prison.

14: Prison

Cárcel f. Edificio donde están encerrados los presos. Fig. Lugar desagradable.

Prison. Building where prisoners are held. *Figurative*: Unpleasant place.

'He did grind in the prison house.' (Judges, xvi, 27)

In Spanish, *preso* means 'prisoner'. *Presa* means 'prey'. It seems an appropriate parallel of sound and sense for life in a Mexican prison, for Mexican prisons have long been notorious even in the Spanish-speaking world for their brutality and harshness. Prisoners, *presos*, are prey, *presa*, of violence and disease, of malnutrition and corruption. And of sexual abuse:

> On the 14th of February, 1998, Juan Jorge Contreras Jurado, 'El Grande' ['The Big Guy'], a member of *Los Rebeldes*, led various other prisoners in a sexual assault on a nineteen-year-old internee who had just entered the prison to serve a sentence for rape.
>
> For this assault Judge María Catalina Ruíz Pacheco found 'El Grande' guilty of rape, along with the paedophile Javier Córdova Robles, Rubén Anaya Martínez, and Antonio Maldonado, for which they all received a six-year sentence.
>
> The victim said in his statement that 'El Grande' pestered him to have sexual relations with the internees in his cell, saying that 'all the prisoners go through the same thing'.

Nevertheless, the youth would not give his consent to sexual relations, and he was therefore subjected to them by force.

After the assault, the affected man decided to inform the prison authorities what had happened . . . Although the detainees denied the charge, the victim showed signs of sexual penetration according to the results of examinations given to him. (SENTENCE AGAINST 'EL GRANDE', *El Diario de Juárez*)

'El Grande' undoubtedly spoke a great deal of truth when he told the nineteen-year-old that '*Todos los reos pasaban por lo mismo*' – 'All the prisoners go through the same thing'. Sexual assault must be a daily fact of life for many prisoners too weak to defend themselves against it. And that is true of prisons not just in México but throughout the world. In many countries, prisons are rape-factories, mass-producing male-on-male sexual assaults at every hour of the night and day on every day of the week. This fact, and the unimaginable mass of pain and indignity that can be inferred from it, had been mostly ignored – except as material for jokes – until it was realised that rape-factories can also be rapist-factories. The female response to rape is often internalised and directed against the self: depression and self-recrimination leading in some cases to anorexia and self-mutilation. The male response to rape is often externalised and directed against others: rage and a desire to take revenge. When those who raped him are beyond revenge, the raped male may redirect his anger against accessible targets, and seek to forget his own humiliation and degradation in the humiliation and degradation of others – others such as men weaker than himself inside prison and women outside it after his release:

Blinded by their victim-centric view of women, the antipornography feminists overlooked the fact that most rape victims are men – and the fact that some substantial number of these male victims are likely in turn to attack women. According to conservative estimates, more than 290,000 men are sexually assaulted in jails and prisons every year [in the United States], while the Bureau of Justice Statistics estimates that 135,000 women are raped annually. Even if the latter figure is understated, as some critics charge, it is indisputable that there is an epidemic of male prison rape – an epidemic that preys not only on men behind bars, but also on women in the outside world. Consequently, according to Stephen Donaldson, president of Stop Prisoner Rape, 'the fight against rape in our communities is doomed to failure . . . as long as it ignores the network of training grounds for rapists: our prisons, jails and reform schools.' (*Defending Pornography: Free Speech, Sex, and the Fight for Women's Rights*, Nadine Strossen, Abacus, 1996)

Such sexual abuse might seem to be among the many dangers faced by a sex-killer like Sharif, a middle-aged intellectual, when he was sent to prison in Juárez. In the hierarchy of prison-life, in México as elsewhere, the rapist-killers of women rank just above the rapist-killers of children. Both are at the very bottom of the hierarchy, recipients of all the violence and abuse the majority of prisoners above them in the hierarchy are able – or allowed – to mete out to them. Sharif could surely expect to be in constant danger of beatings, stabbings, slashings, scaldings, threats, contaminated food and water, and could surely expect to live against a psychic background, day in, day out, of the unrelenting hatred and contempt of his fellow inmates.

And yet Sharif, in another of the mysteries associated with his case, never seems to have been at risk from any of this. He seems to have moved freely inside the *CeReSo*, to the extent, as we have seen, of being able to sell orange juice to other prisoners. His height and physical presence undoubtedly helped him avoid some trouble, and the remainder may have been removed by his charisma. People had believed Sharif an innocent victim of injustice in the past, and may have done so again when he was imprisoned in Juárez.

Less physically imposing and less charismatic prisoners than Sharif, accused of the same, or much lesser, crimes would undoubtedly have suffered a great deal. But then conditions are bad for most prisoners in Mexican prisons, and what criminals find in prison when they are convicted are no isolated phenomena in the Mexican judicial system. Another of the twisted laughs to be raised by the Comedy of Terrors in Juárez can be found in the fact that the only one of the criminals to have made no complaint of police brutality and maltreatment is the protagonist himself: Abdul Latif Sharif Sharif, the author and inspirer of the crimes, and the man without whom they might never have taken place. Sharif's alleged minions, *Los Rebeldes* and *Los Choferes*, the men he is said to have hired and brought into the crimes, have all accused the authorities of torturing them into false confessions.

Each member of 'El Tolteca's' alleged accomplices among the *Los Choferes* was able to present his own story of torture and his own set of injuries to the Juárez media following his arrest:

VICTOR MORENO RIVERA
He said that the police covered his head with cloths and after that poured water into his nostrils. 'With an electric riot-baton they shocked me in the private parts, they beat me, and kicked me all over my body,' he said. 'A man with light-coloured hair, he was the one who shouted at me to sign what he said to me . . . I felt afraid of dying.'

JOSÉ GASPAR CEBALLOS CHAVEZ, 'EL GASPY'

Showing more than ten burns on his abdomen, severe bruises behind his left ear, and marks of blows all over his body, the twenty-five-year-old José Gaspar Ceballos, alias 'El Gaspy', said that he was illegally deprived of his liberty on Wednesday at 9:15 ... 'First they kicked me in the genitals and beat me, then a police officer hit me with a torch in the head, here,' he said, pointing behind his left ear. The young man lifted his shirt and showed more than eleven (*sic*) burns on his abdomen that had been produced by electric discharges, he claimed.

BERNARDO HERNANDO FERNÁNDEZ, 'EL SAMBER'

He displayed grazes on his right arm, as well as severe bruises on his abdomen and wounds inside his mouth ... 'The police took me to the State Academy of Police and beat me. They put a plastic bag over my head and suffocated me, they also poured water into my nostrils so that I would confess to killing the women, and I did it when they beat me harder ...'

AUGUSTÍN TORIBIO CASTILLO, 'EL KIANI'

The last of the detained men showed a severe bruise on his stomach around his navel, as well as severe bruises on his shoulder and face ... 'They took all of us to the [State] Academy [of Police] and we were put into separate cells with the police beating us ... I denied everything they said I had done, but they were kicking me all over my body, and because they said they were going to "disappear" all of us, I signed what they said to me.' (*El Diario de Juárez*)

One might assume this physical evidence of maltreatment is good evidence of *Los Choferes*' claims that they are innocent men tortured into making false confessions. One would be naïve to do so. Like almost every other feature of the crimes, *Los Choferes'* injuries admit of multiple interpretations. Perhaps they are guilty men tortured into making true confessions. Perhaps they made confessions under some pressure, and were then handed over by the police to be worked over by fellow prisoners primed by news of what the men had been arrested for. Perhaps they even handed themselves over to fellow prisoners to be beaten up with the deliberate intention of making accusations of torture and brutality against the police. The idea has been circulating since, at the latest, the release of the film *Dirty Harry* (1971), in which the villain has himself beaten up to provide proof of an accusation of brutality against the eponymous policeman pursuing him.

And the idea – or an adaptation of it, at least – has been made reality in at least one prominent case of serial rape and murder:

> The 'Railway Rapist' began to operate in 1982 . . . He threatened his victims with a knife, tied their hands, and raped them with a great deal of violence . . . In January 1986, the body of nineteen-year-old Alison Day was found in the River Lea . . . She had been raped and strangled . . . In April 1986, fifteen-year-old Maartje Tamboezer, daughter of a Dutch oil executive, was . . . also raped and strangled. Her attacker was evidently aware of the most recent advance in forensic detection, 'genetic fingerprinting', by which a suspect can be identified from the distinctive pattern in the DNA of his body cells. The killer had stuffed a burning paper handkerchief inside her vagina. (*The Serial Killers: a study in the psychology of violence*, Colin Wilson and Donald Seaman, p. 29, Virgin Publishing, London, 1990)

The man responsible was called John Duffy, and the vulpine cunning shown by him here was evident again after he came to the attention of the police and was interviewed by them:

> When the police tried to conduct a second interview, Duffy was in hospital suffering from amnesia, claiming he had been beaten up by a mugger. The hospital authorities declined to allow him to be interviewed. Since he was only one of two thousand suspects, the police did not persist. (*Ibid.*, p. 30)

Later, however, he came to the top of this list of suspects, and police investigations into his background revealed a 'fellow martial arts enthusiast' who:

> admitted that Duffy had persuaded him to beat him up so he could claim loss of memory . . . Five of [the surviving] rape victims picked him out at an identity parade, and string found in the home of his parents proved to be identical with that which had been used to tie Maartje Tamboezer's wrists. (*Ibid.*, p. 30)

This may have been the strategy adopted by *Los Choferes*, and the possibility represents another bifurcation in the *Laberinto de Espejos*, the Labyrinth of Mirrors, that the crimes in Juárez seem to represent.

15: Desert

Ruido m. Conjunto de sonidos inarticulados y confusos.
Noise. Meaningless and confused sounds.

Tune a suitably old-fashioned radio to a spoken-word station. Then, slowly, turn the dial until the voices disappear in static. Then, very slowly, turn the dial back again. When do the voices reappear? Is there a point at which they are there, and yet not there? A point at which they flicker in and out of the static like salmon fighting upstream in rapids, flashes of silver in white foam, transient, meaningful patterns surrounded by permanent, meaningless chaos?

I have just tried it with a suitably old-fashioned radio, and there is such a point. A point of transition, on the cusp between law and disorder, on the boundary between light and dark, at the border between meaningfulness and noise. A border reminiscent of another: that between México and America. For the murders in Juárez are, it seems to me, analogous to this experiment in mixing words and static. Some of the murders are like static: random, unconnected with each other, like separate grains of blond sand heaped by the wind. Other murders are patterned: non-random, deliberate, connected to each other as part of a whole, like a human bone lifted from that heap of blond sand. The sand falls away in separate grains, and the bone is left in the hand, white, whole, and meaningful.

The problem is, of course, to discern which murders are grains of sand and which murders solid bone, which murders the work of unrelated individuals and which murders the work of a serial killer or the gang hired by him. Perhaps one can apply again the concept of serial killing as career or profession. Or, let us say, the concept of serial killing as *art*. One can study the technique of a great artist and see individuality, uniqueness, in the pattern of his brushstrokes, in the deployment of his pigments, in the arrangement of his figures, in the choice of his themes. In short, in his *modus operandi*: his method of working.

Like an artist, a serial killer uses his hands, and often instruments too, and he works on something analogous to a canvas or block of marble: the body of his victim. He often deploys fluids – blood, semen, spittle – or sculpts and rearranges his material with blows, cuts, scratches, bites. Or extend and modify this metaphor of art, and see the serial killing of Juárez as ballet: a dance of death enacted in the real time of real life, on a stage as wide as a city – because it *is* a city – and with a permanent curtain-fall for one of the partners in the *pas de deux*.

And see from this how, like an artist or dancer, a serial killer can so arrange the elements of his art as to achieve uniqueness and, in the ensanguinated terms by which some will willingly judge him, greatness. This has come to be recognised by the forensic psychologists, who have devised a system known as 'profiling' by which the evidence of behaviour in a crime is matched to personality and used to predict lifestyle or patterns of future behaviour that may allow the police to hunt down and arrest the perpetrator. This field was developed and has been brought to its highest pitch of perfection in the United States, where both resources and subjects for study are readily available. This American expertise in profiling was, belatedly, lent to the police and judicial authorities of Juárez:

> On March 8 [1999] three FBI agents are expected to arrive in Juárez to assist the local authorities in their

investigation. The experts will be from the Behavioral Sciences Unit in Quantico, Virginia, and will hopefully be able to create a psychological profile for the serial killers and other criminals that may be involved. (BORDER REACTS TO 184 MURDERED WOMEN, Anne Marie Mackler, *Frontera NorteSur*, March 1999)

The FBI's offer of assistance was made before the arrest of *Los Choferes*, which came about by chance, not by psychological profiling. Perhaps this is because the murders in Juárez are, as yet, something unique in the annals of serial killings, though familiar in the field of art to which I have compared serial killing. Sharif, like da Vinci or Michelangelo or Raphael, founded a *school*. Even now some great paintings and drawings cannot be ascribed with certainty to an individual artist, but have to be labelled 'school of'. That famous 'human proportions' drawing co-opted for the British television series *World in Action* – the naked man standing legs and arms outstretched in a square and circle. Is it by da Vinci or a pupil of da Vinci? No one knows. Similarly, are some of the crimes in Juárez by Sharif or a pupil of Sharif? No one knows. And psychological profilers, working from the equivalent of half-a-dozen brushstrokes rather than a canvas-full, may never be able to differentiate such multiple-perpetrator murders overseen by a single psychopath.

Particularly when, as in Juárez, these half-a-dozen brushstrokes of which each serial crime is composed are overlaid and surrounded by the brushstrokes of incidental murders: pregnant women killed by their boyfriends; wives subjected to one drunken blow or kick too many; casual rapes turned into casual murders. There is a hiss of white noise through which a voice narrating a larger tale can barely be heard, a sentence scrawled in blood that is three-quarters-obliterated by a splattering of random gouts. Or a scattering of white bones in blond sand. When the stinks and colours of putrefaction have faded, the flesh melted away, and the wind heaped sand over the remains, it is sometimes very hard to find where a victim lies in the desert, and there is a great deal of desert around Ciudad Juárez. A very great deal indeed.

Desert

Desierto m. Lugar arenoso, árido y despoblado.
Desert. Sandy, arid, and unpopulated place.

For he had commanded the unclean spirit to come out of the man. For oftentimes it had caught him: and he was kept bound with chains and in fetters; and he brake the bands, and was driven of the devil into the desert. (Luke, viii, 29) [I have followed the translation in the King James Bible, save for the rendering of *deserta* as 'desert'.]

National flags tell stories. The Mexican flag is a tricolour: three vertical stripes of green, white, and red. That tells a story of rebellion and revolution, for it was adopted in the struggle for independence in 1820 as a conscious echo of the *tricolore français*. But on the central white stripe of the *tricolor mexijana* there is a crest – a picture. The picture of an eagle. It is sitting on a cactus, biting at the neck of a snake that it clutches in its right claw.

The story here is harder to read, lying outside European culture and history in Aztec mythology. It is the story of the founding of México City, when wandering Aztecs were shown this tableau of animals and plant as sign of divine favour for the founding of a new city: an eagle, a snake, and a cactus. Two desert animals, and a desert plant. That the Aztecs chose them as symbols of their capital city, and the state of México as the crest of its national flag, tells us that desert casts a long, long shadow on Mexican history and the Mexican psyche.

Even so, México is not entirely a desert country: it has tropical and temperate rainforests too, in the south, and lakes and rivers in both the south and the north. In part, perhaps, the obsession with desert is a reflection of how others see México. And the most important 'other' is, of course, the United States: to Americans, México is a desert country because that is how it appears from their point of view – literally. Look south from the United States into México and you see desert, whether you stand in the extreme east, and Texas, or the extreme west, and California. The very names of these southern states – and nearly all their neighbours: Colorado, Nevada, New Mexico (Nuevo México), Arizona – are Mexican, for the United States grew at México's expense during the wars and border disputes of the nineteenth century. And these once-Mexican states are famous for their heat and their deserts, facts sometimes reflected in the names they were given in Spanish by their former owners: California was named the 'hot-furnace' for its climate, Colorado the 'Coloured State' for the vivid tinctures of its desert landscapes.

In part, then, México sees itself as others, including Americans, see it. And others see desert. But this might remain largely true even if the landscape along the border of the United States and México were lush green and humid, and Mexican deserts were further south. For there is something about desert that fascinates the eye and the mind. A vastness. A stillness. And an omnipresent whisper of death. A whisper that sometimes rises into a shriek. To look into a desert is to look into death. One's own death. Deserts are not places for human beings. That is why they are called deserts: they are deserted, *despoblado*, empty of people. They are too harsh, too fierce, for habitation, places to be hurried through or fought against from the foothold of a spring or well or river.

This is why they so fascinate the eye – or the lens. Films like *Romancing the Stone* (1984) or *Shark* (1968), the latter of which may have given birth to the first rumours

of the 'snuff-movie' (publicity for the film included the
probably apocryphal claim that a stunt-diver was killed by
sharks during filming: see H. David Baldridge's *Shark
Attack*, Everest Books, 1976, for further details. Publicity
for the eponymous *Snuff* itself, of course, claimed that the
movie 'could only be made in South America, where life is
cheap') were made in México but not set there, for
cinematic representations of México, from the underground to the mainstream, are overwhelmingly of
northern México and desert. There are Westerns like *The
Magnificent Seven* (1960), for example, in which a
'Mexican village hires seven American gunmen for
protection against bandits' (*Halliwell's Film Guide*). But
perhaps the most famous films of this genre are in the
short cycle that began three decades ago with *A Fistful of
Dollars* (1964), continued with *For a Few Dollars More*
(1965), and ended with *The Good, the Bad and the Ugly*
(1966). The first is summarised in this way in *Halliwell's
Film Guide*: 'An avenging stranger, violent and mysterious, cleans up a Mexican border town.'

The film created a sub-genre that would quickly coarsen
into such titles as *A Town Called Bastard* (1971) (also
known as *A Town Like Hell)*, which is summarised in this
way in *Halliwell's Film Guide*:

> Mexican revolutionaries massacre a priest and his
> congregation and take over the town. Ten years later
> a widow arrives seeking vengeance. Sadistic western
> with an opening massacre followed by twenty-two
> killings (count 'em).

The guide also notes that *A Town Called Bastard* and
A Fistful of Dollars were, respectively, an all-British
production and an international collaboration between
Italy, Germany, and Spain. These films are México as seen
by other nations, and other nations see México through

American eyes, looking south to border towns set amid desert. Suitable places, and a suitable backdrop, for the enactment of the swift, bloody death by bullet or knife that symbolises the slower, dehydrating death always offered by a desert: death by thirst or sunstroke.

And here we find a further element of the macabre call of the desert. It will kill you but not destroy you, take your life but not always your flesh and very rarely your bones. The same deadly heat and sun may mummify you, sucking all the moisture from your body and leaving it unpalatable to the scavengers and bacteria that would swiftly dissolve and dismantle and scatter your remains in wetter, cooler climates. And even if your body is discovered in time by desert scavengers, they will strip your flesh but leave your bones to be bleached by the sun. The Mexican desert whispers death, and displays it, for white bones show up well against red sand.

As do black wings against blue sky. Death can be seen in the desert even when it is very, very far off. It can be seen in the sky, in a loose-edged wheel of descending vultures, hubbed on a tiny patch of death in the midst of desert *mesas* or canyons, *arroyos* or *playas*. All Spanish words, all taken into English from the Spanish of México. México is desert, and desert is México. Even to Mexicans. But Mexicans draw distinctions. There are deserts, and deserts. There is the desert of Sonora, and the desert of Chihuahua. And the desert of Chihuahua can kill not just with heat but also with cold:

Temperature ranges are extreme, varying from 40°C (104°F) in midsummer to well below freezing in winter. (*Northern Mexico Handbook*, Joe Cummings, p. 8, Moon Publications, 1998)

Juárez is in the Chihuahuan desert. And however much its inhabitants try to shut out this fact, however widely the city spreads, encircling and shielding itself with shanty-town outriders in all directions, the desert's presence will remain inescapable. In Juárez the desert is never very far away as the crow flies. Or as the wind blows:

> I head downtown. A wind whips across Juárez. The city often sprawls under moving walls of dust since so little of it is paved. The whores are out, sixteen- and seventeen-year-olds. There is no way to tell if they are full-time prostitutes or factory workers making an extra buck. ('While You Were Sleeping', Charles Bowden)

In nineteenth-century London, fog cloaked the movements of the serial killer known as Jack the Ripper; in twentieth-century Juárez, dust has cloaked the movements of the serial killer Sharif Sharif and his hirelings. Even at a distance, the desert has provided cover for killers who will then dump their prey to its wide, gritty, dusty embrace. It is almost as if the desert has assisted in sacrifices to itself, swirling its substance over negotiations between prostitutes and kerb-crawlers, over cars driving off with prostitutes on board, masking struggles, confusing the direction of screams and cries for help, soaking up and covering splashes of blood by the roadside.

And later, when the bodies of murdered women have been dumped to the embrace of the desert, there is still work for it to do. For it and its master the sun:

> Jaime Bailleres has projected a beautiful black carved mask on the screen. The head is tilted and the face is smooth with craftsmanship. The hair is long and black. It takes a moment for me to get past this beauty and realise that the face is not a mask. She is a sixteen-year-old girl with a forgotten name ... The girl's skin has blackened in the sun, and the face

contracted as it mummified. She was kidnapped, raped, murdered ... The lips of the girl pull back, revealing her clean, white teeth. Sound pours forth from her mouth. She is screaming and screaming and screaming. ('While You Were Sleeping', Charles Bowden)

The desert is waiting to do to all the inhabitants of Juárez what it did to this one young woman. If it can it will, in time, have all of them dead, desiccated, mummified, silently, deafeningly screaming to the blue ultimate iris of the sky and its glaring golden pupil: 'Juárez will run out of water completely in five years unless something is done.' ('While You Were Sleeping', Charles Bowden.)

And will something be done? Yes, perhaps. For the rich. Those who have. In the Mexican desert, those who have protect themselves very harshly against those who have not. Cactuses have water, for example, and protect themselves against those who do not have it with flesh-tearing thorns and spikes:

The forbidding teddy-bear cactus (*Opuntia bigelovii*) has been described as being armed with 'ten million cambric needles, set on hundreds of loosely jointed spindles'. (*Wildlife of the Deserts*, Frederic H. Wagner, p. 165, Windward, Leicester)

The rich of Juárez have money, and protect themselves against those who do not have with the human equivalents of thorns and spikes:

[A] paper [in Juárez] wanted a soft feature on the lives of the rich, so one Saturday a photographer and his editor strolled through an enclave of wealth looking for the right image. The photographer brought along his wife and two children. As a rabbit hopped across the lawn of a mansion, the camera came up. Suddenly two bodyguards appeared with AK-47s, and one said, 'Give me that fucking camera.' They forced the photographer face-down on the pavement with the automatic rifles at his head. Then, in front of his wife and children, they beat him about his head, ribs, and genitals. Police stood nearby and watched. ('While You Were Sleeping', Charles Bowden)

This savagery arises everywhere there is fierce competition for scarce resources, in nature or the human world. But in the desert there is savage competition *between* species; in Juárez there is savage competition *within* a species. Some citizens have more than others. Some few citizens have hugely, grossly more than many others. Juárez, like all of modern México, brings to mind in its income distribution one of the *teocallis*, the pyramids, of ancient México. But it is an inverted pyramid. A few, at the top, have a very great deal; very many, at the bottom, have almost nothing. Juárez is a desert of pain, where a very few have more water than they could drink in a lifetime, and very many have barely enough water to survive a day.

16: Pain

Dolor m. Sufrimiento, padecimiento físico. Aflicción, pena.
Pain. Physical suffering. Affliction, punishment.

'An hour of pain is as long as a day of pleasure.' [*Gnomologia*, Dr Thomas Fuller (1732)]

Have you ever lost a limb? Suffered third-degree burns? Gone a fortnight without food? A week without water? Caught smallpox, dysentery, or cholera?

Very probably your answer to each question will be a simple 'No'. The answers of your parents, and your grandparents, and your great-grandparents, would very probably be the same. The odd thing is that if you ever do have to experience one of these things, your body will know what to do. Only this is not so odd. Climb the tree of your direct ancestors and you will sooner or later find someone who did have to experience one of those things. And who survived and had children. Sooner or later you will find someone else who had to experience another of those things. And who survived and had children. And someone else who had to experience yet another of those things. And who survived and had children. And so on for each and every one of those things, many, many times over, stretching back beyond human beings into primitive hominids, primitive primates and insectivores, primitive mammals, and on, back into reptiles, fish, worms, unicellular organisms.

And that is why your body – and mine – knows what to do if it experiences life-threatening injury or deprivation or disease. Ancestors are, by definition, people who survived and had children. Their bodies knew what to do when the world attacked them. If their bodies had not known what to do, then they would have died and not had children. But they did not die and they did have children. And those children, and *their* children, and *their* children, already had, at birth, that implicit bodily wisdom bequeathed them by their parents, and *their* parents, and *their* parents.

As well as something perhaps even more important. For even someone whose body knows how to react to life-threatening injury and disease is better off avoiding them. Injury and disease are physiologically costly, and though they may not end life they may shorten it, and so lessen the number and quality of one's offspring. The safest thing is to avoid injury and disease, and the best way to avoid them is an ability to experience pain:

> People who are born without the ability to feel pain provide convincing testimony on the value of pain . . . Many of these people sustain extensive burns, bruises and lacerations during childhood, frequently bite deep into their tongue while chewing food, and learn only with difficulty to avoid inflicting severe wounds on themselves . . . [One] man walked on a leg with a cracked bone until it broke completely. Children who are congenitally insensitive to pain sometimes pull their own teeth out and have on occasion even pushed their eyeballs out of their sockets. (*The Puzzle of Pain*, Ronald Melzack, p. 15, Penguin, 1977)

Pain helps us to avoid injury by informing us when it is about to begin. It gives us time to react, sometimes *forces* us to react against our will, or before our will can come into play. Our bodies have been built by evolution to supply us, when the need arises, with inexhaustible supplies of pain in many, many different varieties and degrees.

And this is, in some ways, the most horrifying thing about being alive and conscious. Because if our bodies supply us with pain when the need arises, they also supply it when the need does not. When it serves no purpose. Pain is a blindfold gamble played by evolution with the lives of individual animals. Most of the time, the gamble pays off: pain helps an animal survive and breed. Some of the time, the gamble fails. A very young gazelle is caught by an inexperienced cheetah. It is doomed. Pain can no longer provide it with any possible benefit. The cheetah does not kill it cleanly, and begins chewing into its bowels before it is dead. Before it dies the gazelle's body supplies its consciousness with pain that is enormous and utterly useless.

And something similar may await the cheetah at the end of its life. It may have bred many times, been as successful as it possibly can be, but the taps of pain in its body will never be turned off. Finally too old and slow to respond to the spur of hunger pangs, it will nevertheless suffer them, and suffer what comes after them as it slowly starves to death. Examples can be multiplied from nature almost *ad infinitum*, certainly *ad nauseam*, and reach their zenith in the useless, unnecessary pain of the primates, whose evolution has refined the horror of pain in two ways, one of them previously unknown. Primates experience the most acute forms of psychological pain – fear, anxiety, depression – and were responsible for the invention of sadism: the taking of pleasure in the deliberate infliction of pain on other creatures.

Human beings have refined both aspects of this primate heritage even further. They have the ability both to experience and to inflict higher degrees of psychological and physical pain than any other animal in more ways than any other animal. In this, as in so many other things, we are, as yet, the *ne plus ultra*: the limit beyond which there lies nothing. But even among human beings, distinctions must be drawn. The ability to inflict and experience pain is not shared out equally amongst us. Some of us are men and some of us are women. Men are more eager to inflict pain for pleasure, and women more sensitive to its effects. The young gazelle with the inexperienced cheetah suffers greatly, but by accident; the young woman with the experienced sex-murderer suffers more, and by design. Those dozens of deaths by rape and torture in Juárez represent cases in which a gamble that has lasted for many millions of years has finally failed. A human body, exquisitely constructed to guard its own existence with pain, falls into the hands of another human being who derives pleasure from the infliction of pain. The victim's existence is effectively over. Pain can serve no further function, but the taps of pain are not turned off. The victim's suffering is enormous and utterly useless. *Lupus homo homini*. In Plautus' *Trinummus*, act ii, Erasmus quotes as a proverb *Homo homini aut deus aut lupus*: 'Man is to man either a god or a wolf'. Man is a wolf to man. And even more of a wolf to woman.

Because the true sadist can have no better material for his sadism than the body and mind of a woman. Particularly a young woman. Even more particularly a slender young woman, with long hair:

> The six most recent cases involve girls, ages 15 to 17, who closely match the physical description of the nine earlier victims. All 15 victims were in their teens or early 20s, slim and petite, almost always with long dark hair. (SIX NEW SLAYINGS REVEAL THAT KILLER IS STILL ON THE LOOSE, Mark Smith, *Houston Chronicle*, 1996)

But how do these characteristics – femaleness, youth, slenderness, long hair – contribute to a victim's suitability for the attentions of a sadist? Like this. The senses of women are, on average, sharper than those of men. Women can hear softer sounds, detect more fleeting flavours or odours, discriminate with eye or fingertip between more subtle colours or textures. If human senses are characterised as amplifiers, then male senses, by comparison with female, have the gain turned down: the output into the brain and consciousness is reduced from the input provided by the sense organs: eyes, ears, tongue, nose, skin.

This is likely to arise from the different roles assigned to the sexes by evolution: the care and rearing of children, for women, and competition and exploration, for men. And, like the almost universal human capacity to experience pain, it is written in spirals of DNA into our genes:

> The twenty-third pair of chromosomes in females is XX, while in males it is XY. In the presence of the Y chromosome, cell division of the zygote is accelerated, and the medulla of the initially bipotential embryonic gonad differentiates during the seventh week into a testis. The secretion of androgenic hormones from the foetal testis organises both the development of the genitalia and of the brain according to the male pattern. Female differentiation always occurs in the absence of the male hormones. Circulation of androgens [male hormones] *in utero* [in the womb] is known to increase the amount of aggressive behaviour and gross physical activity in primates, and it is likely that these hormones predispose the human male to greater physical activity. (*The Oxford Companion to the Mind*, ed. Richard L. Gregory, Oxford University Press, 1987)

Greater physical activity increases the likelihood of injury, and so men are prepared in the womb to enter the world with coarsened senses, and sensibilities. They are less fearful of pain, more likely to risk it. And more *able*, with larger muscles attached to thicker bones, to inflict it.

These larger muscles on thicker bones account, in part, for the differing shapes and sizes of men and women, and the differing shapes and sizes of men and women, in turn, account, in part, for the differing sensitivity of men and women. Women not only present more sensitive bodies to the world but are also able to receive more stimulation from it. Imagine, for example, that human beings were shaped like cubes. A man might be a cube 2 m high, 2 m broad, 2 m deep. He would present twenty-four square metres of skin to the world for eight cubic metres of body. A woman might be a cube 1 m high, one metre broad, 1 m deep. She would present six square metres of skin to the world for one cubic metre of body. Her skin-to-body ratio is six-to-one; his three-to-one. Stimulation that saturates her consciousness merely dampens his; stimulation that submerges hers only soaks his.

But the use of large and small cubes to represent men and women falsifies reality: men and women are different shapes as well as sizes. The differing shapes increases the disparity in skin-to-body ratios. And a 'slender, petite' young woman has a skin-to-body ratio even higher than the female norm. As a woman she feels any stimulation more intensely, and pain is a form of stimulation. As a 'slender, petite' *young* woman, she feels pain most intensely of all.

But what is the significance of her youth? The significance is that her youth equips her to experience this most intensely felt pain for longer. Her body is stronger, more tightly knit, fuller of life and so slower to drain of it. Her 'long, dark hair' is an extra signal of this, for hair is one of the most powerful indicators of health and youth, or their absence. No matter what the currently fashionable hair-length for women, the women in pornographic magazines almost always have long hair. Its condition indicates their suitability for mating, and their suitability for mating is what places them in a pornographic magazine in the first place. Normal men are aroused by and attracted to healthy young women because healthy young women are likely to be more vigorous and pleasurable sexual partners who will bear and raise healthier children.

'El Tolteca' is reported to have explicitly stated Sharif's taste in victims as this was communicated in instructions to *Los Choferes*:

> 'We had to look for tasty little girls, with nice tits and asses ... We looked for little girls, with properly developed bodies ...' (*El Diario de Juárez*)

Healthy young women, by whom sadists like Sharif, in person or in proxy, are aroused and to whom they are attracted because healthy young women are likely to be more vigorous and pleasurable partners in pain. Though the partnership is not, of course, a reflexive one: XY is not to XX as XX is to XY. XY inflicts pain; XX receives it. It is not always thus in the world of heterosexual sadomasochism. There is a vast oversupply of men who want to be dominated by women: to be humiliated, tortured, made the vessel into which pain is poured rather than the vessel that pours it. To ensure the services of a dominatrix – a woman who will humiliate and torture them – many men have to pay. And many men have the ability to pay: it is a much-remarked paradox of sadomasochism that many rich, successful men, dominant and stereotypically masculine in their professional lives, wish to play the subordinate role in the bedroom. Or the dungeon.

The paradox may dissolve when we consider that it is also stereotypically masculine to seek out new sensations and risks. Subordination is a new sensation, and a risk, to a rich, successful man. Domination is a new sensation to poor, unsuccessful men. Perhaps this partly explains why serial killers – who dominate their victims to the point of death – are so often unsuccessful or unexceptional: drifters, roadsweepers, handymen, clerks. But we must remember that in some ways the greatest serial killers of all time have been politicians, with body counts not in the piddling tens and dozens, but the hundreds of thousands and millions. Their masculine hunger for new sensation is met not by difference but by increase. They have experienced the sensation of domination, and wish to experience the sensation of increased domination. Of domination in harsher, sterner ways, or in different arenas. From powers over life, they want to acquire powers over life and death.

This reasoning seems to apply both to men like Lavrenti Beria (1899–1953), the head of the Stalin's secret police and a monster in his political and his sexual life alike, and to men like Abdul Latif Sharif Sharif, a successful, dominant chemist and a successful, dominant sex-criminal. The two kinds of male sadist – the failure who seeks compensation for his failure, and the success who wants more 'success' – seem conjoined in Sharif's association with *Los Rebeldes* and *Los Choferes*. A rich man imprisoned for rape and murder pays poor men to rape and murder on his behalf. And the story of it reveals another strand of the way male and female characteristics have been woven together in the crimes.

Almost nothing is known of how Sharif captured and murdered his victims before dumping them in the desert. If the confessions of *Los Rebeldes*, and the testimony of 'Nancy', are to be trusted, Sharif's accomplices used cars and buses. The confessions of *Los Rebeldes* are full of street names, changes of direction, travel to and travel through and travel from. Journeys, in short. Something that bus drivers, by definition, make the most important part of their work. And men, on average, are better at making journeys than women: better at changes of direction, better at travel to and travel through and travel from:

> Men and women use their brains differently, it appears. Women are not as good at spatial tasks, but they are better than men at dealing with complex verbal information. Psychological testing had indicated these differences, but now brain imaging has shown that they are caused by men and women using different areas of their brains when they carry out the same tests. (IT IS TRUE, WOMEN FIND MAPS A MAZE, Nigel Hawkes, *The Times*, 25th July 1999)

And so *Los Choferes*, The Bus Drivers, sorted into a driving job by their maleness, were brought into daily contact with *Las Víctimas*, The Victims, sorted into factory jobs by their femaleness: their sharper eyes, more sensitive fingers, more subordinate response to authority and regimentation. Again the crimes seem like a work of dramatic art: a ballet or film in which roles were advertised and competed for, and central casting was evolutionary biology.

And yet a mystery remains at the heart of the crimes. The same mystery is found at the heart of all human existence and action, but crimes such as those of Juárez throw it into sharper, starker relief. Extremes demand and challenge explanations, and it is in the extremes of human behaviour that psychology and neurology are most strongly tested, and are in most urgent need of application. The mystery is this: what is the relationship between consciousness and action? Again and again in this chapter I have made an implicit assumption: that the contents of the mind drive behaviour. The pain of being raped and tortured makes a young woman scream, weep; the pleasure of raping and torturing makes a sex-criminal laugh, ejaculate. And the knowledge or the memory of this pain or pleasure makes it possible that others take action to avoid or re-enact it:

> Before Sharif's arrest, many parents wouldn't let their children go out alone or after dark. Teenage girls cut their hair and dressed in baggy clothes to be less attractive to the mysterious killer. Juárez's busy nightclubs and restaurants reported a drop in business. (SIX NEW SLAYINGS REVEAL THAT KILLER IS STILL ON THE LOOSE, Mark Smith, *Houston Chronicle*, 1996)

The sex-criminals, on the other hand, seek out opportunities to snatch new victims, driven by the memory of the pleasure they experienced last time, or the desire to earn more money. In each case, we explain the actions by reference to the contents of the mind of the individual who undertakes the action. A teenaged girl is fearful of being a victim: she cuts her hair and wears baggy clothes. A bus driver wants another envelope of female flesh, another envelope of cash, and notes each potential new target getting on his bus, where she gets off. Question that teenaged girl or bus driver about *why* she or he does what she or he does, and the answer will be couched with reference to the contents of her or his mind: 'I did it out of fear, desire, greed'.

But in most contemporary philosophy and neuroscience, there seems no need to ascend to this level of meaning: the contents of the mind are effectively identical to the contents of the brain. Fear, desire, greed, and all the other elements of consciousness, depend on the arrangement of chemicals and electrical charges in the brain. Consciousness seems to float on the brain like steam on the surface of the boiling mudpools and fumaroles of New Zealand's

Rotorua district or America's Yellowstone Park: it does not affect what goes on beneath it, and merely echoes changes in that from which it arises.

Why, then, does it exist? If the physical substrate of pain – its representation in brain-stuff – is sufficient, why is there any need for its psychological suprastrate: its representation in mind-stuff? Is the already certain horror of existence – that some pain is unnecessary – only a fragment of the truth? Is *all* pain unnecessary? Can consciousness be compared to a months-old European newspaper appearing at last in a decaying town in the remote Mexican *sierra*, reporting events that the reader can neither participate in nor influence?

Perhaps, perhaps not. But even if consciousness does influence brain-state in some as yet unimaginable way, its importance is already undermined by what has been learned by science about human behaviour. Some of those responsible for violent sex-crime have openly stated that they do such things for the sake of pleasure. The Hungarian train-wreck fetishist Sylvestre Matuschka, for example, is said to have announced, ten days after his arrest:

'I wrecked trains because I like to see people die. I like to hear them scream. I like to see them suffer.' (*The Sex Killers, Thirty fully documented cases of men and women whose aberrant sexuality drove them to kill*, Norman Lucas, p. 5, Virgin, 1998)

There is direct testimony that Guardado Márquez, 'El Tolteca', 'El Dracula', found a similar pleasure in the suffering of others, though at much closer quarters. After his arrest for the rape of Nancy, the Juárez media described how he seemed to drink in the fear of his underaged victim as eagerly as his Transylvanian nick-namesake drank blood. When he and Nancy were left alone on the bus she had boarded late at night to get home from her *maquiladora* job: ' "The Toltec" asked her, smiling, "Are you afraid?", to which she answered, "Yes, please take me home." '

Nancy then described her feelings as the bus droned on into the night, taking her further and further from home, further and further into the deserted outskirts of Juárez:

'I was very afraid during the whole journey, I did not do anything because I could not, my fear was stronger than I was,' she recalls. 'As soon as he had stopped the bus he threw himself at me and grabbed me by the throat very hard, saying at the same time that he was going to kill me, and smiling as he asked me again and again whether I was afraid.

'I do not remember anything more because I fainted,' she says with tears that testify to the brutality Jesús Manuel Guardado Márquez used against her. (*El Diario de Juárez*)

Here we find a perfect vignette of male pleasure in the heightened fear and suffering experienced by the female victim. The words of another young woman raped by 'El Tolteca' emphasise another dichotomy between the sexes. On average, women are more empathetic, better able to identify with the emotion and suffering of others. Once she saw him in prison, the young woman identified only as Susana said:

'I am afraid, but when I saw him I felt pity for him, though he does not deserve my pity. He did a lot of harm to Nancy and me, he killed many girls and he has to pay for what he did.' (*El Diario de Juárez*)

But in one way Susana could not identify with 'El Tolteca', because the feelings he had were alien to her. On average, women are slower to sexual arousal than men and are far less eager for as much sex with as many partners as possible. From Venus, Susana could not make out the depth of the canyons cut out by storms in the surface of Mars:

> 'Now, after seeing what he did to Nancy and me, I believe he did the same to other women. I do not understand why he did it. If he has a wife, why does he go searching for other women?' the victim asked. (*El Diario de Juárez*)

This average difference of sexual appetite between the sexes is a natural phenomenon, easily explained by the relative investment men and women have to place into what has historically been the consequence of sex: pregnancy and children. Over evolutionary time, female human beings have always risked more by having sex, and the brains and behaviour of women have been shaped accordingly. Men, on the other hand, can often lose nothing by sex but a few cubic centimetres of semen, and their brains and behaviour have been shaped accordingly. In general, women are discriminately sexual, men indiscriminately sexual, both adapted to seeking the best advantage of their genes.

But some would go further and claim that the vigour of the male pursuit of sex must, by the truly honest, be coupled with violence, and that it is only in this way that true pleasure can be found in sex. Remember the words used by Hungarian sex-criminal Sylvestre Matuschka to express the feelings of his psychopathic *confrères*: 'I wrecked trains because I like to see people die. I like to hear them scream. I like to see them suffer.' Some of the sex-criminals *manqués* who gloat over crimes such as those committed by Matuschka – or Sharif – would echo, and have echoed, such claims. Neither group is to be trusted:

High P scorers seem pathologically drawn towards sexual behaviour which in the end does not satisfy them. They do not share the neurotic's guilt, and do not show any repression; nor do they show the neurotic's nervousness towards members of the opposite sex. Looking through the inventories of high P scorers, one almost feels that they are addicted to sex as if to a drug, and that this addiction and dependence creates more difficulties for them than it solves. (*Psychology is about People*, H.J. Eysenck, p. 90, Penguin, 1982)

'P' stands for 'Psychoticism', and men like Sharif and the members of *Los Rebeldes* and *Los Choferes* certainly seem to be psychotics whose sexual behaviour has created more problems for them than it has solved. What they or their *aficionados* might say about their motives is not to be trusted, for consciousness does not always tell the truth about the basis of one's actions:

[A] subject is hypnotized and told that he will be awakened after ten minutes. He is further told that some time after this the hypnotist will blow his nose three times. Upon receipt of this signal, the subject will get up, go out into the hall, pick up the third umbrella from the left on the rack, go back into the room, and put up the umbrella there ... When the experimenter blows his nose three times, the [hypnotized and awakened] subject becomes vaguely restless and uneasy; finally, he gets up, leaves the room, picks up the designated umbrella, brings it back to the room and puts it up. When questioned as to the reasons for his actions, he cannot, of course, give the true reason because he is unconscious of it. Instead he will make up as good a reason as he can ... Many of these rationalizations are quite remarkable in their ingenuity, and intelligent people in particular can usually find a good reason for doing almost anything that has been suggested to them under hypnosis. What is more, they apparently believe their own rationalizations implicitly. (*Sense and Nonsense in Psychology*, H.J. Eysenck, p. 41–2, Pelican, 1978)

A rationalisation is an attempt to express the reason behind – and the rationality of – one's actions. In fact, these may be, as in the experiment just described, quite without reason from the point of view of the individual. Not necessarily irrational, but arational: not opposed to reason, but operating by laws outside or beyond reason, unless they are taken in a wider context. In a wider context of laws and police agencies, sex-crime is not a rational way of seeking pleasure unless it can be committed both without immediate risk and without fear of later detection. An intelligent, successful man like Sharif could have obtained legitimate, legal pleasures in abundance during his stay in the United States, but ran the risks of rape and violence against women instead. These risks caught up with him, and he suffered the indignities and privations of incarceration in the American prison system. And perhaps, while he was incarcerated, he suffered rape and violence against his own person. Now he is again incarcerated, and in a prison system even more notorious than that of the United States. Was the pleasure he gained from his crimes sufficient to compensate him for what he has lost?

And even if he replied that it was, and is neither rationalising nor lying, try the thought-experiment of offering him, or some other psychopath with his inclinations, the opportunity to obtain, entirely without risk of possible sanctions, more pleasure than he could conceivably obtain in a lifetime – a hundred lifetimes – of unquantifiable sex-crime. Try the thought experiment of offering him, or some other psychopath with his inclinations, the opportunity of being directly stimulated in the pleasure centre of the brain. This would be pure, unadulterated pleasure. Any admixture of sensation or thought could only dilute and weaken it. It would be available for as long as the stimulation were supplied, and would be available without risk and without physiological cost, for the famous stories about laboratory rats self-stimulating to the point of exhaustion or starvation are false: a self-stimulating rat will reorganise its life around self-stimulation, but not neglect food or grooming. But would Sharif, or a psychopath like him, accept this form of pleasure, given a choice between it and, say, a fresh opportunity to rape and murder a perfect victim?

Presumably no, he would not. He would understand the choice, but be unable to make it in the rational direction: that of direct brain-stimulation and greatly enhanced pleasure. Irrational, or arational, forces operating in his brain below the level of consciousness would impel him in the direction of indirect brain-stimulation through the sense-organs of the eyes and ears and genitals. For him this would mean greatly reduced pleasure. Pleasure that would be impure, tainted with sense-data and with what the American linguist Steven Pinker has called 'mentalese': the raw concept-stuff of pre- or sub-linguistic thought. (See Pinker's *The Language Instinct* for further discussion of this term.) The sadist is seeking power and domination, but these are concepts that are not in themselves pleasurable, merely tokens representing relationships between entities in the sadist's universe. To introduce them into the psycho-sexual discourse of rape and torture may enhance the initial pleasure, but will block its ultimate fulfilment, for it crowds the mind with information that might otherwise be devoted to the pure stuff of pleasure.

But the choice our hypothetical Sharif makes when presented with a verbal explanation of its entailments might alter if he were allowed to *experience* direct brain-stimulation, and so was shown the incomparable pleasure it offered. Here he would, perhaps, realise the irrationality of his previous choice, for human beings are usually guided not by reason but by what they perceive through the sense organs. By what they hear and taste and smell and feel. And by what they see.

17: Light

Luz f. Lo que ilumina los objetos y les hace visibles.
Light. That which illuminates objects and makes them visible.
Fiat lux. Let there be light. (Genesis, i, 3)

It is a well-established rule that wherever visual technology goes, pornography is breathing hotly down its neck. This is as true today with the World Wide Web as it was back in 1839 when reliable photography was first developed. And there is a simple reason for it. Technology has always been invented and controlled by men, and men have always been interested in sex.

They have always been interested in money too. And photography is perhaps the best way yet devised of making money from sex. Drawings are slices of imagination: photos are slices of reality. Drawings take a long time to create: photos are created at the speed of light. Drawings depend on talent and skill: photos depend on competence. Photos are quick and convenient, easy to mass-produce and easy to conceal. They can enhance a quick one off the wrist almost anywhere and almost anytime.

The middle of the north Atlantic during one of the most vicious and one-sided sea-battles ever fought, for example. In July 1942, a convoy of thirty-five Allied merchantmen escorted by nineteen naval vessels sailed from Iceland with arms and supplies for the Soviet Union. It was a semi-suicidal voyage anyway at that time of year, when daylight is almost permanent in the far north, but *en route* news came in that the German battleship *Tirpitz* had broken through a blockade around Norway and was loose on the high seas. The naval escort was ordered to run for cover by the Admiralty and the merchantmen sailed on alone. They did not meet the *Tirpitz* (it was a false alarm), but they did meet lots of German aircraft and submarines. An American ship called The *John Witherspoon* was among the twenty-four merchantmen that never got through, and survivors from it were very lucky to be picked up by a Royal Navy corvette called *La Malouine*. (If anyone's interested, *La Malouine* seems to mean 'The Female Falkland-Islander'.)

They fell asleep as soon as they lay down, at various places in the corvette, and seemed to little appreciate their great fortune. Lieutenant Caradus found one of them asleep in the officers' small bath, and ten more had taken over the wardroom and forced the wine cupboard, and were lying about the floor in a drunken stupor. The bath's tenant awoke when Caradus found him there. The Lieutenant later described: 'He had an amazing collection of nude photographs and obscene flicker photos. He pushed these cards and photos into my coat pocket. It was when I got to my cabin, after stepping over men sleeping in groups in passageways, that I saw what I had been given. Flicking the photos gave the motion-picture effect of sexual intercourse. I nearly vomited.'

The RN Lieutenant returned the man's property to him at once, and was profusely thanked for returning the crew's 'girlfriends'. The seaman said he wouldn't go anywhere without them.

This is a passage from David Irving's history of the disaster, *The Destruction of Convoy PQ.17* (Corgi, 1970), and the differing reactions of the two nationalities involved are very revealing. The British Royal Navy Lieutenant 'nearly vomited' at what the American merchant-seaman was very grateful for having returned to him. Class undoubtedly played some part too – the Lieutenant presumably being middle-class and the merchant-seaman working-class – but it is still likely to have been the case that Americans were in general more familiar with pornographic photographs than the British.

It is also likely that among the pornographic photographs owned by the American crew were some taken or printed (or both) in México. So strongly associated was early American pornography with México that the earliest and most famous examples of it were called after a Mexican border city already notorious for the easy access it afforded American citizens to prostitution and drugs:

> Illustrated pamphlets depicting penetrative sex date back to the 1920s. Eight pages in length, these pamphlets – or 'Tijuana Bibles', as they came to be known – are perhaps the earliest form of comic book. Personalities of the day, whether cartoon characters (like Popeye) or gangsters (like Al Capone), were depicted in a sexually compromising position. The artist was always anonymous; so too the exact origins of the Tijuana Bibles (though it is pretty much accepted that they *didn't* come from Tijuana, more likely Los Angeles or San Diego). 'Thrill to Tales of Graphic Lust!' David Kerekes (in *Critical Vision: Random Essays and Tracts Concerning Sex Religion Death*, eds David Kerekes and David Slater, Stockport, Cheshire, 1995)

Strangely, the European equivalents of 'Tijuana Bibles' were known as 'Port Said Bibles', named from an Egyptian port with a similarly unsavoury reputation for prostitution and drugs. We see reproduced here yet another of the parallels between México and Egypt already discussed in relation to *el egipcio* Sharif Sharif. The parallel in this case is explained by the shared poverty of the two nations, and the ready supply this ensured (and still ensures) of women prepared to strip and be penetrated for the lens.

And Mexican and Egyptian women are prepared to do so despite the strong religious prohibitions placed on such behaviour in México and Egypt by, respectively, Roman Catholicism and Islam. Indeed, devout Roman Catholic women once hid the sexual allure of their hair beneath headscarves in public as devout Muslim women still do now. It seems possible, however, that religious prohibitions may have encouraged rather than discouraged the creators and manufacturers of Mexican and Egyptian pornography. The early history of porn is, for obvious reasons, difficult to trace, but it is generally agreed that in the West it began as a form of anti-clerical satire rather than as an erotic aid.

Evidence for this can be adduced from one of the underground 'classics' of literary porn to emerge from the nineteenth century. *A Man with a Maid*, written, inevitably, by an 'Anonymous' author, is the story of a man called Jack who devises an elaborate soundproofed sex-chamber for the capture and orifice-by-orifice deflowerment of a maid called Alice. Jack then goes on to maids called Fanny, Connie, Betty, and Mollie. All of whom, of course, end up enjoying it. Indeed, they all end up collaborating with it, except Betty and Mollie, who are the mother-and-daughter victims of a six-in-a-sex-chamber rape-romp that ends the book.

As you can easily infer, the book is not remarkable for its realism. You only ever feel that the author is talking about something real once, when he describes his collection of sex photos:

Among these was a series known as the 'Crucifixion', in which a lovely girl (evidently a nun from her despoiled garments scattered on the floor) was depicted bound to a cross naked, while sometimes the Mother Abbess (in her robes), alone and sometimes in conjunction with one of the Sisters, indulged their wanton fancies and caprices on the poor girl's breasts and cunt as she hung helpless! One photograph showed the girl fastened naked to a Maltese Cross, the Lady Abbess had inserted her finger into the Nun's cunt while the Sister tickled the Nun's clitoris! In another photograph, a monk was introduced who, kneeling before the Nun (still fastened on a Maltese Cross) sucked her cunt while his uplifted hands in the attitude of prayer attacked her helpless breasts! Another series, entitled 'La Barrière', depicted various phases in the ravishment of a girl by two ruffians in a solitary part of the Bois de Boulogne. The rest were mostly scenes of Tribadism and of Lesbian love, and interspersed with them were a few representing flagellation by a girl on a girl, both being stark naked! [sic omnia]

'Interspersed' is the right word: it comes from the Latin verb *spargere*, meaning 'to scatter or sprinkle seed', which is what sex photos are really all about, is it not? We can see in the catalogue of sex photos from *A Man with a Maid*, however, that quite different motives may originally have inspired them: the use of monks and nuns as characters in pornography is no longer especially prominent, but must have had a special political and satirical power in nineteenth-century France, a Roman Catholic country with a long history of anti-clericalism. Early Mexican pornography, it might be readily imagined, probably had similar motives, for México is also a Roman Catholic country with a long history of anti-clericalism.

Whatever its origins in satire and politics, however, pornography fulfils a single clear function today: that of masturbatory aid and, some feminists have long suggested, conditioning tool for male rapists. Other feminists have countered this argument with the claim that while masturbation in itself is no evil, pornography also serves to teach young people about things they might not otherwise easily or comfortably learn about. This is what a vulva looks like. This is what a penis looks like. This is what a vulva with a penis in it looks like. And so on. Things young people have not always learnt easily in other ways. Useful and important things, in fact.

The same sorts of things, it might be said, as have been taught by another kind of photo with a hidden history – the death photo. This is what a corpse looks like. This is what a severed head looks like. This is what a pile of human intestines looks like. And so on. Useful and important things too? Well, perhaps. But I do not think curiosity about death can explain all of some people's fascination with death photos any more than curiosity about sex can explain all of some people's fascination with sex photos. Sex remains exciting even when you know all about it. Does the same thing apply to death? For some people, I think it does. One of those people may have been the American magician and escapologist Harry Houdini (1874–1926), who saw a magician perform a cut-up body trick as a boy and:

> remained fascinated by mutilations: he possessed several grisly and much-thumbed photographs of Chinese executions, by beheading and by the death of a thousand cuts. These were images which spoke to his adult obsessions. (*The Life & Many Deaths of Harry Houdini*, Ruth Brandon, p. 22, London, 1993)

Houdini obviously returned to those photos again and again, long after he had satisfied his curiosity about what those kinds of death looked like. Was it because he was one of the people who are excited by photos like that? Perhaps it was. But does 'excited' mean 'sexually excited'? Again, for some people, I think it does, and again, Houdini may have been one of them.

Whether or not he was, his nationality remains, I think, a significant part of the story. Houdini was an American, and the story clearly proves that, whatever his motives, he was able to obtain death photos in pre-war America. There must have been some kind of market for them just as there was for the 'Tijuana Bibles' being sold at the same time. And whatever the true origin of the Bibles, the association of Tijuana with pornography equally clearly suggests that pornography was available in México during the period. But what of death photos? Was there a market for them too in México?

This is much less easy to establish, one reason being that there are far fewer figures from Mexican culture who have received the attention figures from American culture have received, and there is consequently far less chance of relevant facts about their lives being uncovered as in the case of Harry Houdini. But there is indirect evidence that death photos would have been available in early modern México. One is that death photos are available in late modern México, to an extent, indeed, that might with only slight exaggeration be called almost ubiquitous. The fascination of contemporary Mexican newspapers and magazines with the aftermath of traffic accidents and violent crime is well known amongst *aficionados* of trash culture in the United States, but can in fact be read as the Mexican manifestation of a general characteristic of Hispanic and Roman Catholic culture.

Spain, for example, has long been more than half in love with painful death. Bullfighting, as the existence of the Graeco-Latin synonym *tauromachy* suggests, has a history stretching back for millennia, and was exported by Spain to her colonies in the New World:

Bullfights
Each summer, four bullfights are held in Juárez at the
Plaza de Toros Monumental on Av.[enida] 16 de
Septiembre, beside Rio Grande Mall a bit east of
Plaza de Américas. Seating up to 17,000, Monumental is the world's fourth largest bullring, and a major
stop on the professional *corridas* circuit. The annual
season runs April–Sept; the first *corrida de toros* takes
place around Easter and then three more corridas are
held on four Sundays before Labor Day. These are
real Spanish-style *corridas* in which the bull may be
killed by the matador. (*Northern Mexico Handbook*,
Joe Cummings, Moon Publications, 1998)

The matador is an archetypal hero of Spanish-speaking
culture – one book on bullfighting describes how 'a man
metamorphoses into a god of the arena' (*Plaza de Toros*,
Gerard & Co., Verviers, Belgium: *'un homme se
métamorphose en un dieu de l'arène'*). But his name
literally means 'killer', from *matar*, 'to kill', from which is
also derived *matanza*, 'slaughter, butchery, massacre'. As
already described, Roman Catholicism added another
ingredient to this stew of death-and-pain worship at the
Renaissance, when its artists and sculptors began to
represent the gory details of the Passion of Christ and the
martyrdom of his saints with a hyper-realism designed to
cement the allegiance of the faithful and encourage their
attendance at church. One common image of Roman
Catholic iconography remains, for example, the *corazón
sagrada*, the sacred heart, in which Christ folds open the
flesh of his left breast to reveal his blood-dripping,
thorn-pierced heart.

The exportation of such images to México found a
fertile soil for naturalisation and continued growth, for the
native traditions of México contained similar obsessions,
which hybridised with Spanish imports to produce such

uniquely Mexican psycho-cultural artefacts as *el Día de los Muertos*: the Day of the Dead:

> México's third most important festival ... Some of the festivities are held in cemeteries where families clean the headstones and crucifixes of their deceased relatives (*los defuntos*), decorate them with flowers, and play games unique to this fiesta. In some areas the faithful will spend a whole day and night beside the family graves in a cemetery. Even roadside shrines throughout México are laid with fresh flowers and other tributes to the dead. Offerings of *pan de los muertos* ('bread of the dead') and food and liquor are placed before family altars, along with papier-mâché skulls and skeletons. (*Northern Mexico Handbook*, Joe Cummings, Moon Publications, 1998)

Such festivals have nourished a Hispano-Mexican obsession with death and its liquid concomitants that expanded eagerly to occupy the new media of photography, film, and television. One can readily see such things as the following on Mexican television – and at breakfast-time:

> The camera pans a suicide. The man is quite young and wearing a bulky blue sweater. By his feet is a five-gallon bucket. The rope around his neck is tied to a small tree in a city park. His neck is bent but the rope is straight and taut. The camera frames the man and the tree, then zooms in to peruse his body, and quickly does a 180-degree pan around to his neck. The camera zooms in again to one of his feet. It is touching the ground during the hours he spent hanging here alone, the man's neck stretched and now he is firmly planted on the earth again. ('While You Were Sleeping', Charles Bowden)

Such scenes run 'every morning at 7:45 a.m.' on a television station in Juárez as 'a special eight- to ten-minute part of the morning news', and must reflect something about the tastes and propensities of Juárez's inhabitants. Undoubtedly, some viewers must enjoy watching scenes like that, just as they must enjoy newspaper pictures of crash victims and gang murders. But can one pass moral judgments on such pleasures, and extrapolate from them to behaviour? Could, for example, the saturation of the Mexican media by images of death and pain have contributed something to the Juárez serial murders? In short, is there something wrong – and dangerous – about someone who enjoys and is attracted to such images?

For me, the answer is yes. There *is* something wrong with someone like that. Wrong, but interesting too. That people should enjoy looking at sex photos is not really interesting: it is what you would expect. That people should enjoy looking at death photos is not what you would expect. That people should be sexually excited by death photos – as some undoubtedly are – is even less what you would expect. The question raised by it must be: Why?

And the answer must be something to do with maleness. Like technology, culture is created and driven by men, and most areas of culture are dominated by men too. Death photos are part of what you might call splatter-culture, and splatter-culture is created, driven, and dominated by men. It is men who make horror videos, sell them, and watch them, and it is men who trade in and collect death photos. Just as it is men who trade in and collect postage stamps, telephone cards, and child pornography. There are general male characteristics of obsession and acquisitiveness at work in each hobby, but for death photos and child porn I think there are some more particular male characteristics at work too. One of them is, I would say, a greater tendency to perversion, which is based on a greater tendency to neurological abnormality.

As I said previously, there is something wrong with people who enjoy looking at death photos, and whatever is wrong with them must be present in their brains. Male brains are much likelier to be *abnormal* than female brains. Jack the Ripper's brain was abnormal, for example, but then so was Albert Einstein's, it is just that Jack the Ripper's abnormal brain probably owed at least as much to male environment as to male genes. The male environment has always been more violent than the female one, and males get attacked and injured more often. This is true in all cultures, which differ merely in attack and murder rates while always maintaining a higher and lower rate of, respectively, male and female victimisation. The murder rate in México is one of the highest in the world, for example, but only for men.

Murder necessarily entails deliberately inflicted physical injury, but deliberately inflicted physical injury does not necessarily entail murder: some victims of would-be murder survive the attack made against them. And this attack is often made against the head: many victims of attempted murder or less violent assault survive with brain injuries of varying severity, particularly with modern surgical and rehabilitation techniques.

Such brain injuries can cause problems both for the sufferer and for society at large. A serial-killer is even likelier to have suffered a head injury in childhood than he is to have been brought up by God-fearing, Bible-reading parents. (See, for example, Bill Thompson's *Soft Core: Moral Crusades against Pornography in Britain & America*.) Head injuries damage the brain, and damaged brains do not work properly: they make their owners get excited by abnormal stimuli, like sexually immature bodies or dead and decomposing ones.

But even if women were brain-damaged as often and as badly as men, you would still see more male perverts because the brain-damage would already have with men what might be called a head start. Men are naturally more adventurous in and excited by sex, and so are likelier to develop and indulge in fetishes. Which particular fetish is developed and indulged in often depends on chance. The Anglo-German behaviourist Hans Eysenck describes in his *Fact and Fiction in Psychology* (Penguin, 1965) a man who:

> Had received many hours of analytical treatment and had been enabled to trace his abnormality back to two incidents in his childhood. The first was when he had been taken to the park to sail his boat and had been impressed by the feminine consternation manifest when he struck the keel of his yacht against a passing perambulator. The second was when he became sexually aroused in the presence of his sister's handbag . . . Apparently he had masturbated from the age of ten onwards, with fantasies of prams and handbags and particularly of damage being caused to them by their owners. Intercourse, he said, was only possible with the aid of fantasies of handbags and prams. There were two children, and his wife said that he was a good husband and father. The domestic perambulator and his wife's handbag, however, were not immune from attack, and the handbag, filled to capacity and bulging, often provided piquancy to his masturbation. While it was true that handbags and perambulators roused him sexually, his attacks upon them were never accompanied by emission, although he was usually conscious of a release of tension.

Eysenck tells the story as an example of how behaviour therapy provides a triumphant cure for someone facing a prefrontal leucotomy – 'an operation by means of which the frontal lobes are severed from the rest of the brain'

(*Ibid.*, p. 182) – after the failure of lengthy psycho-analysis:

> He had been led to see the significance of these events and to understand that perambulators and handbags were, for him, 'symbolic sexual containers', but the attacks continued. (*Ibid.*, p. 183)

But ludicrous as much psychoanalytic use of 'sexual symbolism' is, it is likely that the idea will retain some value in properly scientific psychology and psychotherapy. Fetishes do arise by chance, but some are less likely to arise by chance than others. Some, in fact, are not likely to arise at all. In *Sex, Violence and the Media*, Hans Eysenck and N.K. Dias describe an experiment in which men were conditioned with pictures of naked women to become sexually aroused at pictures of women's boots:

> An interesting extension would have been to see whether erection could be conditioned just as easily to 'truly' neutral stimuli; it seems likely that such conditioning is easier for stimuli that already have 'symbolic' sexual significance, which may well be the case for knee-length female boots. Relevant research has in fact been conducted, and it appears that it is indeed difficult to condition men to respond to pictures that have no sexual association. Although evidence of slight arousal to coloured circles and triangles was obtained by McConaghy (1967), virtually no response to polygons was apparent in research by Langevin and Martin (1975) even when they used the potentially stronger reward of erotic films rather than pin-ups. (*Op. cit.* Maurice Temple Smith, London, 1978)

It seems reasonable to suppose, therefore, that the male brain is in some way 'programmed' to respond sexually to certain sexual stimuli that can be mimicked or imitated by non-sexual objects. This theory is applicable to death photos. An aroused vulva, for example, gapes, glistens, and oozes. So does a wound. An aroused vulva is red and pink. So is a wound. An aroused vulva is swollen. So is a wound – if it is old enough, or on a corpse. You can see these similarities between vulvas and wounds most clearly in colour photos on glossy paper.

The sort of photos and the sort of paper you get in Mexican pornographic magazines and in Mexican splatter-magazines. The sick thing is that there is at least as much 'aroused vagina' stimuli in the latter as there is in the former: both contain glistening, oozing, and swelling, for Mexican splatter-magazines often show photos of large wounds that gape, glisten, and ooze in red and pink.

You can apply the same reasoning to another kind of photo often shown in Mexican splatter-magazines: a fear-stricken or screaming female face. Part of what some men may enjoy about looking at a face like that is the fact that pain and pleasure, like grief and laughter, can have similar effects. Sometimes, indeed, they can go hand in hand. Or cock in ass:

> My favourite moment, however, has to be when Roxanne is penetrated in the pooper (for the thirtieth time, or something), goes wacko, yet still hangs in there. Hoo-*ray*!
>
> 'Oh-ho-ho,' she moans in mixed pleasure and pain. 'Oh my God . . . Not again. Not again. Not again . . . Oh, GOD! . . . Oh shit! . . .' (Is she having an orgasm or a bad case of the squirts?) Her expressions, of course, are great: a sex-injected look of fuzzy intoxication abruptly contorting into a snarl. [With apologies to Anthony Petkovich (see *Pardon Me, But Your Worm Is In My Crotch: Gregory Dark's Snake*

Pit, Headpress #13). In Japanese pornographic films, apparently, it is a sign of virility for a woman to look pained during sex, because it means the man has a large penis.]

'Contorting' is the operative word, I think: pain, pleasure, and fear all contort the face and in partly similar ways. They all contort the voice, and in partly similar ways too: hence, no doubt, the great popularity of the female scream in splatter-movies, which parallels the great popularity of the female groan in porn movies. But this is about sadism, not necrophilia: sadists like to hurt their objects of desire, necrophiles do not, because they cannot. Which is not to say that a sadist cannot be a necrophile, or vice versa, but I think the two are distinct in some important ways. You can place sadism toward one end of a continuum of male sexual behaviour, which is characteristically proactive and aggressive. Necrophilia jumps a qualitative fence, becoming a new kind of perversion and doubtless representing a greater underlying abnormality in the brains of those who practise it, though still, like sadism and other perversions, being based on biologically normal brain-mechanisms too. Biologically normal for men, that is. Perversions distort or exaggerate what is already present: it is probably almost impossible for brain damage or genetic disorders to create truly new patterns of behaviour.

Homosexuality is an interesting example of this. Culturally speaking it has passed from being a sin through being a sinful perversion to being a lifestyle option; biologically speaking I think it remains what it always has been: an abnormality. And, like other abnormalities, it has always affected more men than women and, in part, for the same reasons: because men are more adventurous in and desirous of sex. Recall the rape carried out by one of Sharif's arrested hirelings in prison:

181

On the 14th of February, 1998, Juan Jorge Contreras Jurado, 'El Grande' [The Big Guy], member of *Los Rebeldes*, led various other prisoners in a sexual assault on a nineteen year-old internee who had just entered the prison to serve a sentence for rape. (*El Diario de Juarez*)

Unable to have sex with a woman, Jurado turned to sex with a man. Violent, non-consensual sex. Rape, in short. And we have already seen that a propensity to rape may be caused by brain damage. A propensity to homosexual rape, and homosexuality in general, may also be caused by brain damage. Some homosexuals are homosexual because there is something wrong with their brains: like paedophiles and necrophiles, they respond to biologically inappropriate stimuli. In fact, it is very likely the case that there are more homosexual paedophiles and necrophiles – and serial killers – than would be expected from the proportion of homosexuals in the general population.

But apart from their choice of partner, homosexuals have not invented any truly new forms of sexual behaviour: they are, for example, still attracted by the same things as heterosexuals: either youth and physical attractiveness or dominance and the ability to protect and provide. Heterosexual men are attracted to the former and heterosexual women to the latter for good biological reasons: because a mate possessing them tends to increase the quality and survival chances of offspring. Homosexuals respond to the same biological imperatives, it is just that they respond in what might be called a misdirected way. This happens elsewhere in the animal kingdom, but human beings generally have more fun with their misdirection, and until recently did not have to suffer for it as other animals sometimes do. As, for example, I imagine one male broad-bodied darter dragonfly once did:

Males of *L.[ibellula] depressa* are rapacious – one was once seen attempting to mate with a hornet! This behaviour was probably released by the orange and yellow markings of the hornet, which resemble those of the female dragonfly. (*The Encyclopedia of Insects*, ed. Christopher O'Toole, p. 27, Guild Publishing, London, 1987)

Just as, for example, the smooth skin and rounded contours of a pre-pubescent male human being resemble the smooth skin and rounded contours of a post-pubescent female human being: an adult male who is attracted to the former and not the latter is running distorted neurological mechanisms, not newly created ones.

But homosexual or bisexual readers will probably think that is more than enough about homosexuality. *Guardian* readers too. Because this is all terribly old-fashioned, is it not, equating homosexuality with perversions like paedophilia and necrophilia and attempting to explain it in pathological terms? It may be, but it may also be true. Attempts to regard homosexuality as an undetermined choice or as a natural inclination or as something that does not need justifying or explaining at all do not seem to me to work very well, just as they do not seem to work very well for an interest in death photos. Homosexuality *is* abnormal, just as collecting pictures of dead people is: you have to admit that before you can go on to discuss behaviour like that and decide what your attitude to it should be.

But you also have to recognise that 'abnormality' is not an all-inclusive and atomic category: it has degrees and qualities. Smoking cigarettes and running marathons are abnormal too, and those things differ from homosexuality just as homosexuality differs from collecting pictures of dead people. An obvious rejoinder that might be raised at this point by liberal readers is that the stress laid on the 'abnormality' of homosexuality is a little rich, and more than a little irrelevant, in a book ostensibly devoted to an examination of the behaviour of heterosexual males responsible for the rape and murder of dozens of young women.

Examine, then, a posting to the same Internet site as has already been drawn upon for postings by Doreen Ramirez and a *soi disant* ex-fiancée of Sharif Sharif from Florida:

> Liked the web site and will put a link to it on my Police Supply Web Site. I would tend to disagree with the 'conventional' FBI Profile wisdom that most serial killers tend to be 'Heterosexual'. While many are, fags tend to be appear in VASTLY disproportionate numbers among serial/sex killers. Just a routine survey of your top 47 serial killers (20 or more) shows at least 18 or 38% were known fags. There were probably more. When you compare this with the realistic figures that fags are only about 1–2% of the male population (NOT 10–15%) we see that homosexuals are VASTLY disproportionately repre-sented among sex offenders/killers. If you eliminate serial killings without sexual overtones it would probably be over 50%. I have always objected to the fact that we are teaching our investigators to generally look for 'heterosexuals' in these cases. This is very misleading and overlooks the highly dispro-portionate numbers of fags involved in sex crimes & murders. [*sic omnia*] (http://www.mayhem.net)

Though these words were doubtless published to provide liberal visitors to the site with a *frisson* of enlightened superiority, the suggestion (though preferably cast in less emotive and pejorative language) deserves to be taken seriously. There is no *a priori* reason that serial murder should be an equal-opportunity profession, as guaranteed (according to a test as widely applied as it is fallacious) by an equal outcome in which minority groups are represented in exact proportion to their representation in the population at large.

It is amusing to speculate, for example, on the sociological convolutions a liberal criminological analysis would have to go through to explain the *over*-representation of blacks in one of the most despised forms of sex-crime: the rape and murder of elderly people. One study of serial murder says this about the British killer Kenneth Erskine, dubbed 'The Stockwell Strangler' by the tabloid press:

> The identifiable racial behaviour link that stamped his crimes [the sodomy and murder of at least seven elderly people, four men and three women] as the work of a coloured man [he was of 'mixed West Indian and Scottish parentage'] was his sexual assault of the elderly; it is the only sex crime that blacks commit more often than whites. No one knows why – it is a statistic established by years of patient behavioural research. Interestingly, the same behavioural research shows that most serial killers are young, male, and white – again there seems no logical reason why – and most serial killers, regardless of colour, commit their first murder between the ages of twenty-five and thirty. (*The Serial Killers: a study in the psychology of violence*, Colin Wilson and Donald Seaman, p. 48, Virgin Publishing, 1990)

This intersection of race and crime, like the intersection of sexuality and crime, is a dangerous topic to investigate or even to discuss, but it may eventually become a commonplace of criminology that different racial and sexual groups have differing propensities to commit different kinds of crime and deviance. It is already a commonplace of criminology that the different *sexes* have differing propensities to commit different kinds of crime and deviance. In almost every case, males outnumber women, often greatly, sometimes grossly.

This particular under-representation of women, and the accompanying glass ceilings that, for example, keep women from occupying senior management posts among the drugs cartels of Latin America, have never been great objects of concern in the media, and yet the explanation for them may also apply to the vastly more familiar under-representation of women (and the accompanying glass ceilings) in finance, business, and academia.

Before this explanation is proposed, it is important to lay out certain very important but little-recognised facts of social statistics and gender-relevant genetics. First, note the relative numbers involved in, on the one hand, serial murder and, on the other, the senior management of international business. The high profile afforded to each in the media tends to blind us to what would otherwise be the obvious fact that extremely few people are involved in them: serial killers, like the CEOs of billion-dollar-grossing multinationals, are extremely rare: over 99.9 per cent of the human race are not part of either category. It is likely, therefore, that serial killers, like CEOs, will be exceptional in some way, or several ways. Another way of expressing this point is to say that they will differ from the average in one or more psychological traits, and will very likely represent an extreme of human psychological variation.

This point is readily recognised for serial killers, who are often referred to in mass-media discourse as 'monsters' possessing some gross abnormality of psyche or morals. CEOs may be monsters, however, in a precisely parallel sense. Given this, we can extrapolate the conclusion that both serial killers and CEOs are likely to be 'over-represented' among any group of human beings whose members display wide general variation as compared to any other group of human beings whose members display less general variation.

This does indeed prove to be the case. Serial killers and CEOs are 'over-represented' among the group of human beings called men as compared to the group of human beings called women. Men are a more variable group in almost every imaginable measure of physiology, anatomy and psychology. There are easy and objective – and surely universally recognisable – proofs of this in such areas as height. There are more tall men than tall women, and among those tall men is Abdul Latif Sharif Sharif:

> 'Man, you're pretty,' said Sharif, as he introduced himself to the girls. The tall, ruggedly built guy with short, dark hair and a mustache often followed up with an invitation. 'How about coming over to my place for a drink?' ... Sharif bolted from his chair, towering over shorter guards who nervously reached for their guns. He was a large, menacing presence who filled the room, a man completely in control, against whom even the prison director seemed cowed. ('MONSTER' BEATS THE SYSTEM, Tim Madigan, The *Seattle Times*, 1999)

According to *The Guinness Book of Records*, the tallest male human being who has ever lived was the American Robert Ludlow, at 8'11" (2.72 m), and the shortest the Indian Gul Mohammed, at 1'11" (57 cm). The tallest female human being who has ever lived was the Chinese Zeng Jinlian, at 8'2" (2.48 m), and the shortest the Dutchwoman Pauline Masters, at 1'9" (55 cm). This represents a range of seven feet (2.15 m) for men, and a range of 6'5" (1.93 m) for women: the female range is ninety per cent of the range for men.

This greater variation combines with a 'differential extremes' phenomenon arising from the greater average height of men to ensure that there are more tall, and far more very tall, men than there are tall, and very tall, women:

> As an illustration, assume that two population groups vary along some dimension – height, for example. Although it is not essential to the argument, make the further assumption that the two groups' heights vary in a normal or bell-shaped manner. Then even if the average height of one group is only slightly greater than the average height of the other, people from the taller group will constitute a large majority among the very tall (the right tail of the curve). Likewise, people from the shorter group will constitute a large majority among the very short (the left tail of the curve). This is true even though the bulk of the people from both groups are of roughly average stature. Thus if group A has a mean height of 5'8" and group B has an average height of 5'7", then (depending on the exact variability of the heights) perhaps 90 per cent or more of those over 6'2" will be from group A. In general, any differences between two groups will always be greatly accentuated at the extremes. (*A Mathematician Reads the Newspaper*, John Allen Paulos, pp. 59–50, Penguin, London, 1996)

Controversy arises, however, and political sparks begin to fly, when one moves from anatomy and physiology to psychology and neurology and examines topics such as intelligence (which one would expect to play a role in the success both of criminals and of executives in big business). Even in psychology and neurology, however, there are tests nearly as indisputably objective as tests for height. An example of an indisputably objective psycho-neurological test would be that for chirality, or *handedness*. Human beings are believed to be the only

188

major group of animals that shows a clear preference for use of limbs or sense-organs on one or the other side, let alone to be one that shows a clear majority preferring to use the limbs or sense-organs on the *right* side. However, this clear majority is clearer among women than among men:

> R.C. Oldfield at the MRC Speech and Communication Unit of Edinburgh University [found that] of 1,128 subjects (394 men and 734 women) ranging in age from twenty to twenty-one, 25.9 per cent of the men and 16.6 per cent of the women claimed a tendency to left-handedness. These figures reflect the same disparity usually noticed between the sexes. (*Living Left-Handed*, Marjorie Iverson, London, 1995)

But why? One strong theory is that lefthandedness is more likely to be a pathological condition than righthandedness, that is, lefthandedness is likelier to represent the opposite of what would have naturally developed without some form of environmental insult such as brain damage. Suppose, for the sake of argument, that ten of every hundred human beings are naturally – genetically – lefthanded and the remainder (ninety of every hundred) are naturally righthanded. Suppose further that 10 per cent (one in ten) of each group changes handedness due to environmental insult. In this case, one lefthander (10 per cent × 10) will become unnaturally – pathologically – righthanded, while nine righthanders (10 per cent × 90) will become unnaturally – pathologically – lefthanded. The result is that fifty per cent of the lefthandedness (9/18) is pathological as opposed to (a very little over) one per cent of the righthandedness (1/82).

The over-representation of men among lefthanders, then, suggests the hypothesis that men are more subject or more vulnerable (or both) to environmental insult such as brain damage. This would in its turn suggest an increased male rate of pathological behaviours such as criminality and sexual perversion, and, by the statistical 'accentuation of difference at the extremes' effect, a gross over-representation of men among the most extreme criminal and sexually perverted groups. Such as, of course, serial killers.

What evidence is there for this hypothesis? A great deal. Slightly more male than female babies are born, but the male death rate is higher in every year of life so that in the United States, for example, white female life expectancy at birth stands at 79.2 years, according to data published in 1995, and white male life expectancy at 72.7 years (*The New York Public Library Science Desk Reference*, ed. Patricia Barnes-Svarney, Macmillan, New York, 1995, 'Life Expectancy by Race, Sex, and Age'). The same actuarial tables reveal how the male death rate accelerates from birth onward, with death rates among white males passing one per a thousand at the age of sixteen, a figure white females will not match until the age of thirty-nine (by which age white males will be dying at the rate of 2.52 per thousand).

The figures for non-white males and females show a similar dichotomy, but at higher levels and with the sex differential even more exaggerated. Non-white males, for example, seem to experience rates of mortality very similar to those experienced in the Third World: a little over twenty in a thousand die at birth, compared to a little over nine in a thousand white males at birth (the figures for females are a little over seven and a little over seventeen, respectively. The conclusion to draw seems to be that, for any given population, the male environment is always harsher, and only becomes more exaggeratedly so as the environment worsens for an entire population. Males, white or non-white, die to a greater extent both in accidents and of disease, in part due to their greater susceptibility to these environmental insults. What determines maleness, for example, might be described as a genetic truncation: the famous XX and XY female and male sex-chromosomes are named for their appearance under the microscope, and the Y chromosome that determines maleness and that is passed down from father to son might be described as an X lacking an arm.

This missing arm means that males are more susceptible to genetic disorders, because, if they receive a defective copy of a gene from either parent, they may be unable to compensate for it with a good copy received from another: the good copy would have been on the missing arm of the Y chromosome. The most famous example of this is haemophilia, a bleeding disease that females can carry and transmit but that almost invariably afflicts only males. A female child receiving the defective gene responsible for haemophilia on one X chromosome is able to compensate for it with a good copy on the other; a male child has no such advantage, and his faulty genotype, or collection of genes, is realised as a faulty phenotype, or the body and behaviour created by the genotype.

What is not commonly realised is that this higher male tendency to suffer from pathological influences may be applicable to much more than stereotypical diseases such as haemophilia. Could not the combination of psychological traits necessary to succeed in the highest level in physics, for example, also be regarded as 'pathological' in some sense? Take Sir Isaac Newton (1642–1727), who no one could deny possessed decidedly above-average powers of concentration and visualisation. One account might describe these powers as unusual, another as abnormal, yet another as pathological. Perhaps the final adjective is the correct one: it is known that Newton's birth was difficult and that he was not expected to survive beyond infancy, let alone into adulthood. His brain, then, is likely to have been subject to environmental insult, and this perhaps explains his 'genius', which was purchased at the cost of normal social development and behaviour: it is also known that Newton's adult behaviour was cold, distant, and solitary, and that his obsessive scholarship also involved years spent investigating alchemy and hidden codes in the Bible. The writer and wit Max Beerbohm (1912–1956) once remarked that he had known no man of genius who had not paid more or less severely for his gift.

The step from Sir Isaac Newton to fruit flies of the genus *Drosophila* might seem to be an over-ambitious one, but there is evidence from animal studies to buttress this hypothesis about how the greater stress of the male environment and weakness of the male genotype increases the variability and pathology of the male phenotype, that is, of male bodies and behaviour (the latter being, of course, mediated by part of the male body, that is, the brain):

In the 1950s the British developmental biologist C.H. Waddington . . . pointed out that organisms are often subject to environmental pressures during their development, pressures that affect their phenotype. It was already known that litters of mice kept on starvation diets during critical times in their development grow up to exhibit a greater range of sizes and other physical characteristics than litters given normal amounts of food. Suppose, Waddington suggested, that this increase in phenotypic variation in a stressful environment was due in part to a greater degree of expression of underlying genetic differences among the litter mates . . . Waddington was able to use *Drosophila* [fruit flies] to demonstrate this. When the eggs of flies were subject to a sudden heat shock, or exposed to ether vapour, the adults that developed from these eggs were more phenotypically variable than adults that came from unshocked [or un-vapoured] eggs. (*The Runaway Brain: The Evolution of Human Uniqueness*, Christopher Wills, pp. 239–40, HarperCollins, London, 1994)

Men, then, display greater variability than women because the male genotype, already more vulnerable to environmental insult than the female, receives more environmental insult in the course of life. More men are therefore found in 'extreme' categories: the very small groups who comprise the most successful sportspeople, chess-players, scientists, business-people, and criminals.

México, as a Third World country struggling to develop, would be expected to expose its entire population to greater environmental stress in the form of pollution, malnutrition, and poverty, and would therefore be expected to produce a greater variety of pathological behaviours, including, perhaps, serial murder. Perhaps. But does this claim not come up against the simple fact that serial murder has been a typically *First* World phenomenon, conducted in rich countries like the United States and the United Kingdom by men like Theodore 'Ted' Bundy and Peter Sutcliffe ('The Yorkshire Ripper') who have good jobs and lives of unremitting wealth and luxury by the standards of the Third World?

This simple fact, however, may not be as simple as it appears. First, the readiness with which the names of American or British or German serial killers are recalled by students of true crime may reflect the greater efficiency of police forces in the First World and the publicity received by men like Bundy and Sutcliffe both while they are committing their crimes and after they have been arrested and put on trial. Consider, for example, the career of a serial killer who is almost unknown by comparison with Bundy and Sutcliffe:

Pedro Alonso López (b. Colombia, 1949) known as the 'Colombian Monster', was reported captured by the villagers of Ambato, Ecuador in early March 1980. He admitted to more than 300 murders of pre-teen girls in Colombia, Peru and Ecuador since 1973. The remains of 53 victims of the 110 admitted to in Ecuador were rapidly detected after his confession. (*Guinness Book of Records 1987*, 'Crime: Most Prolific Murderers')

How many other Pedro Lópezes have there been in Latin America this century? It seems highly unlikely that he is unique in anything other, perhaps, than his total of murders. Note too that he was captured by an unofficial agency, the inhabitants of an Ecuadorian village, not by the Ecuadorian police. Students of true crime might match this with the 'Night Stalker' Richard Ramirez, who, as described elsewhere, was similarly captured by private citizens, but Ramirez had been responsible for only a fraction of López's total of murders, and had already received an enormous amount of publicity.

Given this, I think it must be recognised that serial murder is not a typically First World crime, and may in fact be *more* prevalent in Third World nations like Colombia – which, indeed, seems to brew a particularly strong form of violent psychopathology:

A total of 592 deaths was attributed to one Colombian bandit leader Teófilo 'Sparks' Rojas, aged 27, between 1948 and his death in an ambush near Armenia on 22 Jan 1963. Some sources attribute 3,500 slayings to him during *La Violencia* of 1945–62. (*Guinness Book of Records 1987*, 'Crime: Murder Rate; Highest')

Serial murder is nonetheless also present in the First World, which evidently contains, therefore, some of the extreme male variants I have suggested are responsible for this extreme form of crime. But what environmental insult is responsible for this extreme variation in the First World, whose serial killers have not been subject to the pollution, poverty, and malnutrition of countries like Columbia? The question can be answered by considering that 'environmental insult' for human beings may include a greater range of phenomena than it does for fruit flies: not just physical effects like pollution and malnutrition, but psychological ones too. Serial killing can and has been explained as, in part, a crime arising from a thirst for status and an enhancement of self-image. The period over which serial killing has emerged as a recognised category of violent crime – 1888 and Jack the Ripper being one oft-chosen starting point for the period – could be seen as one in which unprecedented numbers of male human beings began to live lives of sufficient leisure to allow them the luxury of concern for their position within society, and for the amount of gratification they are receiving from life.

It is here that we see how the mass media could have had an effect on the emergence of the serial killer through advertising and film. The basic premise of advertising in modern capitalism is that consumption leads to happiness – to gratification by the acquisition of more sensations, more friends, more sexual partners. Men like Bundy and Sutcliffe, with sufficient disposable income to attempt to purchase the new way of life offered by advertising, discovered that it was illusory: consumption did not bring happiness. They could therefore be seen as falling back on old grievances now freshly sharpened by a comparison with the hyper-successful male élite presented to them in the Technicolor visions of advertising and the cinema. However enviably successful Bundy's and Sutcliffe's lives were by comparison with those of their ancestors in the Middle Ages or their male counterparts in the Third World, they were miserable by comparison with the lives of James Bond and the male sports stars rising to unprecedented heights of prominence in the 1960s and 1970s in both the United States and the United Kingdom.

Psychologically starving for power and dominance – in short, for success – Bundy and Sutcliffe set out to gratify their artificially created and stimulated appetite for it in the only way they believed was open to them: by the sexual abuse and serial murder of women. Perhaps the career of Pedro López can be accounted for in the same way. Where his putative similarly psychopathic ancestors might have simply been too busy trying to fill their bellies to embark on any form of gratuitous violence, he had sufficient leisure to devote almost a decade of his life to the mass murder of 'pre-teen girls'. Perhaps he was pursuing in the only way he believed open to him a vision of the endlessly gratifying existences of the First World male presented to him in the universally influential creations of Hollywood. To López, the lives of Bundy and Sutcliffe might have seemed paradisical; to Bundy and Sutcliffe, actually living those lives, they were not. Advertising must eternally promise gratification and just as eternally deny its fulfilment, or the capitalism it serves would crumble. Advertising, in short, may artificially stimulate the natural appetites of human beings to spawn monsters.

For the epidemic of obesity in the United States – almost unglimpsed in the propagandistic confections of American television and cinema – can be read as a parallel to serial murder. Human beings have a natural appetite for the gratification offered by food, but capitalism has created an environment in which this appetite can be pursued to gross excess, with results clearly visible in the bodies of many American citizens. And serial killing's sister-crime – the mass-shooting – is easy to read as typically First World, indeed, as typically American. Advertising promises gratification quickly and conveniently, and the mass-shooting is the quickest and most convenient route to the gratification of dominance and power. Here too, however, the 'gratification' is discovered to be illusory, and the mass-shooter's final victim is almost always the mass-shooter himself.

How far the media contribute to violence by their portrayal of violence has always, of course, been a hotly debated question. Although it may be possible, even likely, that some influence is exercised on the participants in a culture by that culture's art and sources of news, it is even more likely that the influence is far from clear-cut and direct. If we set aside, however, the question of how a psychopathic personality is created, we confront a far clearer question: that of how a psychopathic personality is nourished. If an individual has acquired, in whatever way, a taste for portrayals of death and suffering, he would be expected to seek them out. Modern societies, even in developing countries like México, combine the availability of psychopathically pleasurable media with sufficient leisure to consume them.

The question then arises of whether these psychopathically pleasurable media feed the psychopathic appetite or satisfy it. A question simple to frame, extremely difficult to answer. Perhaps the answer varies from place to place, time to time, individual to individual, even from one individual in one place or at one time to the same individual in another place or at another time. In some ways, however, there do seem to be clear statements to be made on the topic. The death obsession of the modern media, seen in exaggerated forms in México, has been at the very least an index of late twentieth-century mass culture. By its very existence it guarantees the existence of death-obsessed individuals with greater or lesser degrees of psychopathology. It is possible to support the right of people to look at moving or still pictures of dead or dying people and still regard doing so as being not only

197

objectively abnormal but also aesthetically unattractive or unpleasant. If readers disagree with that, fine, but they have to provide responses for the points raised in this chapter, the most obvious one being, I think, the sex-bias of this kind of hobby: both kinds of splatter-pics, the death ones and the sex ones, are far more attractive to men than they are to women. That is an objective and easily recognisable fact because there is an objective and easily recognisable difference between the bodies of men and women. Differences between the brains of men and women, or between human brains in general, may be equally objective but are far less easily recognisable – or are not, at the present day, recognisable at all. Nor are many of them likely to be categorical differences: as I pointed out above, perversions are not new categories of behaviour, merely distortions or misdirections of tendencies that are already present. Brain damage cannot give human beings the ability to see in infrared or ultraviolet, but it can affect their ability to see in ordinary red and ordinary violet, as well as all the colours in between. It can also affect their responses to what they see in ordinary red and ordinary violet and the colours in between. Note, however, that brain 'damage' does not have to be physical: it can be psychological too, partly or wholly (physical and psychological brain damage must both have physical effects however. For example, a blow to the head produces changes in brain tissue that can then affect behaviour; being raped doesn't necessarily involve blows to the head, but it can affect behaviour in ways that must also be based on changes in the brain), and I have already suggested that Roman Catholicism and Islam have played a part in creating the psychopathic personalities responsible for the crimes in Juárez.

18: Oblivion

Olvido m. Falta de memoria.
Oblivion. Loss of memory.

'But the inequity of oblivion blindly scattereth her poppy, and deals with the memory of men without distinction to merit of perpetuity.'
[*Hydriotaphia, or Urn Burial* (1658), Sir Thomas Browne (1605–82)]

In 1774 the German novelist and playwright Johann Wolfgang von Goethe (1749–1832) published a book called *Die Leiden des Jungen Werthers*, or *The Sorrows of Young Werther*. It enjoyed great success all across Europe, brought Goethe the first flush of the fame he and his memory have enjoyed ever since, and created a new fashion among its readers. A very strange new fashion: for suicide.

Because that was the fate of the hero of the book, the eponymous 'Young Werther', who elected to kill himself after an unhappy love affair. Readers of *The Sorrows* identified with Werther, and so adopted the solution he presented for the problems of life. Such behaviour – the damaging or dangerous imitation of a fictional character – has sometimes been called the 'Werther Effect' by modern psychologists, and it seems likely that few readers will not have experienced some milder form of it in their own youth, or even later. We want to be like the heroes we encounter in books or on film and video, and so we adopt some aspect of their behaviour: a way of talking or walking, a choice of cigarette or alcohol brand, a glance, a smile, a gesture.

So familiar is this imitation that we forget how very strange it is. Werther never existed, and yet his invented life so impressed those who read of it that some of them adopted the sincerest form of flattery they could offer to his creator. They killed themselves in imitation of a young man who had never existed save as patterns of black ink on white paper. And even readers who did not go so far as to kill themselves were moved by Werther's story. They felt sympathy, sadness, even misery at the sorrows of a young man who had never existed save as patterns of black ink on white paper. This is very strange.

And it extends, of course, far beyond Werther, far beyond Goethe's other creations. Human beings have been moved by art and myth for many tens of thousands of years. Perhaps for many hundreds of thousands, or a million. They have felt sorrow or joy, or fear or delight, at characters and situations that have never existed save as patterns of black ink on white paper, or stylus-impressions in baked clay, or chiselled-out glyphs on stone, or any of the other visual and auditory means human beings have employed to tell stories to each other.

Very strange. But it prompts me to wonder about another strange question. Young Werther never existed. Young Esmeralda did:

Case 16, November 15 [1993] – Esmeralda Leyva Rodrígues ... A long-haired 13-year-old girl, 1.60 m tall, who was abducted while leaving Technical Secondary School 27. She was raped anally and vaginally and then strangled, and her body was found at the rear of Mariano Escobar School next to the Tiofilo Borunda.

The strange question prompted by these patterns of black ink on white paper is this: has Esmeralda Rodrígues, in death, acquired the same ontological status as Young

Werther? Can the emotions roused by her story be distinguished from the emotions roused by his?

The immediate answer might seem to be yes, for Esmeralda Rodrígues has a continued existence beyond that of print and the list of Juárez murder victims published on the Internet. She, unlike Werther, has real friends and family who remember her, who knew her for years, and who felt emotion at her death not by reading about it in print but by experiencing it in reality.

But how many family and friends did Esmeralda Rodrígues have? How many acquaintances? How many shopkeepers or bus drivers who knew her by sight and perhaps by name? Dozens? Hundreds? Thousands? But it is unlikely anyone reading this book knew her. So how do the emotions of the readers of this book differ from those of the readers of *The Sorrows of Young Werther*? Esmeralda Rodrígues, like Young Werther, is known only through the medium of language, and how can one be certain that Esmeralda Rodrígues, like Young Werther, is not entirely invented? There is no way of discovering from the printed word alone that she is not: one would have to be shown photographs, talk to those who actually knew her, perhaps see her gravestone, even, at an extreme, conduct scientific tests on the bones in her grave to prove that they are of a female aged approximately thirteen whose DNA matches that of those still alive who claim to be her family, and who have further documents, further photographs, further witnesses to prove it. And even then, with all this proof, the truth about Esmeralda Rodrígues's death is only decided on the basis of probabilities. It is more likely that she died as she is said to have died than that an elaborate and extremely skilful and expensive conspiracy has been conducted to convince the world that she died of strangulation after kidnap and rape when in fact she died in some other way.

But will anyone ever go to these lengths to convince him- or herself of the truth of Esmeralda Rodrígues's death? No. One can be almost entirely certain now that the truth is as it is presented. Further efforts would change the probability very, very little, in the way that pouring a cup of water into the Pacific Ocean raises its water level very, very little. By all natural and almost all unnatural standards, Esmeralda Rodrígues existed and died painfully and unpleasantly, and the words describing her death and the discovery of her body are true. In some very important way, her ontological status is different from that of Young Werther. She existed; he did not. The emotions aroused by her death are different from the emotions aroused by his.

But one of the differences may be that the emotions aroused by her death are less powerful. Not for family or friends, but for you, a reader of this book. What did you feel as you read those words about Esmeralda Rodrígues? What do you feel *now*, as you read them again?

Case 16, November 15 [1993] – Esmeralda Leyva Rodrígues . . . A long-haired 13-year-old girl, 1.60 m tall, who was abducted while leaving Technical Secondary School 27. She was raped anally and vaginally and then strangled, and her body was found at the rear of Mariano Escobar School next to the Tiofilo Borunda.

Almost certainly you feel far less emotion than you have sometimes felt reading other words or seeing pictures about human beings who, unlike Esmeralda Rodrígues, have never existed. But then these words about Esmeralda Rodrígues are not designed, like the art of a novel or film, to arouse emotion. They are neutral, forensic, scientific, designed to convey information as efficiently as possible, and their effect on the reader will be commensurate with that reader's ability to snag a context against the burrs of meaning lying within them. Someone who is Mexican and *juarense* (an inhabitant of Juárez) will know the probable context of time and temperature for a kidnap taking place on 15 November, and may know the location, even the school; someone who has experienced rape will know the context of fear and pain into which Esmeralda Rodrígues was dragged; someone never raped but who is, or has been, a thirteen-year-old girl might begin to know, a little, what Esmeralda Rodrígues experienced. But the true experience, the full context, the complete measure of sensation was known only to Esmeralda Rodrígues herself, and she is now dead.

So does it matter now that she was raped and murdered? To her family and friends, certainly. But in fifty years' time? In a hundred? Will Esmeralda Rodrígues *then* share the status of Young Werther: someone who exists only in so far as the words telling of her pass into a living brain and dissolve into meaning? Another fictional character, the Winston Smith of George Orwell's *Nineteen Eighty-Four* once speculated thus on a fictional character in *his* – Winston Smith's – fictional universe:

> Comrade Ogilvy, unimagined an hour ago, was now a fact. It struck him as curious that you could create dead men but not living ones. Comrade Ogilvy, who had never existed in the present, now existed in the past, and when once the act of forgery was forgotten, he would exist just as authentically, and upon the same evidence, as Charlemagne or Julius Caesar. (*Op. cit.*, chapter iv)

And what if there are no living brains left in a hundred years' time for those words to pass into? What if the human race becomes extinct? Does Esmeralda Rodrígues then become nothing, the way victims like the following are already almost nothing?

Case 9, October 24 – Name unknown . . . A sixteen-year-old woman, 1.40 m tall, wearing a sweatshirt with braces and a CORONA logo, a brown brassière, white tennis shoes, and coffee-coloured stockings. On the ring-finger of her left hand she had a gold ring with a black stone in the centre of it engraved 'Hidalgo Academy'. She was strangled and was found by the airport inside a plastic bag.

This was a human being with a life and a name, and now she is a *Desconocida* – an 'Unknown Female'. And what of the *Desaparecidas* – the 'Disappeared Females'? And the females identified neither as unknown nor as disappeared, because no one has ever gone to the police to enquire about them? What status do they have? A status *less* than that fictional creation Young Werther? While alive they had something he never had: consciousness and the universe of sensation that goes with it. Once they were dead, that consciousness and the universe created by it were overturned, annihilated, swallowed by nullity like a shining tear falling into black ink, and no words commemorate them now. Paradoxically, they are identified only by the impossibility of identifying them: the victims neither found nor reported missing. In a city like Juárez, with two million people, it is easy for this to happen.

19: People

Pueblo m. Conjunto de los inhabitantes de un lugar or país: el pueblo mexicano.

People. The inhabitants of a place or country: *the Mexican people.*

Many Spanish words are transparent to a speaker of English: they are like familiar faces wearing a little make-up, and you recognise them almost instantly. *Cristal*, for example. *Relación. Foto.* Others are, at first, what might be called translucent: they are like familiar faces wearing a lot of make-up. You do not recognise them instantly. Sometimes you do not recognise them at all. *Cristal* is obviously crystal. *Pueblo* is obviously . . . nothing. Yet it is tied to an English word by rules of derivation nearly as regular as those that tie *cristal* to crystal.

Pueblo is a word that has been distorted by the weight of time: its initial vowel has fractured and bifurcated from an original 'o'; its second consonant has sclerotised – hardened – from an original 'p'; its original second vowel has disappeared altogether, creating a thickened node of consonants in the heart of the word. For the Spanish *pueblo* was originally the Latin *populus*, which passed similarly distorted through French into English as 'people'. In Spanish the meaning has mutated as well: *pueblo* means people, but also village or town: a place where you will find people.

These facts of philology mirror a theory that may cast light on the crimes in Juárez. *Pueblo* has been distorted, fractured, sclerotised, thickened, modulated by the weight of time. These may be precisely the effects people, or a mass of individuals, have on the psychology of the individuals who make up that mass. It has long been possible to predict the adverse effects of overpopulation – over-peopling – from observations of nature:

> In time ... The bluegill population in farm ponds builds beyond the carrying capacity of the water. The fish become stunted, their heads large but their bodies small and thin. (*The Fresh and Salt Water Fishes of the World*, Edward C. Midgalski and George S. Fichter, p. 220, Octopus, London, 1977)

Bluegill are members of the *Centrarchidae* family of fish, as are the predatory North American freshwater fishes known as bass.

> 'I mean ... I sit there having nightmares about not being able to go fishing in the lake and catch bass,' Sharif testified on July 28, 1992, during the first of his deportation hearings. 'I would like to have another chance. I won't let you down, Your Honor.' ('MONSTER' BEATS THE SYSTEM, Tim Madigan, The *Seattle Times*, 1999)

These effects of overcrowding on fish are obvious because they are external. But what of the effects on fish, and fishermen like Sharif, that are not obvious, because they are internal? Scientific investigations have only recently become sophisticated and thoroughgoing enough to attempt to answer this question. The hippocampus is a structure buried in the brain. Invisible from the outside, it regulates emotion and the storage of memory, yet this hidden structure is subject to the effects of 'peopling' that are just as objective as the effects of 'peopling' on the bodies of fish:

If stress persists too long, the hippocampus begins to falter in its ability to control the release of the stress hormones, and to perform its routine functions. Stressed rats are unable to learn and remember how to perform behavioural tasks that depend on the hippocampus. [Investigation] has also shown that severe but temporary stress can result in a shrivelling of the dendrites in the hippocampus. Dendrites are the parts of neurons [brain cells] that receive incoming inputs and that are responsible [for memory]. [It has also been shown] that if the stress is discontinued these effects are reversible. However, with prolonged stress, irreversible changes take place. Cells in the hippocampus actually begin to degenerate. When this happens, the memory loss is permanent. (*The Emotional Brain*, Joseph LeDoux, Weidenfeld & Nicolson, 1998)

But what kind of 'stress' is responsible for this neurological degeneration?

The effects of stress on the hippocampus were first discovered [in] monkeys [who] had lived in a colony as social subordinates to a dominant male. Over several years, some died. Upon autopsy ... It was discovered that marked degeneration of the hippocampus had taken place. There was little sign of any damage to any other part of the brain. This basic finding has now been confirmed in a number of situations. For example, the hippocampus is degenerated in mice living under social stress.

Recent studies have shown that the human hippocampus too is vulnerable to stress. In survivors of trauma, like victims of repeated childhood abuse or Vietnam veterans with post-traumatic stress disorder, the hippocampus is shrunken. (*Ibid.*, p. 242)

In short, the behaviour of other people – child-abusers, enemy soldiers – has an objective, clinically quantifiable effect on a vital part of the human brain. What other effects take place elsewhere? Autopsies conducted on dead monkeys revealed 'little sign of any damage to any other part of the brain', but that is not proof that none had taken place. It is possible, for example, that stress induces changes in living brains that do not leave any trace in the brain after death, at least to current techniques of investigation. What of transient chemical and electro-magnetic changes? And what of changes in the brains not of individuals subject to stress, but of individuals subjecting others to stress? What changes had taken place in the brain of the dominant male in the monkey colony investigation?

What changes take place in the brains of dominant males of the species *Homo sapiens* in *our* colonies? That is, in our towns and cities. In our centres of population; of *empeoplement*. It seems reasonable to assume that some kind of feedback loop exists for dominance as it does for subordination. Subordination produces changes in the brains of subordinate males that presumably mediate subordinate behaviour that leads in its turn to further subordination, and so on. Turn this on its head and one would predict that dominance produces changes in the brains of dominant males that mediate dominant behaviour that leads in its turn to further dominance, and so on. What happens when this feedback loop begins to work too fast? A town or city, crowded with human beings, vastly increases the number of encounters between human beings, and so vastly increases the opportunities for subordinate and dominant behaviour. This is a super-enriched psychological environment: super-enriched with psychic toxins, for the subordinate, and with psychic nutrients, for the dominant. What millennia-dead tribal leader, for example, dominating a few dozen of his fellow humans, could ever have competed for egotism and *folie de grandeur* with Hitler or Stalin, dominating millions? And, to take a less extreme example, it has been observed that British Prime Ministers undergo changes in personality and behaviour during their premiership, becoming more grandiose, more paranoid, more intolerant. These changes arise, it seems safe to presume, from changes within their brains influenced by an environment of continual dominance: continual deferment and obsequiousness by others.

Paranoia and intolerance break out when this 'mutated' brain encounters dissent or criticism, and may be viewed as manifestations of hyper-dominance that attempt to reassert authority and re-create the environment of continual subordination from others. If so, we can perhaps begin to understand the behaviour of serial killers in a new light. They are dominant individuals who have no good opportunity for dominant behaviour. In constant contact with other human beings in the overcrowded colonies of our towns and cities, they are unable to enact the dominant behaviour enjoined upon them by the hard-wiring of their brains. Their brains, then, may begin to mutate, releasing neurochemicals in unnatural quantities or combinations, altering the structures and networks that underlie normal social and sexual behaviour.

And, as I have suggested elsewhere, we must define 'people' in a wider sense in an age of mass electronic communications. Our societies are overpopulated not only with people but also with ideas and images, which must also exercise an effect on the brain and its electrochemical patterns and structure. Human beings can be influenced by words and the meanings they carry, by patterns of coloured ink on paper. One of the clearest examples of this is pornography: written pornography, visual pornography. But again, pornography must bear a wider sense in our modern age: a medium not just for representations of sex, but also for representations of death. Minds and brains are warped by the images of sex and death fed to us in the media, and warped minds and brains then produce more such images in a feedback loop, a vicious circle that creates the fuel that powers it.

And yet we must also recognise that the effects of the modern age upon the psychology of those who, willy-nilly, participate in it are not always imposed upon passive recipients. Sometimes the warped have *chosen* to be warped. Examine pictures of *Los Choferes*, for example, and one sees apparently clear evidence of one of the most terrifying phenomena to have been created in the United States and exported to the rest of the world. It is a particular form of the body-modification we have already seen in notes made on the death of a woman from Juárez:

'Case 16, July 30 [1996] – ROCÍO MIRANDA AGUERO ... Rocío Miranda Aguero, 28 years old, manageress of the night-club Top Capos, was found by children in a 200-litre drum full of corrosive acid, with only her hands and feet remaining undissolved. She was identified by her silicone [breast-]implants.'

This is a form of body-modification chosen by women: an artificial enhancement of a natural female asset: the curved and rounded somatic profile. Men have chosen another form of body-modification: the artificial enhancement of musculature. Advances in modern medicine have given individual human beings the ability to subvert the physiological heritage of their genes – indeed, to rewrite it entirely:

The natural overproduction of human growth hormone during the years of skeletal growth of an otherwise normal human being results in *gigantism*. In other words, and in accordance with current

210

medical knowledge, we know that excess of human growth hormone produces a human giant, for that is how giants are made, generally by nature's 'mistake'. And there seems to be little doubt, therefore, that chronic administration of exogenous human growth hormone also will produce a human giant, and perhaps a giant athlete with gargantuan abilities! (*Hormonal Manipulation*, William N. Taylor, McFarland & Co, 1985)

But this section of a book called *Hormonal Manipulation: A New Era of Monstrous Athletes* has only been reached after its author, William N. Taylor, has discussed a related and much more notorious means of creating larger and stronger human beings: anabolic steroids, 'synthetic derivatives of the natural male sex hormone, testosterone'. Increased size and strength, and the psychological changes that accompany them, are no longer dependent solely on a human being's willingness to train and exercise, and are no longer assigned limits by a human being's genes: increased size and strength can be bought in small bottles and injected. And huge numbers of people, in both the United States and México, have been buying and injecting them. The first people who may have done so, back in the Old World, suggest that this is probably something to be concerned about:

Anabolic steroids were apparently first used in World War II; steroids were said to have been administered to Nazi SS troops in order to make them more aggressive and less fearful of violence. It has been speculated that these early anabolic steroids were used by Hitler and his entire military staff, which may have accounted for, in part, the 'driven', aggressive and violent acts committed by the German military. (*Ibid.*, p. 33)

211

If so, doses of anabolic steroid would have been too late to affect the size of Hitler's body but would certainly have affected the functioning of his mind: as their derivation from testosterone might suggest, anabolic steroids enhance what are regarded as typically male characteristics like aggression, self-confidence, tolerance of pain, and so on. In fact, they can be said to create these characteristics in the first place: the neural mechanisms underlying them are 'built' by them not just in men, but in women too. It is the lower average level of male hormones in women's bodies that explains the lower average level of male characteristics in women's behaviour, just as it explains women's lower average levels of size and strength.

And there is an association between the use of steroids and a vastly increased sex drive. This, coupled with the aggression engendered by steroids, seems a potent recipe for rape – and indeed, it seems to have been so. There are cases of bodybuilders in both the United States and the United Kingdom arrested and convicted for rape, and discovered to have been suffering a form of rape-psychosis brought on by the abuse of illegally purchased steroids. But it seems highly likely that these drugs merely aggravate and exacerbate an underlying psychopathology, merely widen psychic fissures through which the bubbling, acridly steaming lava of sexual violence can pour. 'Bodybuilding' is an explicit expression, in both language and reality, of a desire to remould a body with which one is by definition dissatisfied, and bodybuilding can itself alter the chemistry of the body and brain, and so bring about a change in personality and behaviour. The Yorkshire Ripper, for example, did not so far as is known abuse steroids, but he did bodybuild. Investigations into his childhood have revealed that:

With the indignity of the bullying still fresh in his mind as he finished his teenage years, Peter Sutcliffe decided to prepare himself for possible further problems. He started body-building, which surprised his father, a surprise which was to turn to something close to amazement when Peter developed the strongest grip in the family, easily beating his two-years-younger brother Michael, a much rougher diamond than Peter, at arm-wrestling ... [A friend called Michael Emery described how] 'he was dead keen on keeping fit and had some chest expanders. We used to have competitions with them but Peter could always beat me and his brother, Mick.' (*The Yorkshire Ripper: an in-depth study of a mass killer and his methods*, Roger Cross, p. 46, 49, HarperCollins, 1993)

Why should México be free of similar psychopaths? But they, decades on, and far closer to the cauldron of competitive self-improvement that is the United States, can find chemical supplements for their efforts in the gym and on the lifting-bench. Indeed, the medical history of synthetic endocrinology already reveals disturbing effects in the Third World from use of artificial steroids forced on the Third World by multinational agribusiness. Nations very near to México, geographically speaking, have suffered from the consumption of meat from animals reared according to 'advanced' agricultural techniques imported from – or imposed by – the First World:

Apparently, there is enough residual hormone in the meat and other products subsequently ingested by humans to alter their own hormonal balances. For instance, an epidemic of premature thelearche, with over 2000 young girls from Puerto Rico and the Caribbean Islands, continues to be of great concern. Premature thelearche is essentially premature breast development and enlargement in girls prior to the age of 8 years or so. Researchers concluded that estrogenic steroid contamination of animal feed was associated with the cause of this phenomenon. Furthermore, a large percentage of these young girls showed signs of precocious puberty as young as 2 years of age. These signs included growth of pubic hair, onset of menstruation and advanced bone development, which may ultimately shorten their stature significantly. (*Hormonal Manipulation*, William N. Taylor, p. 46, McFarland & Co, 1985)

These Latin American and Caribbean girls suffered from artificial hormones unwillingly: they ingested them without either their or their parents' being aware of the effects they would have. It seems likely, however, that many men in Latin America have deliberately ingested artificial hormones in pursuit of the hyper-enhanced musculature promoted by such Hollywood stars as Arnold Schwarzenegger and Sylvester Stallone in such films as *Conan the Barbarian* (1981) and *Rambo: First Blood, Part Two* (1985), respectively. Some members of *Los Choferes* seem to have been among the admirers of Schwarzenegger and Stallone. Was abuse of steroids, then, a contributory factor to the rapes and murders in Juárez? If they were, then it seems another example of the truth of the metaphor chosen by Charles Bowden as the subtitle of his book on the city, which is called *Juárez: the Laboratory of our Future*.

Steroid abuse, and even newer techniques of chemically or electronically mediated body-enhancement, seem likely to become even commoner in the future, and the concomitant psychological effects will not, it seems even more likely, be compensated for by any equivalent advance in what might be termed artificial morality. Our ability to modify our bodies is likely to far outstrip our ability to modify our ethics, and what awaits us in the third millennium may be more and more of what has been seen in Juárez. The last laugh may be had by Sharif and his hirelings.

20: Humour

*Humor m. Cualquiera de los líquidos del cuerpo del cuerpo de un animal,
como la sangre, la bilis. Humor negro, gracia que se basa en presentar
como jocosos asuntos que por su naturaleza son muy serios.*

Humour. One of the fluids in the body of an animal, such as blood, bile.
Black humour, humour that consists of presenting as amusing matters
that are by nature serious.

What is the most boring number of one through nine? Not
the Evil One. And it takes two to tango. Three strikes and
you're out. Five senses. Being at sixes and sevens is never
boring. Nor is being behind the 8-ball. Or being on cloud
nine.

What does that leave? Oh, yes, four. What has four got?
Four corners of the world. Which is rather dull. And
mathematicians have solved the four-colour problem. It
turns out that you do only need four colours to colour any
map so that no two adjacent regions are the same colour.
Which means we need a new problem associated with
four. How about the problem of why the classic rock
line-up has four members? Not three, not five, but four:
count them: vocals, guitar, drums, bass.

As in the Who and Led Zeppelin – so it obviously works.
But why? Is it because four is the optimum number for the
organic interplay of creative dynamic tensions in a rock
group? Or because that is what the fans prefer? Or both? Or
neither? I am not sure, but I have a theory. I think it is
something to do with the ancient Greek idea of the humours.

The ancient Greek idea of the humours was that our temperaments are determined by the amount of one or another kind of body fluid, or humour, we have inside our bodies. There were four of these humours: blood, choler, phlegm, and black bile. Translate those, where necessary, back into Greek (or Latin), and you get the four personality types of ancient Greek medicine: sanguine, choleric, phlegmatic, and melancholy.

We still use those terms in English with more or less the same meanings, and one of the things we can use them for is the individual members of the groups I mentioned above. Take the Who: Roger Daltrey is sanguine, Keith Moon choleric, John Entwistle phlegmatic, Pete Townshend melancholy. Now Led Zeppelin: Robert Plant is sanguine, John Bonham choleric, John Paul Jones phlegmatic, Jimmy Page melancholy.

Do you notice any patterns? You should do. The bassists are phlegmatic, just as the drummers are choleric and the lead vocalists sanguine. The humours could be classified on the basis of whether they were hot or cold and whether they were moist or dry. Blood was hot and moist. Choler was hot and dry. Phlegm was cold and moist. Black bile was cold and dry.

So lead vocalists need a hot humour and bassists a cold one. Lead guitarists need a dry one. Drummers need a hot one too.

The Who and Led Zeppelin were both very big groups in their day, and they both did more than their fair share to create the rock myth. That is another Greek word, by the way. Myth comes from μυθος, *mythos*, or 'story'. Specifically, a story about the gods. Gods like Dionysus, the Lord of Misrule and Excess. Also, the God of Loud Noises. Διονυριος Βρομιος, *Dionysos Bromios* – Dionysus the Thunderer. So what have we got? Violence, excess, loud noises. Sounds like the recipe for rock'n'roll, doesn't it?

That is why Camille Paglia suggests in her book *Sexual Personae* that rock is a modern outlet for the impulses whose ancient outlet was the Dionysia, or the rites of Dionysus. She got the idea from Nietzsche, who drew a distinction between the Dionysiac and the Apollonian sides of art. The Dionysiac side of art is irrational, violent, and destructive, the Apollonian rational, controlled, and creative. You need both, and rock supplies the Dionysiac one nowadays.

This idea fits with the idea of the four humours not just because both come from ancient Greece but because both are about excess. The ideal temperament is one in which none of the humours predominates, so the ideal temperament is neither sanguine nor choleric nor phlegmatic nor melancholy. You get one of those when there's an imbalance of one of the humours – an *excess* of one of them. Rock is both Dionysiac and humorous – in the original sense of the word. The Who and Led Zeppelin appealed to so many people because they each contained good examples of individuals suffering from an excess of one of the four humours.

But you do not have to put it in those terms. And should not, in fact, at least not seriously. Nobody seriously believes nowadays that personality type depends on body fluids, so modern psychology does not use those terms any more. It still uses concepts that would be recognisable to the ancient Greeks though: the concepts of extroversion and introversion and emotionality and stability. Put them together and you arrive at four personality types too: the emotional extrovert; the emotional introvert; the stable extrovert; and the stable introvert. They correspond, respectively, to the choleric, the melancholic, the sanguine, and the phlegmatic, or to the hot dry, the cold dry, the hot moist, and the cold moist humours.

The advantage of the modern system of classification, from the scientific point of view, is that it is purely descriptive: it does not try to explain why people behave the way they do, simply to classify them according to how they behave. We still do not know exactly what causes personality differences, so there is no point in using explanatory labels the way the Greeks did.

But if we do not know exactly what causes personality differences, we have some ideas, and those ideas apply pretty well to the Who and Led Zeppelin. One idea is that personality is related to build: *soma* determines *psyche*. Take John Bonham and Keith Moon. They were choleric, or emotional extroverts. They liked sensation and excitement, and both are still renowned for doing stupid and destructive things, Bonzo in particular. In other words, they were both rather childish. Maybe this is because they both had rather childlike bodies. Again, this is an idea that goes back to the ancient Greeks:

> The belief that there is a relationship between physique on the one hand and personality, mental and physical disorders, on the other, is very old indeed; Hippocrates, who lived about 430 BC, already discriminated between the two main types of body build, the long, lean, linear which is often referred to as 'leptosomatic', and the thickset, stocky type, sometimes referred to as 'pyknic'. (*Fact and Fiction in Psychology*, H.J. Eysenck, p. 270, Penguin, 1965)

The significance of these two body types for personality may be that one – the leptosomatic – is typical of adults and the other – the pyknic – is typical of children:

> The new-born [child] has a head which is about 23 per cent of the total size of the child, whereas the adult has a head which is only 13 or 14 per cent of the size of the body. It can be shown that adults with pyknic body build resemble the child rather than the grown-up with respect to this proportion, whereas adults with leptosomatic body build do not resemble children in this way. (*Ibid.*, p. 275)

Bonzo and Moonie both had pyknic bodies like children and both behaved like children, sometimes literally, as when Bonzo, according to the biography by Led Zeppelin's chief roadie, *Stairway to Heaven*, got drunk on a plane and urinated in his seat.

This theory is related to another about there being three main body types, which were classified by a psychologist called W.H. Sheldon:

> The first, which he called *endomorphy*, refers to relative predominance of soft and rounded tissue throughout the body; the second, christened *mesomorphy*, is concerned with the relative predominance of muscle, bone, and connective tissue; and the third, *ectomorphy*, is marked by a predominance of linear dimensions and a relatively large surface area in relation to body-weight. (*The Oxford Companion to the Mind*, ed. Richard L. Gregory, p. 98, Oxford University Press, 1987)

Typical examples of each might be the endomorphic Hardy of Laurel and Hardy, the mesomorphic O.J. Simpson, and the ectomorphic Laurel of Laurel and Hardy. Sheldon then went on to attempt to find correlations between these soma-types and psychology, and suggested that there might be:

> three basic temperamental components, which [he] christened *viscerotonia*, *somatotonia*, and *cerebrotonia*. The first of these is marked by sociability and love of comfort, the second by self-assertiveness verging on aggression, and the third by self-consciousness and diffidence. (*The Oxford Companion to the Mind*, ed. Richard L. Gregory, p. 98, Oxford University Press, 1987)

Now apply these ideas to the crimes in Juárez. Sharif is a mesomorph:

> 'Man, you're pretty,' said Sharif, as he introduced himself to the girls. The tall, ruggedly built guy with short, dark hair and a mustache often followed up with an invitation. 'How about coming over to my place for a drink?' ' ('MONSTER' BEATS THE SYSTEM, Tim Madigan, The *Seattle Times*, 1999)

'El Tolteca' is the same: strongly built and well-muscled. So is another man implicated in the crimes:

> A 40-page document, issued by a Mexican judge when finding Sharif guilty of murder, also detailed Sharif's plot to continue the killings after his arrest. Not long after being jailed, Sharif handed an envelope to one of his jail-house visitors, a member of a Juárez street gang called The Rebels, the judge's document said. The gang member in turn took the envelope to a Juárez pool hall, delivering it to Sergio Armendáriz, a *burly* man more commonly known as El Diablo or The Devil. El Diablo, the leader of The Rebels, opened the envelope and tucked $4,000 into his pocket, gang members eventually told police. ('MONSTER' BEATS THE SYSTEM, Tim Madigan, The *Seattle Times*, 1999)

These three men – *el egipcio, el Dracula, el Diablo* – are mesomorphic. Their victims – the slim, dark-haired girls found raped and mutilated in the desert – have been ectomorphic or leptosomatic. Leptosomatic human beings have been said to be typically introverted, mesomorphic and pyknic ones to be typically extroverted. Among human beings, there is a link, on the one hand, between introversion and traits like diffidence, and, on the other, between extroversion and traits like sociability and aggression. Translate this into another family of mammals: the *Felidae*, or the Cats. Cheetahs are leptosomatic – slender and long-limbed – and are also introverted, unassertive, and solitary except for breeding and cub-rearing, though young males do occasionally form pairs or trios for mutual assistance in hunting. Lions and leopards are pyknic or mesomorphic, and are extroverted, aggressive, and lions, at least, live in permanent family groups, or prides.

In fact all the great cats are pyknic and aggressive, except the cheetah and perhaps the snow leopard, which so far 'as is known . . . does not attack man' (*Wild Cats*, Michael Boorer, Hamlyn, 1969). Boorer also notes, however, that such attacks are 'a possibility, given the lonely regions inhabited by this species of cat'. An article on the snow leopard in *National Geographic* vol. 169, June 1986, describes how a photographer was 'seriously bitten on the right hand' by a snow leopard, but this was after the snow leopard had been trapped, sedated, and fitted with a radio collar. And the most pyknic of them all, the leopard, is probably the most aggressive too. At least, the leopard is the most pyknic great cat in the Old World; in the New World there is a great cat that is more pyknic, more mesomorphic, and more aggressive:

Flanked by two jaguars with inlay eyes and teeth, this wooden bowl would have contained a powerful narcotic snuff, used by shamans to 'transform' into jaguars and hunt unwary souls in the mirror-image spirit realm. (*People of the Jaguar: The Living Spirit of Ancient America*, Nicholas J. Saunders, p. 125, Souvenir Press, 1989)

Jaguars, like Sergio Armendáriz, are 'burly': powerful, solidly built, with large muscles. And like Sergio Armendáriz, they are predators:

The link between Amerindian ideals and the jaguar is made explicit in some indigenous languages where the word for predator is *yai*. This same name is applied to a bird that eats insects, the shaman who hunts the souls of lesser humans and the jaguar which kills tapirs, caymans and deer. All, from the point of view of the unfortunate victims, are predators. And, as the jaguar is the most successful predator, and humans do the labelling, the word *yai* is most often used to describe the fierce behaviour of both. To 'be jaguar', therefore, is to be a successful hunter, whether of forest game or of people. (*Ibid.*, p. 157)

But recall that we can also draw a distinction between leptosomatic and pyknic builds: between adults with adults' bodies and adults with 'children's' bodies: with heads and torsos that are large by comparison with their limbs. Pyknic adults seem to be like children in more than just their shape: research by the German psychologist Klaus Conrad 'may be interpreted to mean that the pyknic tends to be more immature in personality, behaviour, and bodily functioning than is the leptosomatic.' (*Fact and Fiction in Psychology*, H.J. Eysenck, pp. 276–7, Penguin, 1965.)

Extroversion and a desire to be the centre of attention are characteristic of children, for example, just as they were of adults like Hitler (in some moods), Mao, Churchill, and Stalin. Perhaps these men were like children in more embarrassing ways too: enuresis, or bed-wetting, is characteristic of children, as it is of criminal adolescents and adults, who, again, tend to be pyknic in build:

Other characteristics of this group are their very deep sleep, a late cessation of nocturnal enuresis, an excessive or morbidly excitable sexual appetite, and often an immature E.E.G. [electroencephalogram, or brain-wave reading] pattern of brain rhythms. (*Ibid.*, p. 285)

Hitler, Mao, Churchill, and Stalin were, in effect, criminal children playing with adult toys. Not that I blame them for that: if children are allowed to get their hands on adult toys, bad things often happen. The moral seems to be: be careful before you vote for a short supreme leader.

When you are given a choice, that is. The Chinese and the Russians were not, and they wound up with Mao and Stalin. The ancient Romans were not given a choice either, and they wound up with many short emperors with pyknic builds: Nero was like that, for example, as was Heliogabalus, and both of them are still infamous for their immaturity and self-indulgence. Tall Roman emperors, in fact, seem to be as rare as tall leaders nowadays, and to stand out in the same way.

Recall the account of how Sharif dominated a courtroom in Juárez by his physical presence: his size and height. He did this in much the same way that the most spectacularly tall of all Roman emperors dominated the classical world when he came along in AD 235. The story of this emperor – Maximin – may offer insights into the story of Sharif Sharif more than seventeen centuries later:

Maximinus has been represented by ancient historians as of a gigantic stature, he was eight feet high, and the bracelets of his wife served as rings to adorn the fingers of his hand. His voracity was as remarkable as his corpulence, and he is said generally to have eaten forty pounds of flesh every day, and to have drunk eighteen bottles of wine. His strength was proportionate to his gigantic shape; he could draw a loaded waggon alone, and with a blow of his fist he often broke the teeth in a horse's mouth; he also crushed the hardest stones between his fingers, and cleft rocks with his hands. (*Lemprière's Dictionary*, entry for 'Maximinus Caius Julius')

Is this true? Well, yes, in part: the emperor Maximin (235–238) was certainly around eight feet tall and must have had a gargantuan appetite and enormous strength, but these details about him come from the *Historia Augusta* and Julius Capitolinus – 'this wretched biographer', according to Gibbon. (*The Decline & Fall of the Roman Empire*, ch. vii)

Gibbon writes about Maximin as part of *The Decline & Fall*, but I have also come across pieces of writing specially devoted to him: Arthur Conan Doyle's short-story 'Giant Maximin' and Harold L. Klawans' essay 'Giants Among Men'. (In, respectively, *The Conan Doyle Stories*, 'Tales of Long Ago', Blitz Editions, Leicester, 1993, and *Toscanini's Fumble and Other Tales of Clinical Neurology*, Headline Book Publishing, 1990.) It is interesting to compare the two as literary and scientific treatments of a single subject.

For they are both, of course, attempts to interpret the facts of Maximin's life and reign, and both offer moral lessons based on these. And what are the facts? That Maximin was a Thracian peasant whose stature and strength brought him to the attention of the emperor Septimus Severus in about 213; that he served under Severus and his son Caracalla and retired during the reigns of the usurping Macrinus and Heliogabalus; that he returned under Alexander Severus, became popular with the troops and was proclaimed emperor in 235 following Alexander's assassination; that he was assassinated himself in 238 after giving greater and greater expression to a hitherto unremarked paranoia and cruelty.

Conan Doyle explains all this by supposing that Maximin's unusual size and strength gave him ambition; that the ambition brought him into the Roman army; that being in the Roman army corrupted and brutalised him:

The fresh young face was drawn and hardened, with austere lines wrought by trouble and privation. The nose was more hawk-like, the eyes more cunning, the expression more cynical and more sinister. In his youth, a child would have run to his arms. Now it would shrink screaming from his gaze. That was what twenty-five years with the eagles had done for Theckla, the Thracian peasant. ('Giant Maximin')

So when Maximin becomes emperor, he behaves in the only way he now knows: brutally. But Conan Doyle imagines that just before the end he regrets the path he has taken and tries to send his son back to the Thracian hills and the simple life of a peasant. It is too late: the son leaves his father's tent but his severed head returns shortly on the point of a spear carried by one of the assassins who have come to end yet another reign.

'Giant Maximin' is a good story, but its interpretation of Maximin's behaviour is very probably wrong. And the truth was staring Conan Doyle in the face too – Maximin's face. The story ends like this:

I sit in my study, and upon the table before me lies a denarius of Maximin, as fresh as when the triumvir of the Temple of Juna Moneta sent it from the mint. Around it are recorded his resounding titles – Imperator Maximinus, Pontifex Maximus, Tribunitia potestate, and the rest. In the centre is the impress of a great craggy head, a massive jaw, a rude fighting face, a contracted forehead. For all the pompous roll of titles it is a peasant's face, and I see him not as the Emperor of Rome but as the great Thracian boor who strode down the hill-side on that far-distant summer day when first the eagles beckoned him to Rome. (*Ibid.*)

It is a poignant ending – the hair prickled on the back of my neck as I typed it up – but it shows that Doyle, who had trained and practised as a doctor, was not keeping up with the medical journals after he became a professional writer. This is because Maximin's face shows the classic signs of a pathological condition first described by the French neurologist Pierre Marie in 1886: 'a prominent supraorbital ridge above his eyes and markedly protruding lower jaw, called *prognathism*'. (*Toscanini's Fumble*, 'Giants Among Men'.) These are classic signs of a condition called acromegaly:

> It is used to define this now well-known clinical disorder characterised by enlargement of the extremities, especially the hands and the feet, as well as the nose and jaw. Acromegaly not only makes a person uncommonly large, but it also causes a specific pattern of growth at the end of the bones that results in the peculiar body features that characterise all patients with acromegaly. (*Toscanini's Fumble*, 'Giants Among Men')

Acromegaly is caused by a tumour in the pituitary gland, a gland in the brain that produces growth hormone. Depending on when the tumour starts to affect production of the hormone, it can result either in acromegaly alone or in gigantism, in which not just the extremities but the entire body grows to excess. At around eight feet, Maximin must have had gigantism too. The American neurologist Harold L. Klawans explains all this at the beginning of his essay 'Giants Among Men', and so far he has not really parted company from Conan Doyle. He does so a little later, when he explains how a pituitary tumour can account not just for Maximin's abnormal *soma* but for his abnormal *psyche* too:

The monstrous change in Maximinus once he became
emperor is difficult to comprehend on purely
psychiatric grounds, but such changes in behaviour
have been described in patients with tumours
involving the hypothalamus [a region at the base of
the brain containing the pituitary gland and responsible for what is sometimes called the reptilian side of
man's nature: primitive urges and appetites like
hunger, thirst, aggression, lust, and so on]. Such
patients can manifest increased emotional excitabil-
ity, even building up to severe rage attacks, and
aggressive behaviour precipitated by paranoid idea-
tion has been described as a characteristic sign of a
tumour involving the hypothalamus. (*Ibid.*)

Once again we note how damage to the brain can
produce 'damaged' behaviour: cruelty, violence, sadism.
Of course, there must have been many psychopaths with
damaged brains in the Roman Empire during Maximin's
reign, as before and after, but only a few were able to
express this damage in behaviour. A peasant or slave
would simply have been killed as soon as he became a
nuisance in this way; Maximin was able, for a time at
least, to express his brain damage through psychopathic
behaviour because he was the emperor. And he was also
able to do this because, of course, he was a giant: taller,
stronger, more physically imposing than those around
him:

Sharif bolted from his chair, towering over shorter
guards who nervously reached for their guns. He was
a large, menacing presence who filled the room, a
man completely in control, against whom even the
prison director seemed cowed. ('MONSTER' BEATS THE
SYSTEM, Tim Madigan, The *Seattle Times*)

This, as we have seen before, is a description of Sharif on trial in Juárez for the murder of Elizabeth Castro García. Sharif is a tall man: not quite a giant, but certainly of well above average height, particularly in a country like México where malnutrition and disease mean a sizeable proportion of the population never reach their full potential height. Match these facts with facts we have already noted about the Yorkshire Ripper Peter Sutcliffe, who exercised until he built up a strength enabling him to do pretty much as he pleased with the bodies of other human beings. Particularly female human beings, who are on average lighter and weaker than male ones even when there is no advantage of age:

Colleen [Sugden], now Mrs Young, remembers staying at the Sutcliffes' house for the night when she was 10 and Peter nearly 19. She had been standing at the top of the stairs and completely unexpectedly felt herself being lifted up bodily and thrown down to the bottom, where she picked herself up, luckily uninjured, and looked towards the top of the stairs.

'Peter was standing there, staring down at me with those funny dark eyes. He had that silly, sickly grin on his face that was so familiar.' (*The Yorkshire Ripper: an in-depth study of a mass killer and his methods*, Roger Cross, p. 57, HarperCollins, 1993)

It is not sufficient for a serial killer to have the impulse to violence: he must also possess the ability to *enact* the impulse: the cunning and intelligence to hunt down a victim, the strength and physical dexterity to attack her with an overwhelming force that will lessen the chances of a scream or sounds of a struggle reaching the ears of a passer-by. Sutcliffe had the cunning and the strength. So did Sharif. And Sutcliffe, like Sharif, had a black sense of humour. Recall Sharif's suggestion as to the continuing motivation of the serial killer still at work after he, Sharif, had been imprisoned: 'he is mad because they have given me all the attention.'

Sharif was paying for the serial murders to continue when he said this. Compare this dark jest with one of Sutcliffe's: 'I have thousands of people below me where I work now.' (*Ibid.*, p. 50.) Because he was now working as a gravedigger.

21: Exploitation

Explotación f. (1) Acción de aprovechar, de sacar provecho o beneficios de bienes, bosques, minas, fábricas, comercios, etc. (2) Acción de abusar, de aprovecharse.

Exploitation. (1) Action of profiting by, of gaining profit or benefit from goods, forests, mines, fabrics, industries, etc. (2) Action of abusing, of taking advantage.

It can be interesting to watch how your ego affects your outlook on the world. For example, I have lived in England for a long time and I like football, so I am pleased when the England football team wins. I have lived in England for a long time and I am not interested in cricket, so I do not care very much what the England cricket team does. I have lived in England for a long time and I hate rugby, so I am pleased when the England rugby team loses.

I also hate religion. That's why I was pleased to learn that Catholicism and Anglicanism were involved in the massacres in Rwanda in 1995. I don't know the full story but it seems that one side was Catholic and one side Anglican, and, as ever, where there's hatred for other reasons, religion helped to make things more vicious and more difficult to resolve. I'm not sure that both sides were equally to blame, though: there were reports on the news in April, 1998, that two Catholic clergymen in Rwanda had been sentenced to death for a direct involvement in, *inter alia*, the bulldozing of a (presumably Anglican) church while people were still inside it. Well, perhaps

saying 'I was amused' would be a little closer to the truth
– genocidal Anglicanism is an amusing concept, after all –
but in either case it was not a very pleasant reaction.
Those hundreds of thousands of deaths did not mean very
much to me until I learned something about them that
confirmed my negative ideas about Christianity. It *was*
almost as if I was pleased that those people died because
Christianity was involved.

And in a way I was. Just as, in a way, I am pleased that
Hypatia died. Because Christianity, in the form of St Cyril
of Alexandria, was involved in her death too. Intimately
involved:

> Hypatia, the daughter of Theon the mathematician,
> was initiated in her father's studies; her learned
> comments have elucidated the geometry of Apol-
> lonius and Alexandria, the philosophy of Plato and
> Aristotle. In the bloom of beauty and the maturity of
> wisdom, the modest maid refused her lovers and
> instructed her disciples; the persons most illustrious
> for their rank or merit were impatient to visit the
> female philosopher; and Cyril beheld with a jealous
> eye the gorgeous train of horses and slaves who
> crowded the door of her academy. A rumour was
> spread among the Christians that the daughter of
> Theon was the only obstacle to the reconciliation of
> the praefect and the archbishop; and that obstacle
> was speedily removed. On a fatal day, in the holy
> season of Lent, Hypatia was torn from her chariot,
> stripped naked, dragged to the church, and inhuman-
> ly butchered by the hands of Peter the reader and a
> troop of savage and merciless fanatics; her flesh was
> scraped from her bones with sharp oyster-shells, and
> her quivering limbs were delivered to the flames. The
> just progress of inquiry and punishment was stopped
> by seasonable gifts; but the murder of Hypatia has

imprinted an indelible stain on the character and religion of Cyril of Alexandria.

Those are the words of Edward Gibbon (1737–94) in chapter xlvii of *The Decline and Fall of the Roman Empire* (1788), and I sense that Gibbon too would rather Hypatia had died gorily like that than in some other, less painful and less exploitable way. After all, Hypatia was long gone in Gibbons' day but the church was still around, and Hypatia's death was a very good story to tell against the church.

And remains so. That is why it is annoying when her death is taken and turned into an anti-male story instead by feminists. To them, Hypatia was a martyr not so much for science and philosophy on the altar of Christian superstition and bigotry as for intellectual womankind on the altar of male prejudice and misogyny:

Her philosophy of scientific rationalism ran counter to the dogma of the emerging religion of Christianity, as did her womanhood and the authority she held. In a terrorist attack of the sort with which women were to become only too familiar, Cyril, the patriarch of Alexandria in about A.D. 415, incited a mob of zealots led by his monks to drag her from her chariot, strip her naked and torture her to death by slicing her flesh from her bones with shells and sharpened flints.

Hypatia's infamous death signified more than the death of one innocent middle-aged scientist. In Cyril and his bigots, every thinking woman could foresee the shape of men to come.

Those are the words of Rosalind Miles in chapter three (entitled 'The Rise of the Phallus') of *The Women's History of the World* (Paladin Books, 1989) and I sense that Miles too would rather Hypatia had died gorily like that than in some other, less painful and less exploitable way. After all, Hypatia is long gone but men are still around, and Hypatia's death is a very good story to tell against men.

Or is it? I do not think so: I think it remains what it always was: evidence that Christianity is a bigoted and, when powerful, a murderous religion. Yet modern Christians do not necessarily find anything shocking or discreditable in Hypatia's death: Evelyn Waugh's Ambrose Silk muses on it thus in *Put Out More Flags* (1942): 'Religion is acceptable in its destructive phase; the desert monks carving up that humbug Hypatia' (*op. cit.*, p. 60, 1975, Penguin).

One must be careful here not to confuse the character's opinions with the author's – Silk's next example of religion in its destructive phase is 'the anarchist gangs roasting the monks in Spain'. And Silk later refers to 'one of those nasty Jesuits ... They're always flapping in and out the department like jackdaws'. Neither priest-roasting nor prejudice against Jesuits would have been approved of by Waugh himself. But anyone who knows much about Evelyn Waugh can, I think, detect in the character's thoughts on Hypatia not just the author's pro-Catholic bigotry and anti-intellectualism but also his misogyny and relish in gruesome and unnatural death. (For a list of gruesome and unnatural deaths in Waugh's books, see my article 'Total Waugh' in the *Headpress* compilation *Critical Vision*, Critical Vision, Stockport, Cheshire, 1995.)

To Evelyn Waugh as well, then, the worse Hypatia's death the better. And he would have felt no sympathy for her either; Edward Gibbon, much as he enjoyed using her death to attack Christianity, must surely have done; and Rosalind Miles goes beyond sympathy to what might be called identification. Rosalind Miles is certainly a woman, and would regard herself as an intellectual struggling for recognition under a hostile patriarchy, and was doubtless approaching middle age when she wrote *The Women's History of the World*. That may have been why she is careful to describe Hypatia not just as an intellectual woman, but as a middle-aged intellectual woman:

> Hypatia's infamous death signified more than the death of one innocent *middle-aged* (my itals) scientist. In Cyril and his bigots, every thinking woman could foresee the shape of men to come. (*op. cit.*, p. 77)

But if Miles was identifying herself with Hypatia by describing her like that, she was probably also telling the truth: Hypatia was born around AD 375 and would have been in or approaching her forties by 415. It would be interesting to see how much stress is laid on this fact in accounts of her death by younger feminists. Accounts of it by men are not only interesting, but significant too: men cannot identify with Hypatia as a woman, but can at least sympathise with her as a human being or as an intellectual martyr or as a sex-object. The appeal of the first of those Hypatian attributes is a little too general; the appeal of the second is a little too particular; the appeal of the third is just right. To Edward Gibbon the anti-Christian male intellectual, Hypatia is an intellectual martyr but also a beautiful 'maid'; to Charles Kingsley (1819–75), a popular Christian author in the nineteenth century, she is a beautiful maid and rather more. Bear her true age in mind as you read the following account of her death from Kingsley's novel *Hypatia* (1853). To set the scene: an admirer of Hypatia's called Philammon has learnt of the Christian plot against her life and is lying in wait near her lecture-room to warn her of it, already seeing the assassins begin to gather:

> At last a curricle, glittering with silver, rattled round the corner and stopped opposite him. She must be

coming now. The crowd had vanished. Perhaps it was, after all, a fancy of his own. No; there they were, peeping round the corner, close to the lecture-room – the hell-hounds! A slave brought out an embroidered cushion – and then Hypatia herself came forth, looking more glorious than ever; her lips set in a sad firm smile; her eyes uplifted, inquiring, eager, and yet gentle, dimmed by some great inward awe as if her soul was far away aloft, and face to face with God.

In a moment he sprang up to her, caught her robe convulsively, threw himself on his knees before her – 'Stop! Stay! You are going to destruction!'

Calmly she looked down upon him.

'Accomplice of witches! Would you make of Theon's daughter a traitor like yourself?'

He sprang up, stepped back, and stood stupefied with shame and despair ... It was too late! A dark wave of men rushed from the ambuscade, surged up round the car ... swept forward ... she had disappeared! And as Philammon followed breathless, the horses galloped past him madly homeward with the empty carriage ...

Why did the mob, increasing momentarily by hundreds, pour down upon the beach, and return brandishing flints, shells, fragments of pottery?

She was upon the church steps before he caught them up, invisible among the crowd; but he could track her by the fragments of her dress ... On into the church itself! ... On, up the nave, fresh shreds of her dress strewing the holy pavement – up the chancel steps themselves – up to the altar – right underneath the great still Christ: and there even those hell-hounds paused ...

She shook herself free from her tormentors, and springing back, rose for one moment to her full height, naked, snow-white against the dusky mass around – shame and indignation in those wide clear eyes, but not a stain of fear. With one hand she clasped her golden locks around her; the other long white arm was stretched upward toward the great still Christ appealing – and who dare say in vain? – from man to God.

Her lips were opened to speak: but the words that should have come from them reached God's ear alone; for in an instant Peter [a leader of the Christian assassins] struck her down [and] the dark mass closed over her again . . . and then wail on wail, long, wild, ear-piercing, rang along the vaulted roofs, and thrilled like the trumpet of avenging angels through Philammon's ears . . . He could not shut out those shrieks! When would they end? What in the name of the God of mercy were they doing? Tearing her piecemeal? Yes, and worse than that . . . It was over. The shrieks had died away into moans; the moans to silence [and] a new cry rose through the dome.

'To the Cinaron! Burn the bones to ashes! Scatter them into the sea!' . . . And the mob poured past him again . . . (Charles Kingsley, *Hypatia*, 'Nemesis')

Kingsley's Hypatia, lithe and blonde and snow-white-skinned, does not sound at all middle-aged and plainly, indeed, she is not. Is this novelistic licence? Yes: to Charles Kingsley and his Victorian readers, Hypatia's death is charged by the fact of its being a woman's but supercharged by the invention of its being a young, blonde, beautiful woman's. Hypatia was a teacher of Greek philosophy, and was probably Greek or Graeco-Egyptian herself. There even seems to be a tradition that she was Jewish. She is not likely to have had blonde hair or very white skin, and though she may still have been beautiful in 415, her beauty would have been fading and her nubility almost entirely gone.

If the truth had been admitted in the novel, though, her death would have had *pathos* and not *eros*. For *eros* certainly seems to be present there now. The fictional Hypatia was young, and women's deaths are most powerful when the women in question are young. Female death is most powerful then because young women appeal most to our sexual instincts. Myths about the unnatural female death will therefore naturally choose to make the victims young, and the stress laid on the age of a real woman who dies unnaturally will depend on the historian or writer who discusses the death. Rosalind Miles explicitly stated that Hypatia died middle-aged probably because Rosalind Miles was approaching middle age herself and regarded that, with her sex, as a very important similarity between herself and Hypatia. Edward Gibbon avoided explicitly stating that Hypatia died middle-aged probably because he, though well into middle age when he completed *The Decline & Fall*, did not see this as an important similarity between himself and Hypatia: only her intellect and opposition to Christianity could be that. Charles Kingsley explicitly stated the opposite of the truth and made Hypatia young and beautiful probably because Hypatia's intellect was much less important to him and his readers than her sex, and her sex took on most power in a young and beautiful body. To Kingsley, after all, her intellect had led her away from the truth, and the bigots who kill her in the novel are able to do so partly because of her stubbornness and pride. And to Kingsley, her death, though criminal, also seems exciting.

But if Kingsley the Christian exploited Hypatia's death, then so did Gibbon the atheist and Miles the feminist. Atheism and feminism are free of blame for the death itself, it is true, but they apparently encourage some of the same habits of mind in their adherents as Christianity does: Gibbon and Miles would not be as interested in the truth if they did not see in it such a way as to serve their own ends. So is there no message in Hypatia's death? Well no, I think there is. I think it is the message Gibbon saw there: that Christianity is a bigoted and, when powerful, a murderous religion. I think the message Rosalind Miles saw in it is wrong: it was not a blow struck by the male side in the sex-war. But then I am, like Gibbon, a man and an atheist and not, like Miles, a woman and a feminist. But then I hope being aware of it helps me to avoid drawing a biased conclusion.

If you don't think it does, compare the death of Hypatia with the death of Archimedes. Archimedes died in 212 BC at about the age of seventy-five when, according to Plutarch, he was challenged by a Roman soldier to surrender during the sack of Syracuse. Archimedes, engrossed in a mathematical problem, did not respond to the challenge, so the soldier ran him through with his sword. (See Plutarch's *Lives* under 'Archimedes'.) Another brutal death of an intellectual, but not one that feminism would be eager to draw any lessons from. Nor one that has ever inspired a popular novel in which Archimedes mysteriously turns young and blond and handsome. Nor one that many people are likely to find particularly interesting or memorable. If you ask yourself why exactly the opposite is true in each case of Hypatia, I hope you will decide that it is because Hypatia is a woman. I also hope you will decide that feminism, which would wish to draw lessons from only one of those deaths, reveals its partiality and intellectual limitations by doing so.

A world-view that can draw rational lessons from both deaths has to be based on something less crude than a division of human beings into male and female. Better seems to be a division of human beings into powerful and powerless – or rather, into individuals and groups with differing amounts of power and differing propensities to abuse it. The deaths of Hypatia and Archimedes contain messages about power, and power does not belong exclusively to one sex, or to one domain. If Archimedes died as Plutarch said he did, then his death contains a message about politics and war. If he didn't die as Plutarch said he did, then the apocryphal details of his death contain a message about nationalism. Some historians have suggested that the story is meant to point a contrast between Roman brutality and Greek intellect. The Greeks may not have been stronger than the Romans but, by the gods, they were cleverer. And why would Plutarch have wanted to tell a story like that? Why do you think?

Invoking the concept of the ego seems the best way of synthesising all these facts about how our nationality and sex and ideologies condition our reactions to death and the stories we tell about it. Nationalism, like feminism and religion, appeals to the ego: it offers the chance of self-aggrandisement if not in person then by proxy. If I am a Greek, then I like to see the death of another Greek prove something about the superiority of Greeks. If I am an anti-Christian, I like to see the death of another anti-Christian prove something about the evils of Christianity. If I am a woman, I like to see the death of another woman prove something about the superiority of women and the wickedness of men. In each case, I may see the proof even when it is not there or I may invent details to create it. Or alter or misinterpret details if the proof already there is not the one I am looking for. All of these things may have been done with the death of Hypatia to suit the ends of others. In short, her death may have been *exploited*.

This argument can now easily be taken and applied to the female victims of the serial killings in Juárez. And yet they were exploited for the ends of others from well before their deaths. Exploited by their employers in the *maquiladora* factories. Sagrario González, the seventeen-year-old victim after whom the campaigning *ParaSagrario*

Consortium was named, was one of young women who worked in the *maquiladoras*:

> The work they find pays around $3.50 a day, not nearly enough for an apartment. Many of the girls wind up living in shanty towns called 'colonias' with no electricity or running water. Sagrario lived in this shack with her mother and father and two sisters who also work at the American plants. ('Silent Screams in Juárez', ABC's *20–20* current affairs programme, Wednesday, 20 January 1999)

The money is not enough for an apartment but is enough, however, for something else. It has to be, otherwise the women could not get to and from work in the first place: 'The fifteen-year-old girl is a welder at 160 pesos a week (about $21.62 at current exchange rates). Bus fare consumes about half her salary.' (*While You Were Sleeping*, Charles Bowden.)

She pays bus fares for travelling on buses provided and owned by the *maquiladora* factories. In effect, the *maquiladora* workers are being taxed for the privilege of working in the *maquiladoras*.

This tax, and the tax on body and mind imposed by the daily journey on jolting buses, has been rescinded for some of the workers, but only by death. They fell into the hands of Sharif or, later, the accomplices he hired from behind bars, and were grossly exploited for the second time, tortured and raped for the pleasure of the men who had kidnapped them. What truly happened to some of the women who were killed cannot be established, because the only living witnesses – the killers themselves – refuse to reveal it. Autopsies can reveal only part of the truth:

> The autopsy revealed that Susana suffered four heart attacks, probably from the terror she suffered while

she was tortured and raped. (Note, however, that this murder is believed to have been committed by someone not connected with the wider serial killings.)

However, we know that the ordeals of such victims are very likely to have begun with psychological torture. We know this because of one of the victims who survived:

As he was taking her further from home, 'El Tolteca' asked her, smiling, 'Are you afraid?', to which she answered, 'Yes, please take me home.' (*El Diario de Juárez*)

Other young women must have been asked the same question before Sharif or 'El Tolteca' or one of the other killers proceeded to the rape, torture, mutilation, stabbing, and strangulation characteristic of the crimes, exploiting the bodies of their victims for their own pleasure before dumping them on the outskirts of Juárez.

But then, at least, exploitation must surely have ended? No, it was only about to begin again. All the murdered victims must have been exploited by nature in the age-old way, their bodies broken down and assimilated by micro-organisms and scavengers, their deaths giving new life to bacteria, fungi, insects, birds, and mammals in the desert. But before this exploitation by nature was complete, some of the dead victims were discovered by the police or passers-by or searching relatives and their exploitation by human beings began again.

The crimes in Juárez have been a political issue, tipping the balance of state elections in the state of Chihuahua:

The slayings became a national scandal, reverberating as far away as México City. In 1998, Francisco Barrio Terrazas, governor of the state of Chihuahua, was defeated in his bid for re-election, an outcome widely blamed on the mounting death toll in the state's largest city. ('MONSTER' BEATS THE SYSTEM, Tim Madigan, The *Seattle Times*)

The man who defeated him, Francisco Barrio, did so with the help of a promise to solve the crimes:

Esther Chávez Cano, director of NGOs [Non-Governmental Organisations] and Casa Amiga, the new crisis center [please see the acknowledgments at the beginning of the book for further details of Casa Amiga], says that the governor does not have the political will to put an end to this horrible wave of violence. 'No changes are happening . . . why haven't we moved the authorities to fight with us, a dignified fight for the betterment of women?' Chávez claims that the governor was willing to fight for women only as a campaign promise, but now that he is in office, it is all talk. (BORDER REACTS TO 184 MURDERED WOMEN, Anne Marie Mackler, *Frontera NorteSur*, March 1999)

But the exploitation of the young women's deaths does not end with conventional politics: however pure the conscious motives of campaigners like Esther Chávez Cano, it seems obvious that feminist organisations have tried to use them to ends beyond those of simply improving protection for working women. The deaths have been used as evidence of the brutal patriarchal nature of Mexican society, as part of an attempt to combat and overturn *machismo*, and one of the theories to circulate before the arrest of *Los Choferes* was that a gang of *machistas*, enraged at the economic and social advance of a new generation of women, were carrying them out to force women back into the home:

Who's stalking the women of Juárez? Is it a serial killer, narco traffickers? Or is it, as has been rumored, some macho gang angry that so many women are now working? ('Silent Screams in Juárez', ABC's *20–20* current affairs programme, Wednesday, 20 January 1999)

The theory was given ideological underpinnings by Esther Chávez herself in interviews with journalists:

And despite her criticism, Chavez said she thinks the blame for the women's deaths doesn't just rest with police. The 65-year-old retired businesswoman has spent years leading demonstrations, badgering officials, holding the hands of victims' families. She has come to believe that the seed of the violence against women lies in Ciudad Juárez itself. The city has been transformed in recent decades with the arrival of hundreds of assembly plants hiring women. This may have generated a macho backlash, she said. 'Women are occupying the space of men in a culture of absolute dominance of men over women,' she said. 'This has to provoke misogyny.' (THE DEATHS THAT HAUNT JUAREZ, Mary Beth Sheridan, The *Los Angeles Times*, 12 May 1999)

And yet it is possible that such ideas may be of great assistance to agents of patriarchy across the border in the United States. Big business is dominated by men who are hungry for profits and the political power they can wield based on them. As has been pointed out several times elsewhere, American companies have rushed to establish factories and assembly plants in México as a convenient means of avoiding legislation in the United States that, while good for workers, is bad for profits: health and safety regulations, sickness and maternity pay, pension

244

and dismissal rights, limits on pollution and the use of dangerous chemicals and practices in the workplace.

And one of the main reasons they have been eager to hire women to work in their factories and assembly plants is that women are less likely to agitate for the rights enjoyed by their American sisters:

> The Maquilas, as the foreign-owned factories are called, often prefer to hire them because they tend to be more dextrous and less bolshy than the men. ('Mexico's murder town', Tom Carver, BBC, 9 September 1999)

In the final analysis, women may be economically worse off by going to work than they would be by staying at home, where they also avoid the costs of work: injuries, stress, loss of time with family and children. Culture is an extremely complex mechanism that rarely behaves according to the relatively simple notions we have of it, particularly when these are based, as political ones often are, on a projection of one's own ego on to the world. Although they identify themselves as and with women, many – perhaps most – feminists are, I would suggest, actually highly unrepresentative of their sex. Esther Chávez is described as a 65-year-old 'businesswoman'. It must have taken a great deal of self-confidence and determination to succeed as such in México in the past, and I would infer that she is a self-confident and determined woman. These characteristics must have biological underpinnings: neurological underpinnings. In short, Esther Chávez, I suggest, has a brain like a man's. She is attracted to things that men are attracted to – power, money, success, prominence in public life – and yet, identifying herself as a woman, believes that what is attractive to and desired by her is attractive to and desired by other women.

Which is true: there are certainly other women attracted to and desirous of the same things. But I suggest that they are women who, like her, are masculinised. Feminism seems to have been a vast attempt to coerce all women into behaving in a way in which only a few women behave naturally, and, like many organised movements before it, seems to have acquired aims separate from, and even antagonistic to, those that it publicly professes.

One could even see it in Darwinian terms. For example, if feminism gains public capital from violence against women, it has in some sense an incentive to encourage violence against women. If it succeeds in this, feminism as a movement gains while individual women lose. Feminist campaigners like Chávez will therefore be anxious to emphasise the extent of male violence against women even at the expense of logic and objective fact, and even when some of the cases they produce as exemplars do not fit the ideology they wish to apply to them. Among the 129 cases of murdered women whose details were collected by Esther Chávez Cano and placed on the ParaSagrario Consortium's website, for example, is this:

Case 2, February 11 [1994] – Emilia García Hernández Rina . . . A woman who was stabbed and killed in the Mandelón shop, presumably by her female companions.'

And yet, by a syllogism proclaimed elsewhere by the campaigners against the killings, this counted not simply as murder but also as self-abuse:

On the 'International Day of No Violence Against Women', November 25, several mothers of assassinated women rallied in Ciudad Juárez. The mothers of the many women recently found dead in several parts of the city wore black and walked as in a funeral march. They demanded justice and greater police effort to solve the cases. They also demanded that police authorities prevent and combat crime against women. They walked in silence, with posters which said, 'Aggression against any woman is an aggression against all women'. The mothers also carried black crosses symbolising each victim killed in the last few months. ('Mothers Of Slain Women Demand Justice', Ana María Ruiz-Brown, *El Diario de Juárez*)

If this slogan is true, one has to conclude that a woman who attacks or murders another woman is actually committing self-abuse. In fact, the slogan seems to partake much more of propaganda than of truth, and it is implicitly predicated on the assumption that 'aggression' against women is exclusively male. Even if this were true, however, male aggression would not be exclusively directed against women. An equivalent list of men murdered in Juárez since 1993 would be far longer, but there is no incentive for anyone to draw it up, for there is no obvious political or social advantage to be gained from campaigns against the abuse of men. What group, for example, is recording the continuing murders of men in Juárez, or the rape and torture of men that continues day and night behind the bars of prisons in Juárez? And in other parts of México, and around the world? In Russia, for example?:

Twice last year convicts in overcrowded prisons killed and ate their cellmates because they claimed they were hungry and wanted to relieve overcrowding. ('Spectre of Russian past blamed for rise in cannibalism', Richard Beeston, *The Times*, 28 March 1996)

In fact, of course, far from campaigning to relieve conditions in prisons, politicians and other groups campaign to make them harsher: doing unpleasant things to criminals has long been an easy (if not inexpensive) means of gaining votes and increasing one's popularity once in office, and has been so since the gladiatorial days of ancient Rome, and before.

But what if the psychological battering received by prisoners behind bars then increases the likelihood and the severity of further crimes once they are released? What if, as suggested elsewhere, being the target of homosexual rape inside prison increases the likelihood of one's practising heterosexual rape outside it? Such questions are little raised and less discussed, and though reports of the horrors of such places as Russian prisons can be found in the media, they are isolated and fragmentary, pungent *hors d'oeuvres* for the more substantial meat of reports about such horrors as, for example, those once under way in Juárez.

Yet the horrors of Russian prisons – and Mexican ones, and many others – are continual and involve pain and misery being inflicted on many hundreds of thousands of human beings for decades on end. The murders in Juárez involved, at most, hundreds of human beings and lasted six years. Why, then, does the latter attract what *prima facie* – and *ultima facie* – seems disproportionate attention? There have been reports about the Juárez serial killings in newspapers throughout the English-speaking world, from America through the United Kingdom to South Africa and Australasia. Five- or ten-minute reports on the progress of the investigations have appeared regularly on flagship news programmes on BBC radio: PM and The World Tonight on Radio 4, for example. Why?

I would suggest that it's because they meet not only the media's general primary criterion of interest but also a correlative one of being very easy to project one's own ego on to. They involve death and suffering, which is the primary criterion of interest for the media. BBC Radio

1FM is a popular music station and devotes very little time to news, and one could therefore expect to see there the prioritisation of news items that are reddest in tooth and claw. Here is a transcript of the first three items on one Radio 1FM news broadcast from the middle of the 1990s:

> Detectives hunting the killer of five gay men in London have released new pictures of a man they are anxious to question. He's tall with short dark hair seen walking with the killer's last victim. A senior Oxford don has died after being attacked by a swarm of bees. Dr Ralph Johnson is believed to have been tending a hive at the time. Nine black women and children have been burned or shot to death in South Africa's Natal province. Nearly thirty people have died in political violence there in the past 48 hours.

Next, and presumably less important, was news of a nuclear test ban treaty: death avoided, rather than death actualised.

The deaths in Juárez are of course deaths actualised, but in addition they are readily suitable for the projection of the egos of news consumers. The crimes are heterosexual in nature. Most human beings, male or female, are heterosexual, and the crimes in Juárez are an exaggeration of the traditional heterosexual relationship, one might even say a satire of it. The man dominates, the woman submits. Consciously or otherwise, then, male heterosexuals may therefore project their egos on to the dominant male criminals, and female heterosexuals their egos on to the submissive female victims. There is a large market in the media for true crime, and anecdotal evidence within the publishing industry that books about heterosexual male serial killers sell predominantly to women.

All this must be taken into account in the description of how the young female victims of Juárez have been exploited, but there is still one further example of exploitation to mention. Once the *maquiladora* owners and the serial killers, the politicians and the feminists, the journalists and the crime reporters had finished with the young female victims of Juárez, there was one final exploitation awaiting them, one final use of them to meet the psychological, ideological, and financial ends of others, one final vulture swinging down from the harsh, salty, sun-blasted blue of the desert sky to splinter and gulp their stripped-white bones. A book called *Crossing to Kill*.

Appendix

Desparecer v. i. Dejar de ser visible. No encontrarse en su sitio. Dejar de existir.

Desaparecido, da adj. Que no puede verse. Muerto o dado como tal (ú. t. c. s.).

Disappear. (Intransitive verb) Stop being visible. Not be encountered in the usual place. Stop existing.

Disappeared. (Adjective) Cannot be seen. Dead or given up for dead (also used as a noun).

In the 1970s and 1980s the right-wing governments of Central and South America, secure under the umbrella of Reaganite rhetoric and arms-shipments, had a strange influence on the semantics of the Spanish language. Previously in Spanish, as in English, 'disappear' was an intransitive verb: it was something a person did for him- or herself. Nowadays in Spanish, as in the English of reports by organisations like Amnesty International, it can be also something a person has done *to* him or her. The death-squads of Guatemala and El Salvador, Argentina and Chile, 'disappeared' people in tens of thousands: abducted them and then killed them in ways that remain unknown, because their bodies have never been found, having been buried deep in the jungle, or hacked into unidentifiable pieces, or dumped in rivers and lakes and the sea, or even fed to farm animals.

These were *Los Desaparecidos*: The Disappeared. The English translation is gender-neutral, but the form of the adjective and article in Spanish is masculine plural, *-os*, because in Spanish the masculine can serve for both sexes. In Juárez we have unambiguously *Las Desaparecidas*: The Disappeared Female Ones. Enormous as the official body-count of the crimes may appear, it is undoubtedly only a fraction of the true total:

> The authorities announced back in November of 1995 that 520 people had disappeared in Juárez that year and 'an important percentage of them are female adolescents.' ('While You Were Sleeping', Charles Bowden)

That is *one* year's count of the disappeared. Indubitably some of them, even of the female adolescents, are 'disappeared ones' in the older, pre-Reagan sense: runaways, elopers, undiscovered suicides. It also seems indubitable that some of them, particularly of the female adolescents, are 'disappeared ones' in the newer, post-Reagan sense: kidnap victims, rape victims, murder victims.

And consider that even combining the discovered with the disappeared does not allow us to make a true estimate of the female death-toll in Juárez. To be recorded as 'disappeared' one has to have relatives and close friends to note one's disappearance and contact the authorities. Many of the known victims were newly arrived in Juárez, without family there, slipping in and out of employment in the *maquiladoras*, making and losing contact with fellow employees who would think little of a sudden absence from work that stretched on into weeks and months and would soon forget a new name and face. The true female death-toll in Juárez could conceivably have reached four figures in the six years since the first bodies began to turn up in the desert and on empty building-lots.

The thought has a literally narcotic – numbing – effect. The human race cannot bear too much reality, or too many numbers. Beyond a certain point, numbers lose their meaning. One death can be imagined. Ten deaths can be. But a hundred? A thousand? Count off even the one-hundred-and-eighty of the official murder total at one victim a second and you will be counting for three minutes. Say the name of each victim as you count and you might speak for half-an-hour. Add her age, brief details of what she was wearing, where she was found, how she died, and you might speak for an hour or more. It would be physically demanding just to *speak* the list of victims and their details. How much more psychologically demanding to imagine what that list means in grief and pain and wasted life?

Women Murdered in 1993

Case 1, 23 January – Alma Chavira Farel: A young woman who was found beaten, raped, and strangled beside two open drains. She had massive bruises on her chin and around one eye, and was dressed in a white, decorated sweater and blue pants. Campestre Virreyes.

Case 2, 25 January – Angelina Luna Villalobos: A 16-year-old, strongly built, pregnant woman with light skin who was found strangled with the cable from a stolen TV. The murderer was Pedro Fernández, a friend of the murdered woman and her husband.

Case 3, 17 February – Name unknown: On the intersection of Oro and Violeta Street a woman who was found beaten and stabbed to death.

Case 4 – Jessica Lizalde Leon: A female radio-broadcaster who was found shot to death.

Case 5, 21 April – Luz de la O García: Found dead from a beating she received on the intersection of G Street, Prieto and Altamirano.

Case 6, 5 May – Name unknown: A 35-year-old, olive-skinned, dark-haired woman in her fifth month of pregnancy, wearing short trousers, no shoes. She had been raped and strangled, and was found near Satellite Street, en route to Ortiz Rubio.

Case 7, 8 May – Elizabeth Ramos: A 26-year-old woman who was shot and killed by her boyfriend.

Case 8, 13 May – Name unknown: A 25-year-old woman with pale skin and light-coloured hair, wearing denim trousers and cloth shoes. She had been raped and stabbed, and was found in Sierra Juárez, at the foothills of the Cerro Bola.

Case 9, 5 June – Veronica Huitron Quezada: A short-haired, thin woman, 1.78 m tall who had been stabbed and set on fire. She was found on Emiliano Zapata Street, on the way to the illegal rubbish-dump in Anapra.

Case 10, 11 June – Name unknown: A semi-naked woman, age unknown, wearing a denim skirt, white T-shirt, and black tennis shoes who was found raped, stabbed, and with fractured skull in the playground of the Altavista Preparatory School, on a paved surface near the Rio Bravo.

Case 11, 15 June – Guadalupe Ivonne Estrada Salas: A 16-year-old woman, thin, brown-skinned, 1.60 m (5′3″) tall and wearing a short blue denim skirt and blue shoes. She worked in the Magna Flex Industrial Park. The cause of death could not be established. She was found in the Chamizal.

Case 12, 1 September – Name unknown: A woman found strangled and dumped in a car in the Senecu Subdivision. After her body was found on Sunday the Judicial Police were informed. This murder now brings to five the number of unidentified women who have been victims of murder recently and whose cases have not been solved.

Case 13, 17 September – Marcela Santos Garza: A black-haired, brown-skinned eighteen-year-old woman, 1.75 m tall, who had been shot by her boyfriend, Heberto

Cruz Aguilar, and then abandoned in the Red Cross building.

Case 14, 14 October – Mireya Hernández Mendez: A long-haired, twenty-year-old woman, 1.60 m tall, who worked for the Phillips *maquiladora*, and was found strangled in a rubbish-skip at the Juárez Industrial Park.

Case 15, 14 October – Name unknown: A woman who was found dead and in a state of advanced decomposition, and who was estimated to have died a week previously. She was wearing blue overalls with an ID badge from Hipermart [Hypermart, a supermarket chain] in the name of Tomasa Salas Calderón.

Case 16, 15 November – Esmeralda Leyva Rodrígues: A long-haired thirteen-year-old woman, 1.60 m tall, who was abducted while leaving Technical Secondary School 27. She was raped anally and vaginally and then strangled, and her body was found at the rear of Mariano Escobar School next to Teofilo Borunda.

Case 17, 15 December – Yolanda Tapia: A fifty-year-old woman who was found dead at her home on 57th Street 540 with a deep head-wound. A piece of wood had been inserted into her vagina. She had been murdered by her son Jesús Roberto Gil Tapia.

Women Murdered in 1994

Case 1, 11 January – Name unknown: A woman with light brown skin, 1.80 m tall, about 25 years old, and wearing a white flowery blouse, red sandals, beige undergarments, and short pants who was found strangled.

Case 2, 11 February – Emilia García Hernández Rina: A woman who was stabbed and killed in the Mandelón shop, presumably by her female companions.

Case 3, 11 March – María Rocío Cordero: An eleven-year-old girl who was kidnapped before arriving at the Gabino Barreda Primary School in Col. México 68, where she lived. She was found strangled and raped anally and vaginally in a drainage culvert along the Casas Grandes Highway.

Case 4, 30 April – Donna Maurine Striplin Boggs: A twenty-six-year-old woman, 1.64 m tall, with thick brown hair who was found by the Río Bravo in front of the Esmeralda refinery. She had deep stab wounds in her neck, chest, and abdomen, as well as one near her collarbone.

Case 5, 25 April – Lorenza Isela González: A twenty-three-year-old woman who worked in the Norma Bar (Alejandro Maynez, owner of the Zafari and other bars, is implicated in this murder) who was found strangled, with a chest-wound and mutilated fore- and index fingers. She was dumped face-down with her head buried at the 19 km point of the Pan-American Highway, about 2 km from the Customs checkpoint.

Case 6, 12 May – Gladys Janneth Fierro: A twelve-year-old girl who was abducted when leaving the Secondary School Jesús Urueta on the intersection of Constitución and Galeana Street. She lived in Lomas de San José. She was raped and then strangled, and her body was found at the 1 km point of the Juárez Porvenir Highway, behind the radio station.

Case 7, 24 June – María Augustina Hernández: A brown-skinned, long-haired thirty-five-year-old woman, 1.50 m tall, who was found strangled in a wooden shack on the intersection of Isla Saboga and Nogal of Colonia 16 de Septiembre. The presumed culprit is her boyfriend Alfredo Coronado Originles.

Case 8, 8 August – Patricia (alias 'El Burra'): A strongly built, brown-skinned, curly-haired thirty-year-old woman, 1.63 m tall, who had been struck violently in the abdomen and was found in the alley along Guadalupe 300. Possible culprits are Raúl alias 'El Chilango' and Mario alias 'El Marichi'.

Case 9, 24 October – Name unknown: A sixteen-year-old woman, 1.40 m tall, wearing brown clothes, white tennis shoes, and brown stockings. On the ring finger of her left hand she was wearing a gold ring with a black stone. The ring had the inscription 'Hidalgo Academy'. She was wearing a sweatshirt with braces and a drawing of the CORONA logo. She was strangled and was found by the airport inside a plastic bag.

Case 10, 11 November – Name unknown: A thirty-year-old woman, 1.50 m tall, with a brown complexion and a platinum cap on one tooth, and wearing a sweater, a brassière, and shorts. She was raped and strangled and was found in a building site at Guerrero Avenue between Paraguay and Bolivia Streets.

Case 11, 20 November – Guillermina Hernández: A fifteen-year-old woman, 1.60 m tall, thin, with a brown complexion and shoulder-length hair who was raped and set on fire and found at Guadalupe DB. The culprit is suspected to be one Juan Carlos Escageda.

Women Murdered in 1995

Case 1, 10 January – Name unknown: A collection of female bones which was found at the Ejido Sauzal by the Juárez Porvenir highway.

Case 2, 25 January – Cristina Quezada Mauricio: A thirty-one-year-old woman, 1.65 m tall, with long hair and wearing a black and grey sweater and yellow blanket, who was raped and strangled. Her body was found at José Casavantes Street #1168 Col. Fco. I. Madero. The presumed culprit is her husband.

Case 3, 24 February – Miriam Adriana Vázquez: A fourteen-year-old girl, 1.60 m tall, with a black purse and gold chain who was stabbed and raped and found in el Ejido Juan Gabriel. She worked in the *maquiladora* AMSA and lived at Gaviotas Street 17, Col. Granjas de Chapultepec.

Case 4, 17 April – Name initially unknown, but later identified as Fabiola Zamudio: A thirty-five-year-old woman, strongly built, with a brown complexion and black hair. Intoxicated. Her body was found at the El Ranchito Hotel.

Case 5, 21 April – Initially unknown, but later identified as Karina Daniela Gutierrez: A twenty-five-year-old woman, 1.59 m tall, thin, and wearing grey leotards. She was strangled and her body was found at the intersection of Hermanos Escobar and P. del Rio Streets.

Case 6, 4 July – Initially unknown, but later identified as Araceli Rosaura Martínez Montanes: A nineteen-year-old woman wearing black jeans, brown boots, and a white blouse who was strangled and found at Granja Santa Elena. The probable culprit has been named as Juan Manuel Cruz Carreon.

Case 7, 16 July – Erika García Moreno: A nineteen-year-old woman, thin, with a pale brownish complexion, black hair, and wearing a white blouse and blue jeans. She was strangled and had marks of violence on her body, which was found behind the Pemex *maquiladora*.

Case 8, 6 August – Gloria Olivas Morales: A twenty-eight-year-old woman, wearing a white T-shirt with the Nike logo and pink, white, and blue Nike tennis shoes, who was kidnapped along with Walter Rios and Alexander Fuentes. She was then strangled. Her body was found on the tarmacadamed section of Jilotepec Avenue.

Case 9, 8 August – Patricia Cortez Campos: A thirty-three-year-old woman, 1.60 m tall, with long hair, who was raped and strangled. Her body was found at C. Velarde and Fco. Campa 331 Streets, Colonia Obrera, and had severe bruising around one ear and on the chest. The police report indicates that she died by poison.

Case 10, 19 August – Name unknown: A seventeen-year-old woman with long hair, wearing green jeans, a white blouse, and white stockings, who was raped. The body was found by the Casas Grandes Highway. Later she was identified as Elizabeth Castro García.

Case 11, 20 August – Glora Escobedo Piña: A twenty-year-old woman, 1.65 m tall, with a brown complexion, long hair, and wearing a T-shirt and black brassière. She was raped and strangled by her stepfather Miguel de Jesús Montelongo León next to the three conduits at De la Pena 1158. Her body was found undressed from the waist down and bleeding from the genitals.

Case 12, Case 13, 22 August – Names unknown: Three unidentified women whose bodies were found at the 20 km of the Casas Grandes Highway. 1) A twenty-year-old woman wearing a dark green blouse; 2) An eighteen- to twenty-year-old woman whose decomposed body was found face-down 25 m to the south-east of the first corpse, dressed in a pale pink jacket; 3) A sixteen- to twenty-year-old woman. A cause for the deaths of the three women has not been established.

Case 14, 27 August – Name unknown: A twenty-five-year-old woman wearing a blue blouse, grey denim shorts, black underwear, white stockings, and tennis shoes who was shot in the chest and stomach. She was found at Mercury 902. Later she was identified as Miriam de Los Angeles Deras.

Case 15, 2 September – Name unknown: A seventeen-year-old woman with long black straight hair, wearing a blue blouse, blue jeans, white stockings, and tennis shoes who was later identified as Silvia Elena Rivera Morales. She disappeared on the 11 July 1995, on her way to the Iberoamericana preparatory school. Her body was found raped and strangled in the Lote Bravo with its right breast severed and its left nipple bearing the marks of human teeth.

Case 16, 5 September – Name unknown: A twenty-four-year-old woman who was found at Zacate Banco at the 20 km point of the Libramiento Highway, *en route* to the Airport. Her hands had been tied with the straps of a woman's handbag. She had a deep wound in her right arm, her right breast had been severed, and her left nipple had been bitten off.

Case 17, 5 September – Name unknown: The decomposing body of a woman with long wavy black hair who was found at Lote Bravo. Cable had been tied to her left wrist and she was dressed in a decorated blouse and Jokko jeans.

Case 18, 10 September – Name unknown: A thirteen-year-old girl, thin, wearing Lee jeans, a red vest, white stockings and underwear, and tennis shoes. She was raped and stabbed. She was found at the Lote Bravo with her neck broken, her right breast severed, and her left nipple bitten off.

Case 19, 11 November – A fifteen-year-old girl whose name was initially unknown, but who was later identified as Adriana Torres Márquez: She was wearing tennis shoes when she disappeared, which is the only identifying description unmatched against the body. Her skull was intact, she had brown hair and was wearing black shoes, dark-lensed glasses with gilded rims, silver Red T. 28 trousers, a denim jacket, a brassière, and white socks. Her neck was broken, her right breast severed, and her left nipple had been bitten off. Her body was found on the Casas Blancas Highway behind Granja Santa Elena.

Case 20, 18 November – Name unknown: An eighteen-year-old woman wearing black trousers with grey trousers underneath, and a grey waistcoat. She had bled to death. Her body was found at Poblado Loma Blanca.

Case 21, 23 November – Ignacia Morales Soto: A twenty-two-year-old woman, thin, 1.63 m tall, with a brown complexion and long hair. She had been stabbed in her left side and had severe bruising all over her body, which was found at Granja Santa Elena along the Casas Grandes Highway. The suspected culprit is one Juan Escajeda.

Case 22, 15 December – Isela Tena Quintanilla: A fourteen-year-old girl, thin, with black hair and wearing purple pants, a black blouse, black tennis shoes and a *Virgen del Cobre* medallion. She had been tied up with the same knot used for Elizabeth Castro [García] and had been stabbed. Her body was found at the sports field owned by the Pemex *maquiladora*.

Case 23 – An initially unknown woman who was later identified as Elizabeth Gómez: She was twenty-nine years old, 1.60 m tall, thin, with black wavy hair, and wearing a copper-coloured blouse, a blue jacket, and black shoes. She was found with her skirt lifted to her waist and her blouse opened to expose her breasts. According to the municipal police she had been stabbed. Her body was found at the sports field owned by the Pemex *maquiladora*.

Case 24 – Laura Ana Inere: A twenty-seven-year-old woman killed by a firearm according to the municipal police. Her body was found in the Municipal Cemetery.

Women Murdered in 1996

Case 1, 9 February – Name unknown: A raped and strangled *tarahumara* [Indian] woman who was about thirty years old. She had also been stabbed several times with an unidentified object and was found in the 'Garita de metales'.

Case 2, 9 March – Name unknown: A girl about ten years old, 1.20–1.30 m tall, with a blonde streak in her hair. She had been stabbed at least eight times with a sharp object and was found at the 27 km point of the Casas Grandes Highway, Lomas de Poleo.

Case 3, 12 March – Names unknown: A thirteen-year-old girl found at Lote Bravo and a girl aged between sixteen and seventeen who was 1.64 m tall, with a brown complexion and wearing a white brassière and short trousers. She had been strangled and her body was found at Lomas de Poleo.

Case 4, 19 March – Name unknown: A sixteen-year-old girl, thin, 1.59 m tall, with long black hair held under a handkerchief. She had been stabbed, with a wound in her elbow and thigh, and another 8 cm deep elsewhere, but died by strangulation. Her body was found at Lomas de Poleo.

Case 5, 23 March – Name unknown: A sixteen-year-old woman, 1.60 m tall, with black hair and wearing a blue blouse and a green brassière. She had been stabbed and mutilated, and her body was found at Lomas de Poleo.

Case 6, 29 March – Veronica Guadalupe Castro Pando: A sixteen-year-old girl with brown hair and wearing a T-shirt and black trousers. She had been stabbed and mutilated, and her body was found at Lomas de Poleos.

Case 7, 29 March – Name unknown: A woman who was about eighteen years old and who had been tied up with one of her own shoelaces. She had been stabbed and mutilated, and her body was found at Lomas de Poleo.

Case 8, 8 April – Name unknown: An eighteen-year-old woman wearing an identity badge from the Phillips *maquiladora* in the name of Rosario García Leal. There were signs that she had been stabbed, mutilated, and raped.

Case 9, 28 April – Name unknown: A woman about twenty-eight years old whose body was found in an abandoned building on Galeana Street. She had wounds in various parts of her body and her blouse had two knife-holes in it.

Case 10, 7 June – Name unknown: A twenty-three-year-old woman who worked as a dancer at La Bahía Bar. She was murdered by her fifty-year-old husband Tomás Sandoval Rodríguez, who entered the bar, shot her without saying anything, and left. She was known as 'Aracely'.

Case 11, 10 June – Name unknown: A seventeen-year-old woman, 1.70 m tall, thin, with brown hair and wearing a black T-shirt, a beige brassière, white underclothes, and size 3 shoes. Only her bones remained when she was found at the 25 km point of the Casas Grandes Highway, but her T-shirt had knife-holes in it.

Case 12, 26 June – Silvia Rivera Salas: A twenty-one-year-old woman killed at Antonio Perez 334, Colonia 1 Septiembre, by her husband. She had been stabbed twenty-one times. Her husband was playing football when he saw the police arrive. They asked him what happened and he calmly confessed to the crime. Oddly the parents of another woman called Elizabeth Ontiveros López first identified the body as that of their daughter, but Elizabeth López turned up later and told the police that she had been with her boyfriend and was not the deceased. The police exhumed the corpse for further inquiries and identified the husband as the killer. The couple had two children, one four months old, the other two years old.

Case 13, 8 July – Name unknown: A girl between sixteen and seventeen years of age, 1.60 m tall, with dark hair 0.25 cms [sic] long, whose bones were found at the Lote Bravo, one kilometre from the 21 km point of the Pan-American Highway. An earring was found with the bones but no clothing. The victim was killed in the same place she was found because dried vegetation was clutched in her fist that matched the vegetation of the area. The probable cause of death was blows to the head or three stab wounds in the chest.

Case 14, 10 July – Name unknown: ... At Capulin 7146 Colonia Revolucion. A seventeen-year-old girl, 1.60 m tall, weighing 52 kilos, with a brown complexion and long dark hair whose body was thrown in the Río Bravo. She had arrived from Zacatecas five days previously and had an appointment on 8 July in a *maquiladora*. When she did not turn up her worried parents reported her missing by telephone. She was dressed in black jeans and a mustard-coloured blouse and had died by strangulation.

Case 15, ? July – Gang members stab a young girl, the daughter of someone nicknamed 'Bomberto'.

Case 16, 30 July – Rocío Miranda Aguero: A twenty-eight-year-old woman, manageress of the nightclub Top Capos, was found by children in a 200-litre drum full of corrosive acid, with only her hands and feet remaining undissolved. She was identified by her silicone [breast-]implants. She had been abducted by a group of seventeen people. In the same house there were a female servant and a two-month-old baby, the daughter of the murdered woman, both of whom were miraculously saved by hiding.

Case 17, 10 August – Sonia Ivette Ramírez: A thirteen-year-old girl, 1.56 m tall, with brown eyes and complexion, and wearing short yellow trousers, a white floral blouse, black shoes, and white socks who was raped and brutally murdered at Falcón 7497 Colonia Industrial. Her corpse was found in the back of Technical Secondary School 48 a few metres from the headquarters of the State Judicial Police. The girl had left her home at six in the morning to accompany a sister who worked in one of the *maquiladoras*, and never returned home.

Case 18, 15 August – Soledad Beltrán: A twenty-four-year-old woman known as Yesenia whose corpse was found beside a sewage canal near Loma Blanca. She had been in Juárez for five years and worked as a dancer in one of the dancehalls. Her murderer has not been identified.

Case 19, 19 August – Name unknown: A young woman about seventeen years old, wearing jeans, a white brassière, and white underclothing who was stabbed and had her throat cut. She was found in the mostly deserted Colonia Erindira (though one newspaper says Col. Arturo Gamiz) behind the slaughterhouse and was wrapped in a green bedspread with yellow and white patterns. She had three stab wounds on one side of her face near her throat and another near her ear. The police said she had not been raped but later the file on the case was revised and it was revealed she had indeed been raped, although no reason was given for the earlier mistake . . . She was buried in the public cemetery on the 13 September 1996.

Case 20, 15 August – Alma Patricia O Leticia Palafox Zamora: A seventeen-year-old girl who was stabbed to death at Mercurio 1948, the home of her parents, by someone believed to be her twenty-seven-year-old boyfriend, Ernesto Gómez Cordero, who said that he did it because she was going to marry someone else. She had two sons.

Case 21, Case 22, 30 September – Names unknown: Two women who were killed on their way to San Augustín and found by a motorbiker on a track built for motorbikes. One of the women was wearing pants and slippers, and the other was also dressed in casual clothing. They had both been shot and although unidentified at first were later identified as thirty-year-old Victoria Elaine Parker Hopking and forty-eight-year-old Perla Parker Hopking. They are believed to have been involved in the trafficking of drugs.

Case 23, 31 October – Name unknown: The decomposing corpse of a woman was found this Tuesday in El Sauzal del Valle de Juárez. She had been dead for about 15 days and was dressed in pants and a blouse with white and blue stripes. Her fingernails were painted with red nail-varnish and she had long, light brown hair. Her age will be discovered at autopsy, as may the cause of her death.

Case 24, 2 November – Leticia de la Cruz Banuelos: A thirty-year-old woman who was working as a prostitute by the Bar Rancho Grande and was murdered by gunshots to the left side of the chest. Two men drove up in a dark-coloured car, called out to one of the women, killed her, and drove off. They have not been identified and their whereabouts are unknown.

Case 25, 14 November – Leticia Garia Rosales: A woman of about thirty-five years of age was found in a ravine beaten to death. She was apparently the victim of attempted rape. Her pants were below her waist, which is what leads to this supposition. The autopsy will determine whether or not she had been raped. She had been beaten on her face and various other parts of her body. The presumed murderer is one Juan Salazar García.

Case 26, 18 November – Name unknown: A woman between twenty and twenty-five years of age who was found floating in the river. She may have drowned and was nude below the waist. She was wearing a white blouse with blue patterns, white socks, and a black brassière. She was 1.70 m tall, strongly built, and had long, dark brown hair and a tattoo on her wrist.

Case 27, Case 28, 7 December – Brenda Lizeth Najera: A fifteen-year-old girl who disappeared on 27 November with Susana Flores Flores (*sic*), a thirteen-year-old girl. They were found murdered with two gunshots to the head inside a house on Magnolia Street, near the corner of Filipinas in Infonavit Tecnológico. Both had been raped, and Brenda also showed signs of having been tortured. The girls lived on Libertad Street, and disappeared on their way to Ricardo Flores Magón primary school. The autopsy revealed that Susana had suffered four heart attacks, probably due to the terror of being raped and tortured. It is believed that the culprit is Edgar Cisar Sánchez, Brenda's boyfriend, who may have fled to the United States.

Women Murdered in 1997

Case 1, 11 March – Cinthia Rocío Acosta Alvarado: The body of a raped and strangled minor was found near the city dump in a desert area south of the city known as Valle Dorado (Golden Valley). She had been partly buried about 300 m to the north of the main road that leads to the city dump near the 25 km point of the Casa Grandes Highway. The body was found by a farm worker on horseback. Reports by the authorities say that she died by strangulation and blows to the head, hands, and legs. She had been raped and had been dead about a month. Tests will be carried out to determine if the body is that of Cinthia Rocío Acosta Alvarado, a ten-year-old girl who disappeared on 7 February 1997, between three-thirty in the morning and eight-thirty in the evening from 18 de Marzo Street, Colonia Raúl García.

Case 2, 14 March – Ana María Gardea Villalobos: The body of an adolescent girl later identified as eleven-year-old Ana Villalobos was found in the Cerro Bola. She had been raped and stabbed and had bled to death from fifteen wounds in her chest and neck. The corpse will be examined in an attempt to establish its identity [which has now been confirmed as given above]. Evidence indicated that she had been raped and murdered by a single individual but a group of young men have now been detained as her possible murderers.

Case 3, 21 March – Maribel Palomino Arvizo: The remains of a nineteen-year-old woman were found in the Valle de Juárez. It is believed the body is of Maribel Palomino Arvizo, who lived in N. Casas Grandes. She had five wounds in her neck and had been in the place where she was found for two to three weeks. She shows signs of having been raped. The body will be turned over to relatives once tests confirm her identity.

Case 4, 21 March – Name unknown: The body of a young woman of about sixteen years of age was found at about seven in the evening on fields outside the town of El Sauzal Nuevo. She was in an advanced state of decomposition and is estimated to have been killed a week previously. She was found completely naked wearing only a single earring. A blue piece of underclothing and a white sock were found near the body.

Case 5, 29 March – Silvia Guadalupe Díaz: At about three in the afternoon the decomposing body of a woman was found on the road about 2 km south of the El Sauzal Viejo cemetery. She had been killed about forty to sixty days previously, and is believed to have been strangled. She had been missing since 7 March after going to the Stracted *maquiladora* to look for work. The initial autopsy revealed that she had knife-wounds in her neck and abdomen, but due to the state of decomposition of her body it could not be established if she had been raped. Farm workers found the body in a ditch in a field about 750 m to the east of the Juárez Porvenir Highway and about 100 m to the north of the local road near Puente Yanez. She was completely nude, but underclothing and a *maquiladora* overall were found near her body. She was 1.65 m tall and had long dark brown hair tied with a dark green ribbon with a metal fastener at the end. She had a white piece of hair elastic on her right wrist and a small pendant earring in her left ear. The victim is identified as Silvia Guadalupe Díaz, who had been missing since 7 March. She leaves a boy of three months and a girl of three years. Her husband is Padro Montelongo. Her mother-in-law Margarita Rodríguez revealed that her daughter-in-law left her address on Wednesday and that the last time she was seen was near a *maquiladora* in an industrial park at the 5 km point of the Casas Grandes Highway. This murder is similar to those that have taken place in the Lote Bravo and the Lomas de Poleo.

Case (?) – A woman who was murdered in Colonia Dublán and was found towards the end of March. Her name is unknown, but it is believed that she is one of the women who have disappeared in Cd. Juárez. Her remains are believed to have been in the open for between six months and a year. She was 1.50 m tall, thin, with short, dark brown hair and was wearing light brown boots with a Bonnyour brand label, blue jeans, a white blouse printed with a picture of a bear and the word SKY, short white stockings, and a white bodice. Tests were carried out to see if the remains were those of Rocío Rincón, whose disappearance in 1991 had attracted nationwide attention. The mother of the missing woman appeared on the 'Real Life Cases' TV programme, hosted by Silvia Pinal, and her picture was put on milk cartons sold in the region to try and get information about her whereabouts.

Case 6, 12 April – Miriam Aguilar Rodríguez: The body of a woman was found yesterday at seven-thirty in the evening behind the 'Embotelladora de la Frontera' company and between silos 11 and 12 of the Com. Fed. de Electricidad by someone on his way to work. A concrete block with traces of human skin was found near the railroad at Oscar Flores and Santo Duron Avenues and is presumed to be the murder weapon. This is the fifth body found in the city. The young woman is believed to have been between nineteen and twenty years of age, although she may have been younger. She was covered with a plastic bag and old bed sheets, had injuries to her face, and her skull had been broken near her right ear. She was dressed in black pants that had been pulled down to her knees. She was 1.65 m tall, thin, with a brown complexion and shoulder-length dark brown hair. The police believed that she was killed where she was found. On 13 April she was identified as sixteen-year-old Miriam Aguilar Rodríguez. The autopsy established that she died from a violent blow to the head and that she had tried to fight off her attacker before her death. Human skin was found under her fingernails, some of which were broken. Her hymen was intact and no traces of semen were found in or on her body. Her family said that she had left home to find work in one of the *maquiladoras*.

Case 7, 16 May – Name unknown: The body of a woman was found yesterday in the town of El Sauz, in the Valle de Juárez. Due to decomposition her age could not be established nor the cause of her death. She was 1.67 m tall, had long black hair, and was wearing dark-coloured pants, black tennis shoes, and a green blouse. A set of keys, possibly for a car, was found in a pocket of her pants. On 17 May an autopsy established that she was between twenty-eight and thirty-three years of age. She was killed by two heavy blows to one temple.

Case 8, 29 May – Amelia Lucío Borjas: A woman was murdered in her home by being stabbed nine times in the chest. She was eighteen years old and was called Amelia Lucío Borjas. She was found lying in a bed at Finix Street 922 in Bosques de Salbarcar. The authorities are investigating the husband, Raúl Saldaña Delgado, who works in a *maquiladora* and is twenty-seven years old. Police have found clothes belonging to the husband covered in blood.

Case 9 – Vernonic Beltrán Maynez: A fifteen-year-old girl who died of bullet wounds shortly after arriving at the IMSS hospital.

Case 10, 19 June – Marcela Hernández Macias: A thirty-five-year-old woman who had been reported missing by her husband was found strangled at the 29 km point of the Casas Grandes Highway. She was found after her husband, Ramón Ochoa Pantoja, confessed to her murder.

Case 11, 10 July – Name unknown: The remains have been found of a murdered woman who is unidentified and may have been killed some months ago. She was found near a sewage canal by the Thermoelectric plant on Juárez Porvenir Highway with her hands tied, a white-and-black glove on her left hand, and a dark-coloured sock on one foot with the Reebok label. Under the glove she had two rings, one on the middle finger, another on the ring finger. She was between twenty-two and twenty-five years of age and had long black hair.

Case 12, 9 September – Martha Gutierrez García: A woman who had been raped and strangled was found completely nude in an empty lot at Colonia Barrio Alto behind a bar in the Ocampo and Mina area. It is believed that she is the eighteen-year-old Martha Gutierrez García. Witnesses said that they last saw her in the company of men nicknamed 'El Chango', 'La Camelia', and 'El Luis', none of whom have been located.

Case 13, 28 September – María Irma Plancarte: The naked body of a tortured and murdered woman wrapped in a bedspread with its feet tied was found inside a black plastic bag. She had been beaten severely around the face and head and was between twenty-five and thirty years old. She was found in the Colonia División del Norte, having been left around one in the morning the previous day on the car-park at Boulevard Zaragoza and Eje Vial Juan Gabriel. It is believed she had been dead for about four days and was left there because her body had started to smell of decomposition. It was not possible to determine if she had been raped. A suspect called Pedro Alberto Muñoz Fernández ('El Coreano') has been arrested.

Case 14, 3 October – Name unknown: The body of a young woman between fifteen and seventeen years of age was found in a ditch near Barranco Azul Street, about 25 m from the railroad bridge on the baseball field. She had been severely tortured before being strangled. Her body had the marks of blows all over it and fifty stab wounds, none of which had penetrated to a vital organ. She has not been identified. One of her legs was shorter than the other. The State Judicial Police have removed all the evidence from the murder scene. All she was wearing was a black blouse with white stripes and a black brassière. She was about 1.70 m tall, of medium build, with a brown complexion and shoulder-length hair.

Case 15, 13 October – María Esther Luna Alfaro: A woman's body was found partly buried and in an advanced state of decomposition on the Pemex sports field, along the Casas Grandes and Barranco Azul Highways. She was 1.78 m tall, with brown hair, and was wearing a white shirt and a white sock on her left foot. She had been stabbed and was later identified by her mother.

Case 16, 14 October – Virginia Rodríguez Beltrán: The body of another murdered woman, Rodríguez Beltrán, was found on Sunday morning in the Colonia Torreón on the intersection of Jaime Nunó and Casavantes Streets. The authorities report that the body shows signs of drug addiction. It was found only an hour before the body in Case 15, above. However, doctors have established that the woman died from a bullet wound.

Case 17, 23 October – Name unknown: The body of a murdered woman was found by the side of a street in the Colonia Palo Chino. She was fully dressed, had a white electric cable around her neck, and an autopsy established that she had been strangled and showed signs of having been beaten. She had been dead for three to four days. She was fully dressed. She was later identified as the thirty-eight-year-old Juana Iñiguz Mares by her daughter, who had reported that she had been missing since 20 October.

Case 18, 7 November – Name unknown: The scattered bones of a woman were found in a remote area along with white pants and underclothing. Dr Enrique Silva Pirez thinks that she died more than two months ago.

Case 19, 8 November – Norma Julissa Ramos: This twenty-one-year-old woman, was shot seven times by her husband, Filix Silva Araujo, a thirty-five-year-old who then fled the area. Police report that he was motivated by jealousy.

Case 20, 17 November – Erendira Buendia Munoz: Another young woman's body was found in an empty building lot along the Pan-American Highway, next to the

Flourex *maquiladora*. More than seven young women have now been raped and murdered in the last two months. The State Judicial Police said she was about eighteen years of age. She was completely naked and her pants and underclothing were found about 5 m from her body. The body was hidden face-up among some bushes . . . On 19 November she was identified by her parents as the nineteen-year-old woman who had disappeared after going to dance at El Patio on Tecnológico Avenue. She had been raped and strangled.

Case 21, 30 November – Teresa Renteria: A bestial crime against a woman. A thirty-year-old woman was brutally stabbed in her home a few days after the 'International Day of No Violence Against Women'. She was separated from her husband and murdered by her current boyfriend because of jealousy.

Case 22, 1 December – Aracely Nuñez Santos: A young woman was found with her throat cut on the bank of a canal in the Colonia Santa Elena. She was found by Juan Ramírez Gurrola, who was out hunting when his dogs smelled decomposition. The body was 5 km from the Casas Grandes Highway, where other women's bodies have been found previously. The victim was face-up, partly naked with her underclothing hanging on one leg below the knee, and with one shoe on and the other lying nearby. She had [five] stab wounds, one in the abdomen, three in the chest, and one in the neck. She had a brown complexion and shoulder-length black hair, which matches some of the previous murders. Four months later, on 7 April, she was identified as Aracely Nuñez Santos, who had migrated from Torreón, Coahuila state, and had only been in Juárez for three days.

Case 23, 2 December – Amalia Saucedo Díaz de León: Another woman murdered and found in the Lote Bravo. A suspect has been detained. She was identified as thirty-three-year-old Amalia Saucedo Díaz de Leon, who worked for UACJ Television and had died from a broken neck and injuries to the spine. She was married and having an affair, according to the police. She was fully dressed and her body did not exhibit any signs of violence, apart from disarranged hair that indicated a possible struggle with her killer. The police believe that she was killed indoors and then dumped in the Lote Bravo, and are unsure whether she was raped.

Case 24, 9 December – Rosa Margarita Arellanes García: A woman was shot at the El Vértigo discothèque and died in hospital. She was identified as Rosa Margarita Arellanes García, twenty-four years of age, and was apparently shot by accident when someone at an adjacent table fired, hitting both himself and her.

Case 25, 21 December – Name unknown: The remains of another murdered woman were found in the Lomas de Poleo. Authorities believe she had been lying there about a year and had been between sixteen and seventeen years old when she was killed. She was between 1.40 m and 1.52 m tall and was found about 1.5 km from the El Oasis ranch by two men looking for recyclable materials. A T-shirt, navy-blue pants, and a black plastic belt were found with the body.

Women Murdered in 1998

Case 1, 3 January – Jessica Martínez Morales: A murdered thirteen-year-old girl who had been missing for ten days was found in the canal behind the Federal Commission of Electricity substation (next to the Flourex *maquiladora*), on the Pan-American Highway. She was identified by her father as Jessica Martínez Morales, who had disappeared on 23 December, when her parents immediately contacted the police. She had apparently been murdered the day before her body was discovered and thrown in the canal, which is about 25 m from the railroad. She was last seen near her home in Zaragoza. The police believe that she had been with her killer for the previous ten days, then murdered somewhere other than where she was found. She appears to have been partly dragged to the area. She was completely nude apart from a pair of earrings and a bracelet, and had bite marks on her right arm.

Case 2, 25 January – Rosalina Vásquez: Another murdered young woman was found yesterday near the Infonavit Oasis, according to the authorities. She had twenty-one stab wounds in her back, neck, and chest and was partly nude, with a belt tied around her waist that had apparently been used to lower her body into the ditch where it was found hidden. This murder is similar to twenty others in the city. The woman was identified as a twenty-year-old Phillips *maquila* worker called Rosalina Veloz Vásquez, who had disappeared on Thursday after leaving for work at the Phillips company. She was identified from a picture provided by her relatives that showed her and her baby son.

Case 3, 26 January – María Isela Nuñez Herrera: The corpses of a man and a woman were found in steel drums half-filled with lye. They were identified as the husband and wife Sergio Zavala, thirty-one, and María Isela Nuñez Herrera, thirty-three. It is believed they were involved in the trafficking of drugs.

Case 4, 27 January – Silvia Gabriela Laguna Cruz: The body of an adolescent girl, sixteen years old, was found raped and murdered yesterday morning about 100 m to the south of the Boulevard Zaragoza. She was found by two passers-by. Her sweatshirt had been pulled up over her breasts and her underclothing pulled down her right leg to the knee. She was wearing socks but her shoes have not been found. Apparently she was raped, then killed with an object found 'nailed' to her lower chest, and had been dead ten to twelve hours. Relatives of the dead girl identified her and said that she had been married only three months before. She had left for work in a *maquiladora* on Saturday at six in the morning, and when she did not return home her parents called the police.

Case 5, 3 February – Ana Hipólito Campos: A murdered thirty-eight-year-old woman was found inside her home partly decapitated and with forty stab wounds. She was discovered by a neighbour, who became suspicious and entered the house, which is on the intersection of Puebla Street and Nuevo León, in the Colonia Lomas de San José.

Cases 6, 7 & 8, 16 February – Names unknown: The remains of two women found in Lomas de Poleo, approximately four km from Colonia Puerto Anapra and scattered over an area about 200 m wide. The skull of one woman had a tooth with a platinum cap stamped 'R'. A black tennis shoe, size 5 'Capricio' jeans, blue pants, and a red sweatshirt were also found by a search party organised for that purpose. On 25 February the police agent Cesar del Hierro reported that the remains were actually of three women and not two, and stated that one set of remains may belong to Raquel Lechuga Macmas, who worked in the Esexx *maquila* and had disappeared on 31 December 1996, after leaving home for work.

Case 9, 16 February – Name unknown: Another woman's body was discovered in the old city dump. She was about 1.50 m tall, thin, and had a brown complexion with short black hair. Her head had been completely crushed by a twenty-kilo rock found about 15 cm from the body. She was wearing blue jeans, a blouse, and black tennis shoes.

Case 10, 17 February – Clara Zepeda Alvarez: A seventeen-year-old girl who lived in the Colonia Colinas de Juárez was killed by shotgun fire during a gang fight. The presumed culprit is seventeen-year-old Jorge Ernesto Ortiz.

Case 11, 19 February – Perla Patricia Saenz Díaz: The body of a twenty-year-old woman was found completely naked in a room at the Motel Fronterizo. She had been stabbed in the chest, possibly with an ice-pick, and was identified as Perla Patricia Saenz Díaz, who is believed to have worked in a downtown bar.

Case 12, 21 February – Name unknown: The body of an incinerated young woman was found behind the railroad near the intersection of Ponciano Arriaga Avenue and Eje Vial Juan Gabriel. The fire brigade had responded to a report of a fire. Police said the body was that of a thin young woman with a small head and small hands. A woman's black belt and a red pen were found 3 m from the remains. There have now been three murders of young women in the same area this year. On 10 March a suspect called Luis Antonio Navarrete was arrested and revealed the identities of other murder victims, though he could only identify this victim as 'Elizabeth'. He implicated two others as accomplices, but they have not been located. He was let out on bail due to lack of evidence and is now regarded only as a witness and accomplice.

Case 13, 18 March – Name unknown: Another woman is murdered. She had been stabbed to death and thrown into an irrigation ditch by the *maquiladoras* at Waterfil[l?]. One identifying mark is a gold tooth on the left of her upper jaw. She had been stabbed at least thirty times around the chest and neck and, although she has apparently been identified, the police, who are treating this murder as a case of domestic violence, will not release any details. She had been dead about thirty-six hours.

Case 14, 17 April – Argelia Irene Salazar Crispín: Another murdered woman's body was found in an advanced state of decomposition on an empty building lot between Eje Juan Gabriel and Ponciano Arriaga. She had been dead about fifteen to twenty days and was dressed only in a black blouse and white brassière that had been pulled up above her breasts. The victim was of medium build with shoulder-length dark hair and was found face-up with her legs flexed. She had no pants, underclothing, or shoes. The young woman was identified on 19 April as the twenty-four-year-old Argelia Irene Salazar Crispín, who disappeared on 6 March, having left at six in the morning to work in a *maquiladora*. She lived with her mother and a sister who looked after her five-year-old daughter while she worked.

Case 15, 20 April – Name unknown: Another murdered young woman has been found by a man looking for cans on an empty building-lot at Boulevard Oscar Flores y Barranca Azul, where two other bodies have been found previously. She had been dead for about a year and was wearing a short-sleeved shirt, a white brassière, black pants, and black shoes with white socks. It was established on 22 April that she was beaten to death, although there were also stab wounds on her body. She was about sixteen years old and worked in the Mallinckrodt Medical *maquiladora*, where she worked for the last time on 12 March 1997.

Case 16, 30 April – María Sagrario González Flores: A young woman's body was found in Loma Blanca. On 1 May it was identified as that of seventeen-year-old María Sagrario González Flores, who worked in the COPCOM *maquiladora*. She had been stabbed and strangled in the same way as other victims of the serial murders, and had last been seen boarding the bus for the long journey home.

Case 17, April/May – Gabriela Edith Martínez Calvillo: A fifteen-year-old girl who was attacked by a gang has died from a knife wound. She was found by a police patrol on the road to La Esperanza. This gang killing is not related to the serial murders.

Case 18, 24 May – Name unknown: A woman was found strangled and dressed in male clothing. A belt that may have been used to strangle her was found in the same place.

Case 19, 27 June – Brenda Patricia Meléndez Vázquez: A fifteen-year-old girl was found raped in the Lote Bravo.

She had been strangled, possibly by a thick belt, had been raped anally and vaginally and had old and new bruises all over her body. She had been dead for about ten hours and was identified by relatives as the high school student Brenda Patricia Meléndez Vázquez.

Case 20, 5 August – Aracely Lozano Bolaños: A woman's decomposing body was found behind a sofa in room 42 at the Campo Real motel. She was twenty-four years old, had been dead between two and three days, and was identified as Aracely Lozano Bolaños, alias 'La Wendy', who worked at the Noche y Día night club on Mariscal Street. She was apparently murdered by her boyfriend out of jealousy.

Case 21, 19 August – Aracely Gómez Martínez: A young woman was murdered in broad daylight on a crowded street. The twenty-four-year-old worker Aracely Gómez Martínez had left work at a *maquiladora* and died on the street near the intersection of Eduardo Romero and Rivera Lara after being stabbed by an unknown attacker who had chased and caught her. The many people in the area did nothing to help her. According to a badge she worked for Phillips. Her husband was arrested in the afternoon and confessed to killing his wife out of jealousy.

Case 22 – Olga Gonzáles López: A twenty-three-year-old woman was shot to death in the Colonia Panfilo Natera on Tepetongo and Pavo Real Streets in a dispute between neighbours.

Case 23, 31 August – Erendira Ivonne Ponce: The body of another raped and strangled woman was found north of the Casas Grandes Highway. She was seventeen years old, had shoulder-length wavy black hair, and was found naked and face-up with her hands tied. She had been violently raped, then killed by a blow to the left of her head with a rock, and had been dead for between twenty and twenty-five days. A skirt was also found in the area but she was wearing only underclothing, which had been pulled down to her knees. She had been identified as Erindira Ivonne Ponce, who disappeared two weeks before after leaving work at a paper recycling company in Foviste Chamizal. She was last seen at five-thirty in the evening on the day she disappeared. The main suspect is her boss.

Case 24, 21 September – Rocío Barraza Gallegos: A State Judicial Police officer working on the 'murdered women' case killed a young woman inside his police car in the car-park at the Police Academy. She was twenty-three years old and had two boys. Rocío Barraza Gallegos worked at the Río Senegal and the Dos Amigos bars.

Case 25, 21 September – A woman had her throat cut with a knife in the Hotel Juárez. She was Dutch [according to] documents found in a pillow-case and was found under the bed stripped naked. It is calculated that she had been dead for fourteen hours. The room had been rented by a man of North American appearance who has not yet been traced.

Women Murdered in 1999

Case 1, 11 January – María Estela Martínez: The body of a thirty-three-year-old woman was found inside a car in the car-park of the Central Bus Station yesterday at about seven-twenty in the evening. An autopsy will be conducted by the police to establish the cause of her death. Initial investigations have found no signs of violence and she was fully clothed. The car keys were not in the ignition. The police have since reported that she was strangled and that they suspect her boyfriend was responsible.

Case 2, 13 January – Patricia Monroy Torres: She was abducted from her home on 8 January and found dead on Tuesday, 13 January, in hills to the southeast of Cd. Juárez. Mrs Torres was killed by two gunshots to the head and was found with her mouth taped shut and a white towel wrapped around her head.

Case 3, 31 January – Name unknown: A young woman about twenty years of age was found murdered on an empty sports lot owned by the Pemex *maquiladora* in Cd. Juárez, where about half-a-dozen other women have been found dead over the last two years. She has still not been identified, although many families have viewed her body at the city morgue. She had been raped and strangled before being left in the desert. A sample of semen was taken from her body and for the first time in the seven years of murders DNA testing will be carried out to try and discover more about those responsible.

Case 4, 16 February – Irma Angelica Rosales Lozano: A thirteen-year-old girl was found naked, raped, and strangled in a drainage ditch at the Colonia Olague yesterday at about four in the afternoon. A plastic bag had been placed over her head and she had been there for about five hours. She worked in a *maquiladora* and had been sent home early. She was found by a boy walking in the area who informed the police.

Case 5, 3 March – Name unknown: Another woman has been murdered and set on fire. She was found along the Casas Grandes Highway on Wednesday night. A new study of the remains have established that she was aged between thirty and thirty-five. Suly Ponce, head of the Special Force Investigating the Murders of Women, said that the identity of the victim had not yet been released, because it was vital to clear the case up before relatives reclaimed the body. She said that pathologists had not been able to discover the height or skin-colour of the victim because of the condition in which her body was found. The woman had been set on fire after she was killed by knife-blows to the chest. One of the wounds had penetrated her heart and another one her lungs, and the cause of death was loss of blood from the wounds. The young woman was murdered twenty-four hours before the discovery of her body, Suly Ponce said. She added the murderer or murderers piled eight tyres on the woman's body and it was believed that a chemical accelerant was poured over her to assist the fire. Due to condition of her body, it was not possible to establish whether she had been raped.

Ponce said that it was only possible to retrieve scraps of the clothing worn by the young woman, but a large earring and three rings were found in good condition. She said that the victim had various pieces of dental work, including three crowns on two pre-molars and a molar, all on the lower left jaw. The woman's body was found on Wednesday night in a brick-kiln in an abandoned farm 500 m above the 29 km point of the Casas Grandes Highway, just before the crossing to Sante Teresa. It appeared that the body had been burnt on Tuesday night.

Case 6, Case 7 – Details of these two cases will be published shortly.

Case 8 (13 under the new administration), 15 March – Gladys Lizeth Ramos Escarcega: The body of a twenty-four-year-old woman identified as Gladys Lizeth Ramos Escarcega was found on Saturday afternoon inside a car on Leon and Hidalgo streets in the Airport subdivision. She had been killed by a gunshot to the forehead. The police have implicated a man who visited her on Friday afternoon. A police officer or commercial security guard may be involved, as a belt designed to hold a billy-club, bullets, and other items used for self-defence was found at the murder scene. Although the murderer's identity has been established, he has not yet been arrested as he is believed to have fled Cd. Juárez.

Bibliography

Books.

Aldapuerta, Jesús Ignacio, *The Eyes*, Critical Vision, Stockport, Cheshire, 1995.

Ali, Abdullah Yusuf (1946 translation and commentary), *The Holy Qur'an*, Islamic Propagation Centre, Durban, South Africa, not dated.

Barnes-Svarney, Patricia (ed.), *The New York Public Library Science Desk Reference*, Macmillan, New York, 1995.

Barsamian, David, *Keeping the Rabble in Line: Interviews with Noam Chomsky*, Common Courage Press, Monroe, Me., 1994.

Brandon, Ruth, *The Life and Many Deaths of Harry Houdini*, Kodansha International, 1995.

Brewer, E. Cobham, *Brewer's Dictionary of Phrase and Fable*, no publisher given, 1894.

Cockburn, Leslie, *Out of Control: The Story of the Reagan's Administration's Secret War in Nicaragua, the Illegal Arms Pipeline, and the Contra Drug Connection*, Bloomsbury, London, 1988.

Conan Doyle, Sir Arthur, *The Conan Doyle Stories*, my edition Blitz Editions, Leicester, 1993.

Crampton, William, *The New Observer's Book of Flags*, Frederick Warne, London, 1984.

Cross, Roger, *The Yorkshire Ripper: an in-depth study of a mass killer and his methods*, HarperCollins, 1993.

Cummings, Joe, *Northern Mexico Handbook*, Moon Publications, Chico, California, 1998.

Dworkin, Andrea, *Letters from a Warzone*, Martin Secker and Warburg, London, 1988.

Emsley, John, *Molecules at an Exhibition: Portraits of intriguing materials in everyday life*, Oxford University Press, Oxford, 1998.

Eysenck, H.J., *Fact and Fiction in Psychology*, Pelican, 1965.

Eysenck, H.J., *Psychology is about People*, Pelican, 1982.

Eysenck, H.J., *Sense and Nonsense in Psychology*, Pelican, 1978.

Eysenck, H.J., and Nias, D.K.B., *Sex, Violence and the Media*, Maurice Temple Smith, London, 1978.

Furst, Peter E., *The Encyclopedia of Psychoactive Drugs: Mushrooms: Psychoactive Fungi*, Burke Publishing, London, 1988.

Gerard & Co., *Plaza de Toros*, Verviers, Belgium/ Esthétiques Nouvelles, Paris, 1964.

Gibbon, Edward, *The Decline & Fall of the Roman Empire*, my edition Everyman's Library, 1910.

Gooch, Anthony, and García de Paredes, Angel (eds), *The Cassell's Spanish Dictionary*, Cassell, London, 1978.

Gregory, Richard L. (ed.), *The Oxford Companion to the Mind*, Oxford University Press, 1987.

Guinness Book of Records 1987, Guinness Books, London, 1986.

Halliwell, Leslie, *Halliwell's Film Guide*, Paladin Grafton Books, London, 1987.

Hanks, Patrick *et al* (eds), *Collins Concise Dictionary Plus*, Collins, Glasgow, 1989.

Hitchens, Christopher, *For the Sake of Argument*, Verso, London, 1997.

The Hutchinson Softback Encyclopedia, editors not given, Helicon Publishing, Oxford, 1992.

Irving, David, *The Destruction of Convoy PQ.17*, Corgi, 1970.

Iverson, Marjorie, *Living Left-Handed*.

Kerekes, David and Slater, David (eds), *Critical Vision: Random Essays and Tracts Concerning Sex Religion Death*, Critical Vision, Stockport, Cheshire, 1995.

Kingsley, Charles, *Hypatia* (1853).

Klawans, Howard L. *Toscanini's Fumble and Other Tales of Clinical Neurology*, Headline Book Publishing, London, 1990.

LeDoux, Joseph, *The Emotional Brain*, Weidenfeld & Nicolson, London, 1998.

Lemprière's Dictionary, my edition Bracken Books, London, 1984.

Lucas, Norman, *The Sex Killers, Thirty fully documented cases of men and women whose aberrant sexuality drove them to kill*, Virgin, 1998.

Mannix, Daniel, *Those About to Die*, Panther, London, 1960.

Masters, Brian, *Killing for Company*, Arrow Books, 1995.

Melzack, Ronald, *The Puzzle of Pain*, Penguin, 1977.

Midgalski, Edward C., and Fichter, George S., *The Fresh and Salt Water Fishes of the World*, Octopus, London, 1977.

Miles, Rosalind, *The Women's History of the World*, Paladin Books, 1989.

Milton, John, *Paradise Lost* (1667/1674), my copy in *The Poetical Works of John Milton*, Ward, Lock, & Co., London, not dated.

Orwell, George, *Nineteen Eighty-Four*, my edition Heinemann, London 1977.

O'Toole, Christopher, (ed.) *The Encyclopedia of Insects*, Guild Publishing, London, 1987.

Paulos, John Allen, *A Mathematician Reads the Newspaper*, Penguin, London, 1996.

Pinker, Steven, *The Language Instinct*, Penguin, 1995.

Potter, Anthony, *The Killer Bees*, Grosset & Dunlap, New York, 1977.

Rider Haggard, H., *Montezuma's Daughter* (1892), my edition George G. Harrap & Co., London, 1925.

Russell, Bertrand, *History of Western Philosophy*, my edition Routledge, London, 1991.

Saunders, Nicholas J., *People of the Jaguar: The Living Spirit of Ancient America*, Souvenir Press, London, 1989.

Seidensticker, Dr John, and Lumpkin, Dr Susan, (eds), *Great Cats – Majestic Creatures of the Wild*, Rodale Press, Emmaus, Pennsylvania, 1991.

Stevenson, Robert Louis, *The Strange Case of Dr Jekyll and Mr. Hyde* (1886), my edition The New University Society, Edinburgh, not dated.

Stockley, David, *Drug Warning: an illustrated guide for parents and teachers*, Macdonald Optima, 1986.

Stoker, Bram, *Dracula*, my edition Galley Press, Leicester, 1988.

Strossen, Nadine, *Defending Pornography: Free Speech, Sex, and the fight for Women's Rights*, Simon & Schuster, 1995/Abacus, London, 1996.

Sykes, J.B. (ed.), *Concise Oxford English Dictionary*, Oxford University Press, Oxford, 1988.

Taylor, William N., *Hormonal Manipulation*, McFarland & Co., Jefferson NC and London, 1985.

Tenner, Edward, *Why Things Bite Back*, Fourth Estate, London, 1996.

Thompson, Bill, *Soft Core: Moral Crusades against Pornography in Britain and America*, Cassell Academic, 1994.

Valenstein, Elliot S., *Brain Control: A Critical Examination of Brain Stimulation and Psychosurgery*, John Wiley and Sons, New York, 1973.

Wagner, Frederic H., *Wildlife of the Deserts*, Windward, Leicester, date not given.

Waugh, Evelyn, *Put Out More Flags* (1942), my edition Penguin, 1975.

Wills, Christopher, *The Runaway Brain: The Evolution of Human Uniqueness*, HarperCollins, London, 1994.

Wilson, Colin, and Seaman, Donald, *The Serial Killers: a study in the psychology of violence*, Virgin Publishing, London, 1990.

Newspapers, Magazines and other sources.

'Silent Screams in Juárez', transcript of *20-20*, ABC TV, Wednesday, January 20, 1999.
Albuquerque Tribune.
Amnesty Journal 77, Jan/Feb 1996.
Bowden, Charles, 'While You Were Sleeping', *Harper's* magazine, December 1996.
El Diario de Juárez.
Encyclopedia Britannica, Britannica® CD, 1999.
Fort Worth Star-Telegram.
Frontera NorteSur.
Houston Chronicle.
Los Angeles Times.
National Geographic magazine for June, 1986, vol. 169, no. 6.
Cape Times.
Seattle Times.
The Times (London).